AFRICAN AMERICANS

THEIR HISTORY

EDITED BY
HOWARD JONES

CONTRIBUTORS:

JOHNSON ADEFILA, TUNDE ADELEKE, LEMUEL BERRY, ROOSEVELT BUTLER, RONALD DATHORNE, DENORAL DAVIS, DOROTHY DAVIS, W. MARVIN DULANEY, CHARLES JACKSON, VEULA RHODES, BUFORD SATCHER, C. CALVIN SMITH, JACKIE THOMAS, RANDOLPH MEADE WALKER, C. J. WHITE, ELMIRA WICKER

AMERICAN HERITAGE ■ CUSTOM PUBLISHING
A Division of Forbes Inc.
60 Fifth Avenue
New York, New York 10011

CIP Data is available.
Printed in the United States of America
10 9 8 7 6 5 4 3 2 1

ISBN 0–8281–1008-5

AFRICAN AMERICANS: THEIR HISTORY

PART I

1

The African Background

Sociological

For centuries African Americans were told that they belonged to a part of the human family that had made no contributions whatsoever to civilization. Africa was portrayed as the most backward and barbaric portion of the globe, devoid of culture, history and civilization. Consequently, Africans and peoples of African descent, were relegated to the lowest wrung of the racial hierarchy. Civilization was identified with Europe, and the beginning of civilization in Africa was associated with the advent of Europeans. The negation of the historical and cultural heritage of Africa legitimized the enslavement, subordination and exploitation of African Americans, and ultimately, the partition and occupation of Africa. It is only recently that Africa is being accorded her rightful place and recognition in the history of humankind. The struggle for this recognition was a hard, bitter and protracted one. For centuries Europeans fabricated the most vicious and negative accounts of Africa, primarily to excuse and rationalize their intrusion into, and plunder of the human and material resources of the continent. The pillage of Africa, and the abuse of the rights, privileges and interests of her peoples acquired the veneer of humanitarianism. Europeans claimed to have found Africans in abject condition, and touched by compassion, they (*i.e.* Europeans), assumed the difficult task of elevating Africans. The historical results of this "humane gesture" were enslavement and colonization. The earliest Africans who became African Americans were impressed with how fortunate they were to have been transplanted from Africa into the Christian and "civilized" societies of Europe and North America.

Europeans came to Africa with a baggage of prejudices within which they placed the new cultures they encountered. The word "Black" was associated with negative and contemptible qualities. It is the color of darkness. It conjures images of the unknown and evil, something dreadful. Negative portraits of blacks were embedded in European thought, as far back as the dawn of "scientific" history. Herodotus, the acclaimed "Father of history," and member of the fifth century Greco-Roman historiography, characterized Africans as savages. The denigration of Africa received added boost in the age of Enlightenment. The intellectual tradition that raised European consciousness on the significance of freedom, liberty and equality—values that upheld the sanctity of the human personality—paradoxically sanctioned the denial to Africans of those libertarian ideals. Africa was dismissed as static, barbaric, destructive and chaotic. Long before any contact with Africans, Europeans theorized and intellectualized on their (*i.e.* Africans) alleged inferiority. European "scientists" placed blacks at the bottom of the racial hierarchy. Third century geographer Solinus in his *Collection of Wonderful Things* described Africans as animals. Enlightenment philosopher, David Hume, in his *Essays and Treatise* (1768), praised western societies, and described Whites as the only race that contributed meaningfully to civilization. G. Hegel, the German philosopher and author of *Philosophy of History,* also depicted Africans as a people without a culture and history. When Europe ultimately encountered Africa, it was relatively easy to identify Africans with the preconceived negative values. The European mind was ill-prepared to concede any positive qualities to Africans. Reports of early explorers and missionaries contain copious references to the "savagery" and "barbarity" of Africans.

Europeans simply resolved their inability to understand the strange cultural and behavioral nuances of Africans by engaging in a process of cultural assassination—complete denial of the reality and essence of African culture/civilization. They conveniently located Africans within the narrow confines of the prejudicial cultural baggages they brought, and refused to acknowledge that Africans possessed the capacity for productive and inventive activities. Africa became "the Dark Continent"—barren, and occupied by savages.

Pre-European Africa acquired the character of Hobbesian "state of nature." Given the state of "lawlessness," "savagery" and "barbarity," that the early explorers and missionaries described, what more was needed than the rescuing and cleansing hands of the Europeans! The slave trade became a benevolent phenomenon, indeed, a historical necessity. The "African savage" had to be saved from a horrible environment, and from self-destructive cultural proclivities. Enslavement became a higher plane of civilization, and those Africans "lucky" to be enslaved were headed for a better way of life, elevated on a pedestal above the "savages" left behind. Pre-European Africa was thus like a **tabula rasa**, *i.e.*, a clean slate. The Europeans came, and began the process of "writing" on this slate, thus inaugurating the dawn of African history and civilization. Colonialism acquired the same justification—a continuation of the "civilization" process begun by enslavement. Its stated objective was to brighten the "dark continent," through a policy of direct occupation.

African Americans were, therefore, impressed, from the very beginning of their ordeal, with the notion of slavery as a benevolent institution, and induced to acquiesce in its practices, and accept and dutifully carry out its instructions and impositions. The propaganda worked so well that many African Americans soon perceived slavery as a necessary stage, albeit a regrettable and painful one, in the process of acquiring a sense of worth and meaning, by imbibing the superior values and traditions of the master class. Little wonder then that years later, African American nationalists would picture themselves as bearers of "civilization" to Africa.

Attempts to debunk Eurocentric views of Africa did not begin until free blacks who struggled to break through the shackles of slavery, and became educated, began to write and publish accounts of their history and experience in Africa and the new world. The struggle to reassert the worth, wealth, and authenticity of the historical and cultural heritage of African Americans was begun by such nineteenth century African American intelligentsia as George Washington Williams, William Wells Brown, Martin R. Delany and James W. C. Pennington. This was carried into the twentieth century by W.E.B. Du Bois, Carter G. Woodson, Benjamin Brawley and Alrutheus Taylor. The Civil Rights Movement of the 1960s intensified this process. In Africa, the relaxation of the strangle-hold of colonialism in the 1960s, created the atmosphere for the rise of post-colonial historiography which challenged and exposed the fallacies and misrepresentations of Eurocentric historiography. The combined efforts of historians, political scientists, sociologists, psychologists and activist scholars and students from many other disciplines in Africa and the United states, succeeded in reopening to the entire world the cultural and historical heritage and realities of Africa.

Africans who became African Americans came geographically from a region that encompassed the whole of West Africa, stretching from Senegal to Angola. It covered hundreds of ethnic groups—Bambara, Angola, Fulani, Mandingoes, Wolof, Asante, Fante, Ga, Ibo, Yoruba, Hausa, Soninke, etc. To appreciate the enormity of the cultural transformation involved in the forcible transplantation of Africans to America, it is necessary to examine the dynamics of the environment from where they were uprooted. Though from different ethnic, linguistic and complex cultural backgrounds, Africans shared certain unifying attributes and values. It is consequently possible to generalize about the African background of African Americans. Broadly defined, there were, and still are, two fundamental environments in the socialization experience of Africans—the socio-cultural and the politico-economic. The two environments are not mutually exclusive, but function complimentarily to shape the personality, views, values and world view of Africans.

The world into which an African is born is a community oriented one. He/she is born into a family, with strong ties to a wider lineage, *i.e.*, other families with whom he/she shares a common ancestry. The lineage is part of a broader community—the village. In many situations, the family and other members of the lineage all occupy the ancestral compound. Every one is linked to the others, both within the immediate family, and in the extended family. The African family is not just the nuclear one, but extends to include uncles, nieces, nephews, cousins, aunts, etc. The system of kinship mandates the assumption of extended responsibility. One is responsible not only for ones immediate family, but also for the welfare of everyone within the extended family. The notion of collective responsibility joins everyone in a relationship of shared responsibilities and obligations.

In traditional African society, the group acquired primacy over the individual in all circumstances. Since individual actions usually impacted the wider group, group survival, and indeed progress, was the responsibility of every member. Individual behaviors were often perceived as reflective of one's background, having significant bearing upon the entire family, clan and lineage. Consequently, the parameter of group action was much wider, and often superimposed upon that of individual action. There was hardly room for individual decisions conceived and executed in absolute disregard of the group. Issues such as the choice of a spouse, or a career, are social decisions deliberated upon by the group. In essence, the parameter of social actions circumscribes the space available for the exercise and projection of individualism. Indeed, individual identity is defined within the context of the group. That is, the individual exists by virtue of membership in a community, and remains meaningless, and perilously adrift in isolation from that community. An Asante proverb aptly describes this situation; "I am because we are."

Traditional African society was strongly gerontocratic. Wisdom was, and remains, associated with age, hence elders were easily recognized, revered, respected and accorded roles as bearers, and transmitters of knowledge and morality. But more significantly, elders were perceived as agents of stability. They settled disputes and intervened in inter-personal and inter-group conflicts. Given this reality, there was no assumption, or presumption of equality. Chiefs, nominated or hereditary, and ethnic elders, chosen or assumed, stood high on the social pinnacle, over and above everyone else. Furthermore, in societies such as the Ibo and Yoruba of southeastern and southwestern Nigeria respectively, one was assigned a place according to one's age group. Age groups, another manifestation of the gerontocratic culture, performed civic responsibilities for the entire community. They assisted in the construction of community projects, and often helped to maintain law and order. They also functioned as media of socialization of their members on civic and social responsibilities.

In traditional Africa, individuals assume their identities within a network of relationships. The African is socialized to acknowledge not only personal rights and privileges, but also duties and obligations to the family, other relatives, and to the community at large. The kinship and lineage networks are sustained by a strong sense of historical identity, ensconced in traditions of origin (tales, fables, parables, etc.), again told by, and received from, elders, who served as repository and transmitters of knowledge. Children gravitate towards elders, humbly and respectfully, with the expectation that through close interaction, some of the wisdom and knowledge would rob off. Oral traditions, pertaining to the origins, and the collective historical consciousness of the community, are entrusted to specialized individuals or groups, recognized as custodians of the official history of the society. These Griots or official state historians are often rewarded for efficient preservation and transmission of the traditions, and equally penalized for poor or shoddy performance of their duties. Not only did pre-colonial Africans have a history, but also an awareness of its significance for the collective survival and identity of the group.

Reality for the African consists of both the physical and metaphysical realms. The ancestors, though dead, remain part of the living present, continually impacting the daily lives of the people.

There is an unending dialogue between the living and the departed. A harmonious dialogue results in survival and prosperity for the community. A state of balance or equilibrium is consequently attained in the relationship between the two. Any sign of unbalance in the relationship with the ancestors portends disaster, which assumes any number of forms—hunger, drought, flood, famine, epidemic etc. This partly explains why Africans practice ancestral worship. Elders of the family, and in many instances, specialized priests and diviners are responsible for performing the necessary rituals for strengthening the relationship with the ancestors. These priests, diviners (and elders), are often relied upon to interpret the mysteries of nature and the universe, thereby enabling the people to live and function, without violating those sacred rules and laws that are indispensable for harmony.

The religious world view is also important. Africans have been described as "a religious people." Most African societies are monotheistic, *i.e.*, they espouse a strong belief in one supreme God—**Olorun**, among the Yoruba, or **Chukwu**, among the Ibo. This is the supreme provider of life. Africans also believe in the existence of spirits, and a host of lesser gods/goddesses that intercede between human beings and the supreme.

Traditional Africa was, therefore, class oriented, with stratifications such as ruling/upper classes, aristocrats, commoners, and in many situations, slaves. Slaves were essentially war captives, or those convicted of serious criminal offenses. A slave could be sold or subjected to forced labor. In principle, slaves were treated harshly, almost like chattels, but in practice slavery in Africa varied from society to society. In certain communities, like the fishing settlements of southeastern Nigeria, the practice allowed a considerable room for elevation and freedom. The career of king Jaja of Opobo remains a striking example of the flexibility of slavery in African society. He was born a slave in the village of Opobo. Through industry and determination, Jaja rose to become the king of his society, and one of the prominent defenders of Nigeria's independence against British imperialism. In Central Africa, recent studies show that chattel slavery existed "in name only." This is due to the relative freedom enjoyed by slaves, and the wide variety of employments they engaged in. They served as local administrators, royal advisers, clerks and messengers, functions that gave the slaves a considerable degree of freedom and mobility. There were many instances of slaves becoming integrated into the families of their masters. At the other extreme was the situation in the Senegambia region in the fifteenth century, where slaves were subjected to hard labor and harsh living conditions. There were also categories of subordination that have often been mistaken by Europeans for slavery. For example, among the Yoruba, the **Iwofa** was a recognized form of debt peonage. An **Iwofa**, the debtor, pledges his/her services, or that of a relative to a creditor for a predetermined period in lieu of payment of a debt. Contrary to European interpretation, the **Iwofa** was not a slave. An Iwofa retained his/her liberty and humanity. There was consequently, a certain flexibility and complexity to the institution of slavery in traditional African societies.

Decision making and conflict resolution began at the level of the family where elders presided. Disputes involving several families were usually settled by representatives of the families. Matters were deliberated upon, and decisions reached after all views were heard. With the exception of "stateless" societies (to be discussed below), leadership and decision-making at the community or village level, was the responsibility of a chief, usually a descendant of the founder or first settlers of the community. Chieftaincy was hereditary in most societies, with the son succeeding his father. In societies with multiple royal families, as in the kingdom of Zaria in Northern Nigeria, political power was rotated among the various royal families. Most African societies practiced patralineal mode of succession, that is, the chief was appointed from the father's line. For example, in the ancient Yoruba empire of Oyo, the **Aremo**, son of the reigning **Alafin** (King), inherited the throne on the death of his father. This practice changed in the seventeenth century, and the **Oyomesi** (council of notables) assumed the responsibility of choosing the **Alafin**. There were, however, matralineal societies such as the ancient Ghana empire, where succession was through the female line. The king was succeeded not by his son, but by the son of his sister. Chiefs rarely administered their territories arbitrarily, or single-handedly. Though highly revered, respected, and in many societies, accorded divine qualities, the Chief usually administered his domain in consultation with a council of advisers and elders.

STUDY GUIDE 1

1 According to the traditionally taught myth, what has Africa contributed to civilization?

2 What area, according to the traditionally taught myth, has been viewed as the most backward portion of the globe?

3 Taught myth would suggest that due to Africa's "backwardness," African Americans should have been glad that what happened to them?

4–5 Inculcating the myth of Africa's backwardness was supposed to have pacified Africans and made them readily accept what two things?

6 Give the "father" of Eurocentric scientific history.

7 Generally, what phrase was used to describe Africa by early western social scientists?

8–17 Give some of the ethnic groups that lived in the region of Africa, from whence came "New World" captives for the European slave trade.

18 YES? NO? Were there slaves in traditional African societies (pre-European)?

19 P.O.W.s were normally assigned to what class group?

Using Eurocentric terms, very briefly define:

20 ALAFIN.

21 AREMO.

22 CHUKWU.

23 IWOFA.

24 OLORUN.

25 OYOMESI.

SUGGESTED READINGS

Nathan Huggins, *Black Odyssey: The Afro-American Ordeal in Slavery.* New York: 1977.

Adu Boahen, *Topics in West African History,* 2nd. edition. Longman: 1986.

James H. Dorman and Robert R. Jones, *The Afro-American Experience: A Critical History Through Emancipation.* New York: John Wiley & Sons, 1974.

John Hope Franklin, *From Slavery to Freedom: A History of African American* 7th. edition. New York: McGraw Hill, 1994.

Lerone Bennett, *Before The Mayflower.* Chicago: 1987.

2

The African Background

Geographical and Economical

The African was equally part of a political and economic environment, which equally defined his responsibilities, obligations, rights, privileges, and remunerations. Pre-European Africa witnessed the rise and development of states, kingdoms, and empires, many of whose imprints remain indelible in the sands of history. In fact, the coastal region of West Africa and its immediate interior, where the majority of African Americans came from, was the geographical setting of the great civilizations of the West, Central Sudan, and the forest region. The rise of the West Sudanese states of Ghana, Mali and Songhay could be explained without any reference to European influence. They all owe their origins to factors domestic to the African environment.

Geographically, all the states emerged in the savanna grassland, an open area that encouraged the movements of people. This area was also a richly endowed region with resources such as gold, ivory, and silver. The Niger, Sankarani, and Senegal rivers covered a considerable part of the region, and furthered the development of communication, agriculture, fishing, and permanent settlements. But perhaps the most important of the factors in the rise of civilization in the West and Central Sudan was trade, in particular the tran-Saharan trade that linked North Africa with the Western Sudan and the forest region to the South. The introduction of the camel to North Africa in the first century A. D. made the conquest of the Sahara desert possible. The Sahara suddenly became a sea of communication as traders packed their caravans from several North African cities such as Tripoli, Fez, Tunis, Tlencem, and Cairo, to embark on the long, hazardous journey to the savanna region, bringing Mediterranean, European, Middle Eastern, and North African goods, such as cloths, ornaments, beads, and bangles, to exchange for the products of the savanna: ivory, gold, slaves, and kolanuts. The savanna region served as the center of trade. Traders from the North and South met there to transact business. Control of this trade brought immense wealth to individuals, and the politically ambitious among them were able to translate this economic power into political power through the conquest and unification of different ethnic groups into larger political entities. Islam also came from North Africa, providing a unifying ideology along with administrative and technical services.

It has also been suggested that the earliest settlers in the West and Central Sudan were migrants forced out by the desication of the Sahara Desert, which began about 500 A. D. The Sahara once sustained settled agrarian communities. Sometime in the sixth century, climatic changes induced desiccation, forcing the inhabitants who were mostly Bedouin Arabs and Tuaregs to migrate in different directions. Some of the migrants moved southward into the West and Central Sudan, and they have been credited with accelerating the process of state formation in the region.

Migration was a common phenomenon in ancient Africa. People moved and changed residences for a variety of reasons. The result, in most situations, was the emergence of organized political entities. The alluring factors that brought migrants to a particular locality could be the availability of rich natural resources, or strategic geographical considerations. Virtually every medieval empire of the West and Central Sudan started as a small nucleated settlement whose economic and strategic significance attracted more migrants. From such small beginnings, the settlements mushroomed, especially as the economy developed and expanded. By the sixth century A. D. some of the settlements began using iron. Iron technology enhanced agriculture and also conferred military advantages that resulted in the creation of chiefdoms and states. The earliest and most prominent of these states was the Soninke kingdom of Ghana.

Trade, both local and long distance, greatly accelerated the rise of ancient Ghana. Ghana was located at the very confluence of the savanna and the Sahara, and being strategically positioned, the kingdom could to play a middleman's role in the tran-Saharan trade. Sometime in the sixth century, the Soninke developed a monarchy in which the king monopolized the trade. Wealth from the trade, especially the gold trade, brought tremendous economic, political and military power. This resulted in the extension of the boundaries of the state.

Ghana was famous for its wealth in gold, hence the name "Gold Coast." Arab travellers such as El Fazzari and Al Yakoubi testified to the abundance of gold and the impact it had on the people's standard of living. Ruled by a semi-divine king who was assisted by a council of ministers, ancient Ghana, for administrative purposes, was divided into two—the metropolitan section, corresponding to the original nucleus, and the provincial, mainly the conquered groups. Though pagan, the king allowed those of the Islamic faith the freedom to practice their religion. The king administered the capital directly, with the assistance of a council, and delegated political responsibility to local leaders in the provinces on the condition that they pledged loyalty to his supreme authority. The king had an army of about 200,000 armed with bows and arrows for defense and maintenance of law and order. He was also in charge of justice and undertook periodic visits to the provinces to ascertain problems and dispense justice. State income and revenue came largely from trade. However, taxation, custom duties levied on foreign traders, and tributes from vassal states were other significant sources of state revenue. As earlier indicated, the Soninke practiced matrilineal succession. The king was succeeded by the son of his sister. They also believed in life-after-death and in the semi-divine character of the king. Consequently, the kings were buried along with their most treasured belongings—ornaments, weapons, vessels, foods and beverages. Like other African people, the Soninke also practiced ancestral worship and performed sacrifices to the dead.

Ghana lasted up to the eleventh century, and began to decline due to a combination of internal and external factors. The most critical internal factor was the absence of ethnic unity or cultural homogeneity. The state was made of different ethnic groups: Soninke, Susu, Serer, Berber, Tukulor, Silla, Diara, Kaniaga, and Tekrur, who all had conflicting languages, religions and cultures. What held the disparate people together was the might of the king. The introduction of the Islamic faith into the kingdom gradually weakened the power of the monarchy and resulted in the disintegration of the state. Due to its pagan character, Ghana became the target of Islamic movements. The Almoravids, an Islamic revivalist movement organized by the Sanhaja Berbers of the Sahara who were dedicated to spreading the Islam religion through **Jihads** (holy wars), conquered Ghana in 1054. This development weakened the state and encouraged the vassals to declare independence. The demise of Ghana created a political vacuum in the Western Sudan. The Malinke of Mali, former vassals of Ghana, soon filled this space.

Mali/Melle started as a small Mandingo chiefdom called Kangaba. The ancient capital Jeriba was situated near the confluence of the Sankarani and Senegal rivers. The early settlers in Kangaba were able to practice both agriculture and trade, and they benefited from a constellation of the same social, economic, and political factors as the Soninke of Ghana. Kangaba was closer to the gold producing regions of Bure and Bambuk over which the Malinke soon asserted control. By the fourteenth century,

Niani, the new capital, and the cities of Jenne, Timbuktu, and Gao had developed into commercial centers. Arab chroniclers left detailed accounts of the wealth, affluence, peace, and prosperity of Mali. Unlike Ghana, the Islamic faith came very early to Mali, and thus played a key role in its rise and development. From the beginning, Islamic jurists, scholars, and administrators helped to shape the future of Mali.

The individual associated with the founding of Mali was Sundiata, 1234–55. Following the eclipse of Ghana, he restored order and unified the various ethnic groups. Sundiata was more of a conqueror; his battles reunited virtually all the former territories of Ghana. And by reasserting authority over the gold producing regions of Bure and Bambuk, he gained control over the tran-Saharan trade. After pacifying the region, he devised an administrative structure. Essentially, he retained the old metropolitan-provincial system, and appointed only able and trusted officials to administer the provinces. Sundiata never quite had time to consolidate his power. He died mysteriously in 1255.

Sundiata was succeeded by several weak rulers—Mansa Wali, Mansa Khalifa, Mansa Gaw and Mansa Mamadu. For a brief period, it seemed as if the empire would degenerate into chaos. This situation was, however, saved by the ascendance of Mansa Musa, 1312–1337, who is considered the greatest of Mali kings. Musa restored peace and stability while continuing the expansionist policies of Sundiata. He tremendously increased the size of the army to more than 100,000 infantry, and 10,000 cavalry, with which he kept peace and unity. He created more provinces and also appointed trusted generals to positions of administrators and governors. All provincial governors were well paid and directly responsible to Musa. To instill a sense of patriotism and more closely identify the people with the state (a realization of the significance of political unity lacking in earlier years), he introduced a system of national honors that recognized and rewarded acts of heroism or patriotism. Musa developed a reputation for impartiality in the dispensation of justice. He appointed judges, scribes, and civil servants to ensure fairness and efficiency in the administration of the state. State income came from a wide variety of sources—taxation on occupations and livestock, custom duties on foreign traders and goods, and tributes from vassal states. Musa's reign is noted for stability and economic prosperity.

Musa's greatest legacy, however, was in the field of religion. Between 1324–25, he embarked on a pilgrimage to Mecca, taking with him wealth of immense value, particularly in gold, which he lavished on charity in North Africa and the Middle East. His pilgrimage not only publicized Mali to the outside world, but brought an influx of Muslim scholars, jurists, clerics, architects, and other professionals. On his return, he ordered strict observance of the Islamic faith and built many mosques and Islamic schools. The cities of Timbuktu and Jenne became centers of Islamic culture and education. Musa's rule has been described as the "golden age" of Mali. He died in 1337, only to be followed by a succession of weak rulers who dragged Mali into decline and collapse by the second half of the fourteenth century.

The last of the pre-colonial states of the Western Sudan was Songhay, which replaced Mali as the most powerful city in the fifteenth century. Songhay developed out of an older and smaller kingdom of Gao, located in Dendi on the fertile plains of the Niger river. The river enabled the early settlers to engage in both agriculture and fishing. The settlers also profited from the tran-Saharan trade, particularly the eastward shift in the trade direction following the collapse of Mali. This shift brought immense wealth to the people of Songhay. The first notable ruler of this city was Sunni Ali, who was often compared with Sundiata, for he, too, was a warrior. After consolidating his domestic position, Sunni Ali embarked on wars of conquest, capturing the breakaway towns of Timbuktu, Jenne, Walata and Kebbi. His wars brought many ethnic groups into Songhay that allowed him to transform the tiny kingdom of Gao into an empire. Sunni Ali also devised an effective administrative system that ensured peace and stability: Provincial governors swore an oath of loyalty to him. He appointed a commander in chief for the navy, which had become an important arm of the military. Ali demanded absolute loyalty and appointed only loyal subordinates to positions of authority.

SUGGESTED READINGS

Nathan Huggins, *Black Odyssey: The Afro-American Ordeal in Slavery.* New York: 1977.

Adu Boahen, *Topics in West African History,* 2nd edition. Longman: 1986.

James H. Dorman and Robert R. Jones, *The Afro-American Experience: A Critical History Through Emancipation.* New York: John Wiley & Sons, 1974.

John Hope Franklin, *From Slavery to Freedom: A History of African-American,* 7th edition. New York: McGraw Hill, 1994.

Lerone Bennett, *Before The Mayflower.* Chicago: 1987.

STUDY GUIDE 2

1 From what general region of Africa did African Americans come?

2–4 Give three valuable resources that were indigenous to the region mentioned in question one (**1**).

5–7 Give at least three rivers in the savanna area of Africa.

8 What desert exist in the area of Africa mentioned in question one (**1**)?

9–11 Name the three major pre-European West African kingdoms.

12–15 What were some of the ethnic groups that made up Ghana?

16 In its simplest terms, define *Jihad.*

17 What was the first outside organized religion that came to Africa?

18–20 Name at least three leaders of Mali/Melle.

3

The African Background

Political

Sunni Ali was succeeded by another notable leader, Askia Mohammed Toure, called "the great." A successful army general under Sunni Ali, Askia Mohammed organized a coup, and toppled the legitimate heirs of Sunni. Devoid of traditional legitimacy, Askia sought legitimacy in Islam. Soon after subduing all opposition, he went on a pilgrimage to Mecca in 1497, on a scale that surpassed that of Mansa Musa. He too exhibited the wealth and affluence of his state in North Africa and the Middle East. He made friends, and established diplomatic relationships with the outside world. He attracted Muslim scholars to Songhay, and insisted upon a strict observance of the rules of the religion. Next, he waged holy wars against neighboring pagan states of Agades, Kano, Katsina and Zamfara. His capture of the salt mining town of Taghaza in the Sahara extended Songhay boundary to its Northernmost limit.

Askia Mohammed encouraged Islamic education with the establishment of up to 150 koranic schools in Songhay. The peace and stability that he established attracted more Muslim scholars and students from North Africa and the Middle East. Timbuktu, Gao and Jenne continued to enjoy economic and intellectual successes, and attracted traders and merchants. The most famous of the institutions of higher education was the famous Sankore University in Timbuktu, which produced some of the leading scholars on whom one relies today for much of the knowledge of the history of medieval Western Sudan—Mohammed Kati, author of *Tarikh el Fattash* (The chronicle of the seeker of knowledge), and Mohammed As-sadi, author of *Tarikh as Sudan* (The chronicle of the Western Sudan).

Askia established an advanced administrative structure, noted for many of its modernizing qualities. He divided the empire into provinces each under a governor. The provinces were further grouped into two major regions—East and West, each administered by a regional commissioner or viceroy. Each viceroy was assisted by a council of advisers. At the capital, which he administered directly, Askia was assisted by a council of ministers, each responsible for a specific branch or function of government—agriculture, forestry, fishing, alien affairs, justice, navy, finance, religion and immigration. Songhay administration had all the trademarks of a modern state. Askia Mohammed was indeed ahead of his time.

State revenue came not only from trade, but also from well organized agricultural estates run by the state. Askia established agricultural estates, scattered throughout the realm. Worked by slaves, the estates specialized in the production of commodities such as corn, rice and fish. Craftsmen were also organized to manufacture boats, spears, and bows and arrows for the military. The state derived more revenue from taxation and tributes than from vassals. Askia imposed a uniform weight and measures, and appointed royal inspectors to the markets to ensure compliance.

Arab travellers who visited Songhay during his reign left vivid first hand accounts of the wealth, economy, and high standard of living of the people. Leo Africanus, a Moorish traveller who visited the Western Sudan, testified to the commercial prosperity, peace and political stability of the region. Ibn Battuta, the muslim traveller, visited the Western Sudan in the fourteenth century and left glowing testimony to the wealth, affluence and industry of the region. Leading Muslim scholars such as Mohammed Kati, and Abdelrahman As-Sadi emphasized the intellectual life, peace, stability and the admirable moral and ethical character of the people. Askia Mohammed died in 1528. His reign was followed by succession disputes that sapped the strength of the state, and unleashed micro-nationalistic aspirations as the constituent ethnic groups sought to declare their independence. With no able leader, external enemies, attracted by the wealth of the region, seized the opportunity to launch attacks. In 1590, Songhay fell to the greed and cupidity of Al-Mansur, the Sultan of Morocco. The Moroccans wrecked havoc and destruction on the Western Sudan, plundered the resources of the region, and opened a period of economic, political and intellectual decadence, totally obliterating the reforms, and accomplishments of the indigenous people.

It is necessary to highlight these three West and Central Sudanese states (Ghana, Mali and Songhay) because, their rise, development and accomplishments could be explained without any reference to European influence, thus debunking the claim that Africa lacked indigenous culture and civilization. In fact, it was not until toward the closing days of Songhay that Europeans began to make their presence felt along the West coast. Though these states had contacts with the outside world through the tran-Saharan trade, the dominant influence in their development was local. European influence came through the West coast, and did not become significant until toward the closing years of Songhay.

To the south of the savanna region, emerged the forest states of Oyo, Benin, Dahomey, Asante. Though these states had earlier contacts with Europeans than their West and Central Sudanese counterparts, again, their rise into prominence had much more to do with domestic circumstances, than with European contacts. For example the several clans that founded Asante empire—Oyoko, Gretuo, Ekoona, Aduani etc., were attracted to the area of modern Kumasi, where they established a number of states that formed the nucleus of the empire, by economic and demographic considerations. Population pressure pushed them out of their original settlements. But the economic and strategic attraction of Kumasi was compelling. This was the area where several tran-Saharan trade routes intersected. It also contained in abundance two of the main items of trade—gold and kolanut. Though the various clans were attracted by economic considerations, perhaps the most important single factor in the evolution of statehood, was the depth of kinship ethos, and how this served to unify the groups, pulling them together in the face of external threat. The outcome was the evolution of kingship, *i.e.* political leadership.

The initial impetus that launched the process of state formation in many parts of Africa was internal. In the case of the forest states, external European influence equally proved decisive in terms of the material and technological wherewithal for state formation (guns and gunpowder). Due to their proximity to the coast, the base of European operations from about the fifteenth century on, the forest states increasingly came under the influence of Europeans. Whereas the Sudanese states of Ghana, Mali and Songhay, rose and flowered without interference from the Europeans, the forest states had, from very early in their evolution, to contend with European presence and intrigues, a factor that portended ominous consequences.

Despite European presence, the forest states were able to evolve strong indigenous institutions that guaranteed political stability. Oyo, Dahomey, Benin and Asante were ruled by monarchs whose powers were deeply rooted in local traditions. They also evolved fairly stable and efficient succession systems that guaranteed continuity. Like the Sudanese states, the forest states were also multi-ethnic in composition, the result of the conquest and absorption of vassals. With the possible exception of Dahomey which practiced a centralized political administrative system, in the other forest states—Oyo, Asante and Benin—the king administered the capital directly, in conjunction with a council of advisers and ministers who constituted the cabinet, while political authority in the provinces was left in the hands of local leaders. In essence, the provinces enjoyed some degree of autonomy—the freedom to retain, and practice their cultural, linguistic and religious beliefs, as long as they acknowledged the supreme authority of the imperial monarch, the **Alafin** of Oyo, and the **Asantehene** of Asante. Dahomey, on the other hand, experimented with a policy of cultural assimilation, and obliterated the customs and traditions of conquered peoples. Dahomey kings insisted upon the universalization of the customs and traditions of Dahomey throughout the empire. This has been called a policy of *Dahomeanization*.

It is clear, therefore, that though the European factor became evident early in the evolution of the states of the forest region, it was not the dominant factor. To explain the rise and development of the forest states one has to consider a constellation of internal and external factors. And more importantly, the institutions and customs that sustained these states, were locally derived and deeply rooted in the traditions of the people. For example, the Golden Stool of the Asante, that represented the national spirit, and unified the various ethnic groups, evolved out of Asante tradition, and was attributed to the leadership abilities of Osei Tutu, who ascended the throne in the late seventeenth century. He not only unified the states politically, but also provided the ideological seal of this unity in the form of a Golden Stool, a divine instrument to which he also linked the monarchy, thus strengthening the divine character of the Asantehene. This national unity was reenacted and strengthened annually through the **Odwirra** festival. Both the Golden Stool and the festival served as the glue that held the states together. Dahomey too developed a unique system, which, though fundamentally different, achieved the same goal of political stability. The policy of *Dahomeanization* imposed a degree of cultural unity throughout the empire. There was also the **Agbadjigbeto** institution, created by king Agaja, 1708–1732. It was used by the king to gather intelligence, and spy on enemies, during wartime, and to disseminate public information. The kings of Dahomey exercised absolute powers, and controlled all political and military appointments. Their pronouncements had the force of law. But the kings (Wegbaja 1650–1685, Akaba 11 1685–1708, Agaja 1708–1732, Tegbesu 1732–1774) could be likened to enlightened despots whose policies were designed to make governance more efficient, and improve the living standards of the populace. There was also a certain uniqueness to Dahomey military. It was the only state to have a female wing, the famous Amazons. Like Songhay, Dahomey had a cabinet system of government, with a Prime Minister (the **Meu**), and subordinate ministers assigned portfolios in taxation, agriculture, commerce, etc. Another unique feature of Dahomey government was that each minister had a female counterpart. The elevation of women to positions of authority in the military and government is indicative of the progressive nature of the government of Dahomey.

Unlike Dahomey, the Yoruba empire of Oyo had a king who was denied absolute power. The Alafin was more of a **primus inter pares** (first among equals), in relation to the **Oyomesi**, the council of notables, which functioned like a modern parliament. The **Alafin** was obliged to consult with the **Oyomesi** before making vital state decisions. The **Oyomesi** was perceived as representative of the interest and opinions of the people. The **Alafin**, **Oyomesi** and other institutions that sustained stability, and gave the common people a sense of representation, resulted from the historical experience of the Yoruba. Perhaps the most remarkable achievements of ancient Oyo was in the arts. The Yoruba began producing works of artistic excellence as far back as the fourteenth century. Archaeological excavations have uncovered numerous works of arts in bronze, ivory, wood and terracotta (burnt clay). The famous Ife bronze heads are noted for their beauty and naturalism. This is also true of the neighboring Benin kingdom, whose famous bronze heads continue to dazzle the imagination all over the world. During the colonial rule, the Europeans stole numerous Ife and Benin arts, and transported them to museums in Europe.

The Ibo society of southeastern Nigeria, another group well represented in the Diaspora, is worth mentioning, if only to highlight the political complexity of indigenous Africa. The Ibo belong to a political tradition defined as "stateless" or acephalus. Included in this class are the Fulani nomads, the Kru of Liberia, the Tallensi of Ghana, the Konkomba of Togo, the Mbeere of Kenya. They are classified as "stateless" because they did not evolve formal political institutions, *i.e.*, identifiable chiefs or political leaders. The Fulani, being nomads, lacked the situational stability to institute formal political institutions. Nonetheless, they maintain justice, cultural integrity and group cohesion, through the extended family organizations and kinship ethos. Fearful of dictatorship, the Ibo discarded completely with formal political leadership. Instead of an individual, the Ibo vested leadership and vital decisions on a council of elders, composed of representatives of the entire community. Or, in much smaller settlements, allowed everyone the opportunity to air their opinions before vital decisions were taken. Though "stateless," these societies had mechanisms for conflict resolutions, and in the case of the Ibo, the decision to discard with political centralization was inspired by consideration for democracy.

The economy of the Sudanese states, and indeed of all the states identified, depended, in the early phases of their history, on subsistence agriculture. But, as seen in the case of the Sudanese states, agriculture was just one among many occupations. The notion of subsistence is often misconceived and overstretched with reference to pre-colonial African economies. The societies produced for both local consumption and trade (both local and long distance). In many parts of Africa, there were daily and periodic markets, which served to bring people together from far and near to transact business. The diversity and complexity of the African geographical feature sustained a diverse economy. Agriculture was widespread in both the savanna and forest region. Trade, especially the tran-Saharan trade, linked the North with the Central Sudan and the forest region. No society was totally isolated and static. The Fulani and Tuaregs, herders of camel and cattle, roamed the open savanna. The Soninke, Susu, Malinke, Tekrur and Sorko, engaged in a multiplicity of occupations—fishing, agriculture, cattle-rearing and hunting. Artisans and craftsmen engaged in numerous productive and industrial activities—weaving, pottery, woodwork, metal-work. Blacksmiths melted ores and forged implements such as knives, axes, and weapons of war.

A fundamental and fascinating aspect of the operations of pre-European African political entities pertains to the maintenance of law and order. This is significant in the light of the contention that these societies lacked any basis for stability and order. That pre-European African societies did not have written or codified laws, did not mean that they were lawless and chaotic. These societies relied heavily on customs and traditions that evolved through centuries of usages and have attained a degree of respectability and universal acceptability as viable mechanisms for conflict resolution and the maintenance of stability. In most cases, the king was the custodian of the tradition, and the dispenser of justice, a notable example being pre-Islamic ancient Ghana. In his executive capacity, the king in traditional African society could delegate judicial authority to loyal subordinates who functioned as judges in lower courts, with provisions for appeals from the lower courts to the highest court (usually the king's in the capital). Oyo, Benin, Dahomey and Asante, all had courts set up in the various provinces to deal with grievances, and maintain law and order. Consequently, though not guided by written laws, Africans were not "lawless," as often suggested by apologists of slavery and colonialism. Customs and traditions defined individual and group responsibilities, and set reasonable limits on behaviors that are in conformity with what were deemed conducive to societal growth and balance. In the states of the West and Central Sudan, particularly Mali and Songhay, customary laws functioned side by side with Islamic laws—the **Sharia**. Islamic jurists and clerics introduced Islamic jurisprudence. The fact that these laws might have been harsh (measured by modern standard) in their daily applications, does not obliterate or negate their existence. Pre-colonial Africans had recourse for legal redress.

It has been suggested that the traditional world of the African was an inward looking one, that it did not adequately prepare Africans for the changes to come. But, it was also a world that satisfied the basic need to survive, and provided support mechanism that shielded individuals from the trauma of isolation. And, it was a world that satisfied the need for identity and survival, and gave reassurance of stability and order, and provided a value system that was inclusive. When the force of change eventually came, Africans, readers are told, did not initially quite realize its very essence and character. After overcoming the initial shock of encounter with Europeans, Africans settled down to relate to them on terms dictated by their traditions, which enjoined hospitality to visitors. They extended open arms to the Europeans, visitors, who, in the African worldview, deserved to be well treated and protected. They gave the Europeans some space on which to erect their dwellings. This gesture of hospitality proved the undoing of Africa!

SUGGESTED READINGS

Nathan Huggins, *Black Odyssey: The Afro-American Ordeal in Slavery*. New York: 1977.

Adu Boahen, *Topics in West African History*, 2nd. edition. Longman: 1986.

James H. Dorman and Robert R. Jones, *The Afro-American Experience: A Critical History Through Emancipation*. New York: John Wiley & Sons, 1974.

John Hope Franklin, *From Slavery to Freedom: A History of African-American*, 7th. edition. New York: McGraw Hill, 1994.

Lerone Bennett, *Before The Mayflower*. Chicago: 1987.

Study Guide 3

1 Who succeeded Sunni Ali as king in Songhay?

2 Give the location of Sankore University.

3 Who was Leo Africanus?

4 The Oyoko, Gretuo, Ekoona, Aduani, *et al.* all helped to form what kingdom?

5 The "golden stool" directly relates to what ethnic group of people?

6 Give the title of the monarch of the Asante kingdom.

7 What gender usage in the Dahomeon kingdom made it very unique?

8 What is terracotta art?

9–10 Rather than codified law, pre-European African societies depended upon what two factors to produce an orderly society?

4

The Enslavement Process

Saunders Redding indicated that because of the nearness, there were always disagreements among the west African kingdoms that led to intertribal wars. Instead of killing the conquered, oft times, captives were taken and turned into slaves (p.o.w.—prisoners of war). This meant that prior to the coming of Europeans, slavery was indigenous to Africa. Economic "have not" became another avenue to slavery. One might sell oneself and one could be ordered sold. But, in this native African slavery, there was no color badge of inferiority. Eventually, the Europeans took this already well developed indigenous African slavery and simply expanded and polished it—making it work better and more profitable. For example, in the Senegambia region prior to the coming of the Europeans, there had been developed centers of trade like Timbuktu, Gao, and Jenne had developed. The Mandinka became the dominant tribal group in this area. It was also these Mandinka who cooperated with the Europeans and became the "middle men" in the slave trade. They simply exchanged goods (slaves) they already had. According to Dawda Faal, Mandinka had become so sophisticated in the slave business that slaves were divided into two groups—domestic slaves and trade slaves. They never sold domestic slaves. These persons were considered somewhat a part of the society and could not be removed. Among others who developed from this domestic slave group was the griot, the oral historian of the society. The trade slaves had been captured in war or bought in regular commerce—these were the folks sold to the Europeans.

According to the Europeans, negroes* had seen the "New World" earlier than 1619. One African, Pedro Alonso, sailed with Columbus on the *Nina*. Africans were with Balboa when he sighted the Pacific Ocean. They were also with Hernando Cortez in Mexico. And they were with Ponce de Leon in Florida. Hardly any of the explorers have gained more popularity than Esteban, the Moor who originally was with the Cabeza DeVaca expedition.

Portugal began exporting Africans to Europe around 1442. By the end of the 1400s (fifteenth century), Portugal had made an agreement with Spain to supply the Spanish colonies with African slave laborers due to Portugal now controlling all of Africa. This agreement was known as the *asiento*.

*The term NEGRO is used interchangeably with African because the early Europeans used the term simply to mean black. In other words, NEGROES were black people. Another usage was that NEGRO referred to people who came from the region of the Niger River.

According to the Europeans, Portugal had gained control of Africa as a result of the 1493 Papal Line of Demarcation. This imaginary line was modified in 1494 by the Treaty of Tordesillas. Under the Treaty of Tordesillas, Spain was given control of all non-Christian lands in a line from the north pole to the south pole (370 leagues west of the Cape Verde Islands). Portugal received control east of that line. This line affected the "New World" in that modern day Brazil jutted out over that line and Portugal received Brazil, while Spain gained control of all else in the Americas.

The Englishman, William Hawkins sailed to Africa's Guinea Coast in the early sixteenth century and got involved with the slave trade. France, Holland, Denmark, *et al.* thereafter got involved. By 1517, in an effort to save the Native Americans from annihilation by Spanish enslavement, Spanish Catholic Church Bishop Bartolome de Las Casas urged the Spanish crown to allow each Spaniard in the American colonies to import twelve Africans as laborers. Many regard this as the formal opening of the slave trade in the "New World." By the seventeenth century, the Dutch, French and English had taken control of the slave trade in the "New World." The same was true in the eighteenth century. Europeans' initial involvement in African slavery came as a result of pragmatism and greed. Upon the Europeans entering Africa, those who did not find gold and silver were disappointed. Unfortunately, Africa did not have readily available the precious metals for the Europeans to take back home to Europe in order to acquire instant wealth. These Europeans decided not to go back home empty handed; so they took back with them, among their various booties, human cargo. These captives, the human cargo, would be sold in Europe as household servants. Because the economy in Europe did not call for large field crops that could be upkept with an unskilled labor force, Africans taken to Europe could only serve as domestic laborers. The Christian church in Europe did not frown upon this practice because, after all, these slaves were heathens and through the practice of slavery they would be brought to God. For those still not accepting this practice, the Africans were then described as being not equal to the Europeans in their development, and therefore, one was enslaving not true men, but inferior beings. This Christian Nationalization soothed the conscious of those who felt some guilt.

Because of indigenous slavery, some African coastal tribes had a number of persons already enslaved. When the Europeans approached them in regard to selling these persons, the Africans did not really perceive of their slaves as really changing conditions. But, there was a real change. In indigenous slavery there had not been the color consciousness. Color was not a factor. But in European slavery, color became very important. The only persons at the time who were slaves held by the Europeans were black. In indigenous African slavery, a bondsman might earn his freedom and eventually marry the chief's daughter and might eventually become leader of the group. This could never happen in European slavery. In a previous chapter, one saw where this actually happened.

After the coastal settlements sold their native slave population, it became necessary to satisfy the European appetites for more slaves by moving this trade in human cargo farther and farther into the interior. Even though historians are still debating over this matter, it appears that sometimes interior groups were raided and the cargo was forced to reach the coastal holding pens by trekking to the coast. Slaves were sometimes marched to the coast in single files often referred to as coffles. This whole episode on the African coast was referred to as the African Trek. In the coffles, men, women and children may have been chained together with galling neck bands, leg irons, etc. and marched along, often to the coast. On the coast, the dehumanizing process that had begun with slave raids in the villages and on the trek in the coffles now continued. Sometimes all the captives were stripped naked so their new owners could inspect them to see what their new commodity was really like. In the more sophisticated holding pens, the cargo was separated by age and sex.

In the holding pens, the commodity might be sold in parcels to various ship owners in the region. So that the new owners might later be remembered, as well as to retain the thought of what the commodity looked like at the time of his/her sale, the commodity was branded. Though this was galling and very debasing to the Africans undergoing this experience, the Europeans understood that this was all practical and necessary. After all, when the slave was to make a six weeks to three months journey aboard ship, the slave might become emaciated and not look to be a very saleable commodity, but the brand would also tell what the slave formerly looked like when captured and could possibly look like again, if properly fed and fattened. The price of the commodity varied on the African coast in the holding pens. In the eighteenth century, an African might bring a price of twenty pounds sterling.

The slaves were now lined up to be taken to the ships waiting off shore. Large fishing boats might have been used to transport the slaves from the holding pens to the ships. This became very traumatic for many of the Africans who did not live on the coast because they had never seen this much water before. Some passed through a "door of no return" never to see African soil again.

When they arrived at the waiting ships the Africans sometime became aware that they were just more of the cargo being loaded on the said ship. When the cargo at this port was picked up, if the ship's capacity was not yet reached, other ports-of-call were made. This procedure might take another three weeks. In the meantime, the African slaves already on board the ships, being held as slaves, were in the holds of ships that were very foul in odor—defecation sometimes all over the floors. Blood, mucous, urine, vomit, etc., all created the scenery of these captives' world. It was true that on the high seas one could smell a slave ship long before such became visible. Ship owners demanded that ships be filled with twice or more the cargo capacity of slaves. After all, it was known a large amount of the cargo would die before reaching the New World. Schools of sharks would often follow slave ships because there was food (bodies of Africans) to be had all along the way. On some ships Africans were allocated the space of 2'x2'x6'. Of course, such a space allotment indicates that the cargo was lying on its back most of the time. Once the quota of the ship was filled, the journey to the New World, known generally in the seventeenth century to the nineteenth century as the "middle passage," began. The "middle passage" was that part of the enslavement process that took place on the Atlantic Ocean. The "middle passage" itself, the time of sailing from Africa to the "New World" might take from three weeks to three months. And, the dehumanizing process just became more intense.

On the initial voyages in the seventeenth century, the Africans might have been allowed the "freedom" to roam the ships, but not so on later voyages because too many had decided that they would rather face death than to leave the shores of Africa. So although the enslaved Africans could see the water around the ships and knew there were sharks, they preferred to dive in that water than leave Africa. Because the Europeans were losing too much of their investment this way, later ships were equipped with netting, which was comparable to modern day chicken wire. Eventually the cargo was placed under lock and key in the holds of the ships. So once again the captives faced putrid, rat infested cargo holds. The Europeans also developed a psychological warfare with the Africans: Some African captives thought that by facing death, their souls, at least, would return to the African shores. The Europeans realized that, again, too many deaths were cutting into their profits. Something had to be done, and it was. Dead Africans were beheaded, and the Africans observing these corpses were told that because these bodies had been beheaded, the souls could not find their way back to Africa.

On these voyages, the Africans might have been fed once a day, and that was in the afternoon. The African might have been fed in groups out of vat like containers. Each person had to "root hog root" or eventually die of starvation. The Europeans criticized these Africans for a lack of etiquette in eating, but at the same time the Europeans never thought they created the conditions under which the Africans were acting merely to survive. The food on these voyages consisted mostly of uncooked meal and water made into a mush called gruel; it was similar to modern day cush (cush-cush). Sometimes the meal to make this gruel had been picked up in South Carolina or another agriculture producing American colony and kept on the ships as ballast for four to six months prior to its use as fodder for the slaves. These ships had been in the warm tropical or semi-tropical regions of Africa. Therefore the meal often spoiled; worms and weavers also infested the meal. These worms became a regular part of the food for the slaves. This was fortunate! These worms provided the slaves with, perhaps, their only source of protein. Middling (bony fish) from New England, which had been used as ballast for the ship, after having been packed in barrels, was also fed to the slaves. Some voyages also fed their cargo beans which had also been packed in barrels and used as ship ballast. The "good" ship captains gave their cargo a variety of food. Now, one should not forget, even for the ship mates, these voyages were not bowls of cherries.

The final part of the enslavement process was "seasoning." Normally, when one refers to seasoning, one thinks about changing the composition of meat.

Well, that was exactly what this process was supposed to do: The enslaved Africans would eventually come to see themselves as property and no longer as human beings. Normally, for the enslaved destined for North America, "seasoning" took place in the West Indies. Seasoning might have lasted from six weeks up to a year. That all depended on the person being seasoned. One was not properly seasoned until one saw oneself as being totally dependent, helpless, and less than human. In seasoning, the slaves were conditioned to the food, the work, and most importantly, to their new position in life.

Some food in the West Indies was the same as the food one had in Africa. Plantain was tropical. There was also the similar, but different banana. Mango was another common fruit. Europeans did not eat the inside of cows, and especially not hogs. The chattel took this meat that was to be disposed and turned it into edible delicacies. Today, we know many of these dishes as "soul food"—hog hash, how maw, chitterlings, cow tripe, etc. The chattel also gathered certain wild vegetables to supplement their diets such as pepper grass, poke salad, etc.

Although punishment helped in learning how to properly perform tasks, many of these Africans held in slavery were already familiar with agricultural labor. They realized that in thinning out the crops, not every stalk of vegetation should be cut, but certain ones should be left standing. The slaves could not run away while working alone in the fields because on their heads they wore bells held in place by leather straps. The bell contraption resembled a small Christmas tree.

But the real role of punishment might have consisted of licks across the back laid on with a braided cowhide whip. Sometimes the punishment became even more sophisticated and vile. For certain crimes, especially those threatening the master class or those signaling that the slave had not accepted his position as a helpless slave, punishment might have consisted of: (1) being severely whipped on the back, and then having salt rubbed in the welts to increase the pain; (2) being tied by the arms to a tree branch with the feet off the ground, and having weights then tied to the legs. (This latter method was used so that the captive would not be permanently damaged, but once the numbness wore off that was produced in this state, immense pain set in all over the body; (3) being tied down with wet leather bands to stakes driven into the ground. Once the sun began to dry the leather straps, the leather contracted causing unbearable pain. If one chose, this punishment could be used to kill the victim. (One is used to seeing this in Hollywood produced movies with the Indians placed in the role of vile fiend perpetrating this crime.) (4) Then there was always just plain killing. Sometimes killing would be done just to destroy the captive, but often it was done to set an example for the remaining captives. Burning alive or quartering alive (taking four horses and tying one to each foot and each hand and then whipping the animals to pull was done to really deliver a message.

However, if one made it through seasoning, one was then ready to be sold to mainland America—(what would become the United States and other countries). Not all Africans underwent West Indian seasoning, some African novices were brought directly into the American British colonies.

SUGGESTED READINGS:

Lerone Bennett, Jr., *Before the Mayflower.*

Benjamin Brawley, *A Short History of the American Negro.*

Basil Davidson, *A History of East and Central Africa.*

John P. Davis, *The American Negro Reference Book.*

Dawda Faal, *Peoples and Empires of Senegambia: Senegambia in History—AD 1000–1900.*

John Hope Franklin, *From Slavery to Freedom.*

Greene, Lorenzo J. *The Negro in Colonial New England.*

Roland Oliver and J. D. Fage, *A Short History of Africa.*

Benjamin Quarles, *The Negro in the Making of America.*

Saunders Redding, *Americans from Africa: They Came in Chains.*

STUDY GUIDE 4

1 *YES/NO*? Did pre-European slavery exist in West Africa?

2 What made indigenous African slavery so radically different from European slavery?

3 According to European historians, who became the noted African on the voyage of Christopher Columbus's *Nina*?

4 Name the European given credit for having "discovered" America.

5 Name the European given credit for having first sighted the Pacific Ocean.

6 Name the moor on the Cabeza DeVaca expedition who went on to gain fame for his escapades in the southwestern part of what is now the United States.

7 In what century did Portugal begin exporting Africans to Europe?

8 What was the name of the agreement that Portugal made to supply the Spanish colonies with African slave laborers?

9 What 1493 European agreement divided the unknown world (unknown by and according to Europeans) between Spain and Portugal?

10 What 1494 provision "legalized" the above (**9**) agreement?

11 What American country did Portugal come to control as a result of question **9**?

12 Bartolome de LasCasas held what position around 1517?

13 Why did Europe not develop a great need for African bondsmen?

14 *YES/NO?* Did the European church frown upon the practice of holding slaves?

15 What name was given to the files by which interior slaves marched to the coast?

16 How long was the journey, for African bondsmen, to the "New World"?

17 What was an average price for a coastal West African slave in the eighteenth century?

18 The journey of the African "slaves" from Africa to the Americas from the seventeenth to nineteenth centuries was known by what name?

19 What name was given to the meal and water mush some Africans ate on the voyage to the Americas from Africa?

20 "Seasoning" conditioned one to what three things?

5

The Diaspora

The presence of Africans in the "New World" might have predated Christopher Columbus by about 2,000 years. Remains or sculptures with African features have been found in South America, Central America, and North America. By the year 1492, African conquest and imperialism were ending in Southwestern Europe, and Columbus was exploring the Caribbean. Myth has it that the people of Hispaniola informed Columbus of Africans who had visited their land many years before him. One might conclude, as William D. Piersen does in his volume, *From Africa To America,* that Africans came to the Americas in three waves:

1) Explorers from Africa sailing for African nations
2) Africans as parties of European exploring expeditions
3) Agricultural laborers (persons held in slavery)

Africans were brought not only to what would become the United States, but to many other would be countries such as: the Caribbean, Central American, North American, and South American. But while the Christian Europeans were exporting Africans to the "New World," Arabs (Muslims) were exporting Africans, those held as slaves in the central part of the continent, to markets in Arabia, India, Iran, and elsewhere. According to Robert Fogel and Stanley Engermann in their book, *Time On The Cross: The Economics of American Negro Slavery,* although from about the middle of the fifteenth century to nearly three-fourth of the nineteenth century, nearly ten million Africans held in slavery were exported. Only six percent of all Africans exported from Africa came to what became the United States. On the other hand, Brazil received nearly forty percent, the British Caribbean Islands received about seventeen percent; the French Caribbean Islands about seventeen percent; Spanish America about seventeen percent; and the Danish, Dutch and Swedish Caribbean Islands about six percent. While what became the United States received over half a million Africans, Cuba, Haiti and Jamaica received more. And, of course, Brazil received about six times as many as the would be United States. However, receiving over a hundred thousand Africans were not only the above mentioned countries, but also Barbados, Colombia, Guadeloupe, Guyana and Surinam, Martinique, Mexico, and Venezuela. Today, one would be hard pressed to find a person of pure African ancestry in Mexico, but strangely enough, prior to 1620, according to Colin Palmer in his book, *The First Passage,* most Africans who arrived in the Americas went to Mexico. The Latins were not nearly as race conscious as the Anglos. They easily interbred with the Africans. Also, in the non-Anglo Saxon colonies, the inhabitants from "back home" (Europe) tended to be all males, and this lack of females helped spur interracial breeding.

Portugal was the first of the European countries to begin exporting slaves from Africa. She was followed by Spain. England followed suit in the mid-sixteenth century. No matter what island or mainland colony Africans were taken to, they were not robots that simply operated on receiving white thoughts in a purified form. They were beings who took orders from their white masters and/or compatriots, sometimes changing these radically but always giving them back in an "African way" that made the orders work best for them the Africans. Thus, they sometimes came up with inventions, and at other times, they came up with lasting ideas that helped shape their immediate societies.

European conquest in the Americas opened a wealth of mining and vast agricultural lands. The Europeans only needed laborers who could withstand the heat and diseases of their "New World" region. According to Piersen, of all persons held in slavery and taken out of Africa, fourteen percent were children, thirty percent were young women, and fifty-six percent were young men between the ages of ten and twenty-four years of age.

The price for Africans held in slavery fluctuated. Supply and demand governed the market to a degree, but price also depended on the personal agenda of the African middle men. Goods such as guns, textiles, hardware, liquor, shell money, etc., were used in exchange for the bondspeople. According to J. D. Fage in his book, *A History of Africa,* in the eighteenth century on the Guinea Coast, the average price for a bondsman ranged between the equivalent of today's money of $75 to $125. The norm for the Africans involved in the slave trade was not to sell their fellow countrymen, but outsiders.

In the "New World," Africans helped to clear the land, plant and harvest crops, build fortifications and homes, etc. Whatever was needed, they helped to fulfill that need. By the beginning of the sixteenth century, the use of the term black had become almost synonymous with slave. The first European country with colonies in the "New World" to make use of these Africans was Spain. The Spanish had a great need for laborers in their colonies and who better to fulfill that need than the Africans.

Although not necessarily enforced, the Africans brought to Mexico and all countries southward (mainland Central and South Africa), and eastward (the Caribbean Islands) the Africans were now under a slave code or group of laws commonly referred to as the *Partidas (Las Siete Partidas*). These laws existed in the Spanish and Portuguese colonies. The laws outlines the rules under which the slaves would work and live, and the rights of the bondsman. Different from the Anglos who lived in what became the United States, the Portuguese and Spanish developed their laws after living many years with the persons they held in slavery. Under the English, the Africans were simply property and had no real protection under their *Black Codes.* But the Spanish and Portuguese laws accorded the Africans protection by stating how a master was expected to treat the slave. Furthermore, the Spanish and Portuguese laws outlined ways by which Africans held in bondage might acquire their freedom. But as time passed, the laws were added to and became more rigid. In part, this came because the masters felt this need to have more and more protection from the larger and more dominant servile class of Africans and Indians.

Chronologically in history, when we look at the history of the African community in the "New World," we can understand the "why" as to why additions were made to these laws. In 1444, kidnapped Africans were taken to Lisbon as slaves. But not until 1502 or thereabouts was African slavery introduced into Hispaniola. And it seemed very soon afterwards, Africans began to show their dislike for the system. In 1522, the first recorded slave revolt occurred on Hispaniola.

Socially, there could have not have been a real African "community" when the Africans were first brought to the "New World" by the Spanish. The Africans came from different ethnic groups and in many cases, did not even speak the same language. When the eventual Cuba imported a hundred thousand more Africans than did the eventual United States, one wonders why the African American population today exceeds the Afro-Cuban population in real numbers. Fogel and Engermann point out that life was much harsher in the Caribbean Islands than on the mainlands. Africans were exposed to many more diseases. There was dysentery, malaria, smallpox, tetanus, yellow fever, etc. There was poorer food and more intense work. One wonders about the role of two other possible factors. Could the initial population have been basically male only? And, even when there were females, how much emphasis was placed on procreation and creating a domestic slave population. Secondly one wonders, if the masters felt so driven to make a profit that they held to the theory that it was cheaper to buy another slave and work the present one to death, than to humanely treat the current one?

Though these were Catholic countries in the Caribbean, Central, and South America and though the Catholic Church was more familiar with slaves than the Protestant Churches, the number of Catholic Churches and clergy were fewer than in Protestant North America. Therefore, less attention was paid to the spiritual care of the individual bondsmen. Non-protestant area held bondsmen were allowed to retain more of their native African religious practices. Plus, the Catholic Churches themselves held a number of slaves.

In a little more than a decade of experience (1528–1538), the most celebrated moor/African made historical exploits in the southwestern part of what would become the United States. His name was Estéban/Estevanico or "Little Steven." Estéban had become a survivor from the Pánfilo de Narvaez expedition. Unfortunately, he was killed by Zuni Indians in 1539.

Slave revolts continued to occur. In 1537, a slave plot was discovered in Mexico. Increasing the number of African slaves, in 1542, the Spanish crown abolished Indian slavery. This came as a result of the urging of men like Catholic Bishop Bartolomeo de Las Casas. His mission was to save the Indians from complete destruction, but it opened the way for the exclusive use of black African bondsmen.

In 1550 the first African bondsmen arrived in Brazil at Salvador (Salvador de Bahia, Brazil). Two years later (1552), Brazil's neighbor, Venezuela, experienced a slave revolt. In 1595, the colonizer of Venezuela, Spain, granted its first *Asciento,* the right for other non-Spanish flag flying vessels to supply its "New World" colonies with Africans held in slavery. In 1612, the Spanish held colony, Mexico was rocked with a slave revolt at Mexico City. In this same country, in 1617, San Lorenzo de Los Negros received a charter from the government of Mexico becoming the first all-black settlement in the Americas.

Much of what became the United States changed because of the 1619 incident at Jamestown, Virginia. In August, twenty Africans were purchased from a Dutch captain and became the first permanent African settlers in the English mainland colonies.

The Danish islands of both St. Thomas and St. John experienced slave uprisings. In Portuguese Brazil, African bondsmen set up their own country, the Palmares Republic, between 1630 and 1697. Things became so hectic in Jamaica during the 1700s that a treaty was made with the maroons (Africans that had broken the chains of slavery and formed their own community). A much larger happening occurred on January 1, 1804. Jean Jacques Dessalines proclaimed the country of Haiti free. Thus, this became the first Republic in the "New World" controlled by Africans. Things seemed to have been looking up for Africans in the "New World." On February 6, 1820, the *Mayflower of Liberia* set sail from New York and landed in Sierre Leone. This began the resettlement of black Americans back in their African homeland. Then, on July 26, 1847, Liberia was declared a free and independent country. For African Americans held in bondage, the "day of the Jubilo" (freedom from slavery) arrived in 1865 with the ending of the American Civil War.

Brazil abolished slavery in 1888; Cuba abolished slavery in 1886, but clouds appeared on the horizon in the 1880s. In 1884, the Berlin Conference partitioned Africa among the European countries. As a partial result of slavery, Africa had become ripe for colonialism of the European governments.

Because of sugar, by the beginning of the nineteenth century, slavery had ceased to be profitable in the West Indian Islands. The slave market then shifted to the mainlands. By 1792, Denmark abolished the slave trade. Great Britain abolished the trade in 1807. And by 1808, the United States was following suit by closing her ports to the entry of anymore African slaves. By the second half of the nineteenth century, France had abolished slavery in 1848. The Dutch did so in 1863. The United States abolished slavery in 1865. And most of the South American countries abolished it at the time of their revolution for independence.

The need for laborers in mining and agricultural enterprises had opened the doors to African slavery in the "New World." African slaves had initially been used in the copper and gold mines of Hispaniola. Then, when silver was found in Mexico, they were used there. Sugarcane added to the use of the slave laborers. But, as Benjamin Quarles noted, the commercial revolution and the industrial revolution caused it to cease to be profitable any longer.

Suggested Reading:

Fage, J. D. *A History of Africa.*

Fogel, Robert W. and Stanley Engermann. *Time on the Cross: The Economics of American Negro Slavery.*

Franklin, John Hope. *From Slavery to Freedom.*

Palmer, Colin A. *The First Passage. Slaves of the White Gods: Blacks in Mexico, 1570—1650.*

Piersen, William D. *From Africa to America: African American History from the Colonial Era to the Early Republic, 1526–1790.*

STUDY GUIDE 5A

1–3 What were the three waves under which Africans might have come to the "New World"?

4–5 Give the two western monotheisms that were involved in the African slave trade.

6–8 What specific markets are mentioned in this chapter to which the Arabs exported African bondsmen?

9–10 Name the authors of *Time on the Cross: The Economics of American Negro Slavery.*

11 Give the percentage of Africans that, according to the above mentioned book, were exported to the United States from the sixteenth to the nineteenth centuries.

12–16 Give the percentage of Africans that the above mentioned book states were exported to:

12 Brazil

13 British Caribbean Islands

14 French Caribbean Islands

15 Spanish America

16 Danish, Dutch, and Swedish Caribbean Islands

17–28 Name some contemporary countries mentioned in this chapter to which Africans were exported as slaves.

29 Name the author of *The First Passage.*

30 Were Latins or Anglos more race conscious?

31 Name the first European country that began exporting bondsmen from Africa.

32–36 Name some European countries that engaged in African slavery.

37 What percentage of children were exported from Africa as bondspersons?

STUDY GUIDE 5B

1 What percentage of young women were exported from Africa as bondspersons?

2 What percentage of men?

3–7 Name some of the goods exchanged for bondsmen on the African coast.

8–12 What kind of labor was performed by the Africans in the "New World"?

13 Why were Africans initially needed in the "New World"?

14 What was the reference for laws under Portugal and Spain of the code under which bondsmen lived?

15 What were the laws generally called in the United States under which bondsmen generally lived?

16–18 Give some reasons why the Caribbean Islands population tended to be more stagnant than that of places like the United States.

19 Give the name of the Moor/African who explored the southwestern area of what would become the United States.

20 Name the Catholic clergyman that opened the way for the use of mass African bondsmen while trying to save the Indians.

21 What name was given to the right to carry African bondsmen to the Spanish "New World" colonies?

22 On a permanent basis, when did Africans first arrive in the English mainland North American colonies?

23 In what country was the Palmares Republic established?

24–28 Name some of the contemporary countries that experienced slave uprisings.

29 Jean Jacques Dessalines proclaimed the independence of what country?

30 In 1847, what African nation declared its independence?

31 In what year did the United States abolish slavery?

32 In what year did Cuba abolish slavery?

33 In what year did Brazil abolish slavery?

34 What 1884 Conference led to the partition of Africa?

35–36 In what two general economic pursuits were bondsmen needed in the Americas?

6

Eighteenth Century African American Accomplishments

At the beginning of the eighteenth century, slavery as a legal institution in the United States had been in existence for about four decades. By then, a vast majority of African Americans were already serving a lifetime of bondage. The various southern states had taken practical steps to ensure that their slaves did not enjoy any rights and privileges whatsoever. Thus, such rights as that of suing in courts, serving as witnesses, owning property and even the right to marry, were systematically nullified through a series of laws enacted by the various state assemblies between the 1660s and 1705. In the latter year, all existing laws dealing with slavery were consolidated into a single act which has been described as the Slave Code. It was under the incarcerating effects of this code that African American bondsmen were to continue living for the rest of the eighteenth and the better half of the nineteenth centuries, respectively.

Not all African Americans lived as bondsmen during the period under consideration. There was a small minority of them who were regarded as "Free Negroes." The status of these so-called free Negroes was, however, adversely affected by the increasing severity of the slave laws. Thus, for instance, in 1705, a statute was passed forbidding Negro ownership of white Christian servants. The statute also declared automatically free any white Christian servant whose master married a Negro. Such legislation as these directly led to a deterioration of the status of the free Negro population.

In spite of the degrading and restrictive condition of their existence, a number of African Americans recorded several outstanding accomplishments during the eighteenth century. Their struggle to achieve has been nothing short of heroic in view of the fact that all avenues to knowledge and wealth were shut against them on account of their color. Unlike all other ethnic groups in America, the African Americans have had to contend with extraordinary odds in their bid to prove themselves equally capable of achieving greatness. The various accomplishments of African Americans were characterized by their desire to forge a separate independent existence of civilized thought and creativity. This struggle for independence produced outstanding achievements in several areas of intellectual endeavor, including: poetry, autobiography, science and mathematics, astronomy, survey and medicine. Blacks also extended this struggle to cover the critical areas of economic independence, the establishment of separate educational and religious institutions, benevolent and fraternal organizations, etc.

In this chapter, there shall be an examination of these areas of black American accomplishments by focusing on a number of outstanding African Americans who have made significant contributions towards the struggle for the independence of their race.

Literary Accomplishments

Despite the fact that African Americans were denied opportunities to receive formal education, there emerged during the 18th century a number of them who achieved remarkable feats in their respective areas of specialization. The first black author was a New York bondsman known as **Jupiter Hammon**. Despite his handicapped situation in slavery, Jupiter's poem—*An Evening Thought: Salvation by Christ, with Penitential Cries*—was good enough to be published in 1760.

Nearly three decades later, another significant work by a black man was published in the form of an autobiography. It was the life history of **Olaudah Equiano** (or Gustavus Vassa as he was later referred). His book was titled *The Interesting Narrative of the Life of Olaudah Equiano, or Gustavus Vassa, the African* (1789). This publication turned out to be most valuable as a source of information on traditional socio-cultural life of the Igbos in the southeastern part of modern Nigeria. It also provides the reader with intimate accounts of the horrors of slavery, including the capture by kidnapping of innocent Africans; their march from the interior to the coast where they were sold to strange white creatures (whites), and their journey into the new world. It is also an autobiographical account of the deplorable condition of slaves in the West Indies and the United States.

Perhaps the most popular pioneer black author was **Phillis Wheatley (c. 1754–1784)**. The true significance of Wheatley's accomplishment lay in the fact that she made her remarkable contribution to scholarship at a time when few women (or men for that matter) read books. It was at this time that she published her *Poems on Various Subjects, Religious and Moral* (1773). This work has been rightly identified as the first volume by a black woman and the second book by an American woman. Although she did not write from the perspective of a black woman dedicated to the liberation of her race, Phillis Wheatley symbolized the truth embedded in the American Declaration of Independence which, among other things, underscored the equality of all human races. As a young slave girl (she was only seven years old in 1761 when her master, John Wheatley purchased her off the auction block), she did not enjoy the advantage of formal school education. Yet, by dint of hard labor and determination, and in less than two years of her stay with the Wheatleys, Phillis had attained a remarkable degree of proficiency in the art of reading and writing. Approximately ten years later, Phillis began to attract national and international attention for her brilliant performance as a poet. One of her early poems was dedicated to George Washington in celebration of the latter's appointment as the Commander-In-Chief of the American army. Although the president and the rest of the reading American public recognized and applauded the poetical talents of "Miss Phillis," it was in Britain that the young author found instant publicity for her works through an English publisher.

Phillis Wheatley's outstanding achievement did not only prove that all men are created equal, it also served to debunk the myth that Africans and peoples of African descent are incapable of any significant contribution to human progress, a Eurocentric view point which was invented to justify and rationalize Europe's imperialistic and exploitative designs for Africa. Phillis was a shining example of those colored people of unmixed African blood who according to Martin R. Delany, "Shone the brightest in the earliest period of our history."

Mathematics/Astronomy/Navigation

Another outstanding African American of this period was **Benjamin Banneker (1731–1806)**. His grandmother was Molly Welsh, an indentured servant who, following her freedom, got married to one of the two slaves she procured and eventually emancipated. One of the four children born to this interracial couple was Banneker's mother, Mary, who, like her mother, also married an African American.

Unlike Phillis Wheatley, Banneker enjoyed the privilege of attending a local school with black and white children in Maryland. Like Phillis Wheatley, however, Banneker developed a keen interest in learning, especially in the field of mathematics and astronomy. Banneker easily demonstrated such remarkable proficiency in his chosen field of specialization that he was appointed to serve on the Commission of the United States Civil Engineers which was charged with the responsibility of surveying the new national capital city of Washington, D. C. Banneker's invaluable contribution to the success of that project obviously attracted much attention from the general public at a time when the prevalent stereotypical view of the black race was that they were devoid of any significant mental endowment. This was a viewpoint to which one of the nation's most notable founding fathers, Thomas Jefferson, publicly subscribed. As one of the local newspapers, the *Georgetown Weekly Ledger* rightly observed, Banneker's outstanding performance on that prestigious commission was a conclusive proof that Mr. Jefferson's view was absolutely without foundation.

In addition to being recognized as an expert surveyor, Benjamin Banneker distinguished himself as a reputable astronomer when, in 1792, he began to issue an annual almanac which was comparable to Benjamin Franklin's *Poor Richard's Almanac.* His devotion to the study of mathematics also earned him so much national recognition that his expert opinions were constantly being solicited by other eminent mathematicians across the country.

Banneker did not restrict himself to purely academic endeavors only. Unlike Phillis Wheatley, he turned his attention to the contemporary social problems confronting his race and boldly assumed the role of political activist and protest leader. He specifically pointed out the contradiction and hypocrisy implied in the nation's struggle for political independence from Britain on the one hand, and the flagrant violation of his people's fundamental human rights and privileges, on the other. He did not mince words in his denunciation of this social ill in a letter he addressed to Thomas Jefferson in 1791. In his opinion, Jefferson's participation in the enslavement of black people was not only fraudulent and violent, but also criminal. Banneker's fearlessness as a political activist, coupled with his outstanding intellectual accomplishments as an astronomer and surveyor earned him a well-deserved place on the honor roll of "Founding Fathers and Mothers" of African America.

In the area of exploration and navigation, it is often not well appreciated that African Americans were actively involved in opening up the new world for settlement in the early days of this nation's history. Even long before the eighteenth century, Africans were known to have taken part in the much celebrated discovery of America by Christopher Columbus. It is on record that one of the ships used by Columbus had for its captain one **Pedro Alonso Nino**. Perhaps the best known black explorer during the period covered in this chapter was **Jean Baptiste Point du Sable**, a black man who came along with French explorers to New Orleans in 1765. He was also known to be a successful trapper and explorer around Lake Michigan. He is popularly recognized for his pioneering effort in opening a trading post on the lake's shore. It was this trading post that later developed to become the modern city of Chicago.

MEDICINE

In the field of medicine, African Americans in the days of slavery had established for themselves a high reputation as seasoned physicians whose services were always in popular demand not only within their own community, but also among the white slave owners all over the antebellum South. It was in Boston, Massachusetts, however, that one of the most spectacular medical feats was performed through the expert advice of an African slave named **Onesimus**. Onesimus was a bondsman of the noted clergyman, Cotton Mather. In April, 1721, there was an outbreak of small pox epidemic which claimed about 844 lives in Boston before it subsided. Strangely enough, however, none of Cotton Mather's slaves died of the disease. This aroused the minister's curiosity. Upon investigation, Onesimus attributed his immunity to a traditional African remedy which he prescribed for dealing with the Boston epidemic. Onesimus' preventive medical prescription consisted of injecting the blood of a small pox patient into a healthy person's blood stream through an incision made on the skin. According to Onesimus, this procedure was capable of guaranteeing a life-long immunity from small pox for the person who underwent the treatment.

The traditional prescription was so appealing to Rev. Mather that he tried to sell the idea to Dr. John Woodward of the British Royal Society and ten other Boston physicians. All of those contacted by Mather in writing rebuffed him and his strange medical idea. He then turned to one Dr. Zabdiel

Boylston who readily embraced this novel idea. On June 4, 1721, Dr. Boylston inoculated his six year old son in accordance with Onesimus' prescription. It was a courageous step on the part of Boylston in view of the fact that the majority of the people categorically insisted that this inoculation was bound to further spread the killer disease. In fact, records indicate that infuriated mobs attacked the homes of Mather and Boylston. Nevertheless, both of them remained undaunted. Eventually, 280 people were inoculated and only six died! This was a clear vindication of Rev. Mather and a convincing proof of the efficacy of Onesimus' African prescription. The tragedy of the African American experience in slavery, however, is that, whereas nobody knows where Onesimus was buried, today, an epitaph on Boylston's tomb in Boston reads that he "first introduced inoculation into America."

Another African American medical genius of the eighteenth century was **James Durham.** In 1778, at the age of twenty-six, Durham was acclaimed to be the most learned physician in New Orleans. He had been a male nurse. Through the encouragement of his owner, he saved up enough money to purchase his freedom. Eventually he became the first African American, on record, to practice medicine. From New Orleans, he moved to Philadelphia. Dr. Durham was not only a well qualified medical practitioner, he was also highly proficient in speaking English, French and Spanish. His professional efficiency was readily acknowledged by the head of the medical profession in the country at that time, Dr. Benjamin Rush. To the latter's utter amazement, Durham proved to be more knowledgeable than him so far as healing of disease was concerned.

Independent Organizations

The genius of African Americans found expression not only in literary pursuits and medicine, but also in the founding of religious and economic institutions whose ultimate goal was to achieve the much desired freedom and independence that had for long been denied to them. Ironically, it was the Christian church that turned out to be the bulwark of racial discrimination during the period of slavery. It is therefore not surprising that the African American strategy for gaining independence involved an assault on the white dominated church during the revolutionary years. As early as 1774, African American slaves had begun to petition for a much needed opportunity to worship their God in an atmosphere devoid of the master's repressive control, and therefore, an environment conducive to the proper worship of God. Their protest soon began to yield concrete result in the form of the establishment of separate black churches, especially among the Baptists in the South. Several of these were a church at Silver Bluff, South Carolina, the *Harrison Street Baptist Church of Petersburg,* Virginia (1776) and the *Negro Baptist Church, Savannah, Georgia* (1779).

The struggle for independence among black Methodists owed much to the pioneering efforts of **Richard Allen** and **Absalom Jones**, two of the highly revered founding fathers of African America. **Richard Allen** was the most famous of the African American preachers of his day. His preaching career began while he was still a bondsman. Upon his emancipation, he continued to pursue his evangelical efforts with such vigor and enthusiasm that he soon gained recognition as a great preacher within the Methodist Episcopal Church. Through his efforts, the black membership of St. George's Methodist Episcopal Church in Philadelphia increased so much so that overcrowding at the Church became a real problem which necessitated the rebuilding of the Church. Given the numerical strength and sincere commitment of the African American members of the congregation, it is reasonable to assume that their contribution toward the building project must have been truly significant. Yet, in the new seating arrangement made after the completion of the building project, the blacks were made to vacate their seats on the main floor and henceforth occupy certain gallery seats above. This clear demonstration of racial discrimination in the House of God effectively sowed the seed of confrontation which was to erupt at a later date.

The occasion for the inevitable confrontation was a dramatic incident that occurred during a regular worship service in November, 1787. Allen and his colleagues had apparently occupied gallery seats which were not assigned to them. This was an "error" which an observant but overzealous trustee of the Church would not tolerate. Hence the attempted forcible ejection of the black worshippers. In a spontaneous reaction to this disgraceful incident, Richard Allen and his followers withdrew enmass from the white-dominated Church and proceeded to develop their existing *Free African Society* (founded earlier on April 12, 1787) into two separate black churches, namely, *St. Thomas' African Episcopal Church* which was dedicated on July 17, 1794, with **Absalom Jones** as Pastor, and *Bethel African Methodist Episcopal Church*, founded on July 24, 1794, under the leadership of **Richard Allen**. Whereas St. Thomas' remained affiliated to the white dominated Episcopal Church (which continued to discriminate against blacks in matters as attendance at annual conferences and membership of governing boards), Richard Allen's Bethel Church was established to guarantee for black people true independence from white domination.

The dramatic withdrawal of African worshippers from St. George's marked the beginning of the Independent Black Church Movement in America. The peculiar characteristic features of this movement can be identified in the original statement of purpose adopted by the Free African Society. From all indications, the Society was formed primarily to meet both the religious and social needs of its members. This pattern of religious commitment with a double focus was to characterize the Black Church henceforth. The revolutionary movement initiated by Allen rapidly spread from Philadelphia to other cities: Baltimore (1787), Salem City, NJ (1800), Wilmington, Delaware (1813), etc. It was the union of these various independent churches that gave birth to the *African Methodist Episcopal Church (AME Church)*, which was inaugurated in April, 1816, with Richard Allen as its first Bishop.

The struggle for religious independence among African Americans was complemented by an equally strategic struggle to attain economic self-sufficiency through the establishment of social and fraternal organizations. The leading black pioneer in this regard during the period was **Prince Hall** of Boston, Massachusetts. A leather-dresser by profession, Prince Hall followed in the footsteps of Richard Allen and Absalom Jones by seeking to carve out a separate identity for blacks within white dominated institutions. The prevailing climate of racial relations at this time was rather hostile to the idea of accepting blacks as equals in any given institution. Thus, Prince Hall's attempt to obtain a charter from American Masons for establishing a black lodge in Boston was rebuffed. In his frustration, he turned to England for assistance and there, in 1784, he obtained an English charter for a Boston Lodge.

Four years earlier, in 1780, African Americans in Newport, Rhode Island, had formed the African Union Society which represented the first black mutual benefit society, many of which were to spring up all over the country soon after Prince Hall's pioneering example of 1784. These societies were organized to provide African Americans in the urban centers with services and functions which individuals could not possibly afford. These included such things as—burial of the dead, care of the sick, and support of widows and orphans. As has been indicated earlier in the case of the Philadelphia Free African Society, it was organized with the express purpose of taking care of the sick, orphans and widows. This, and many other societies (like the Daughters of Ethiopia, the Angola Society, the Sons of Africa, African Lodges of the Masons) deliberately labeled themselves as "African" in order to establish their unique African cultural identity.

The emergent black leadership, both in the church and in the various mutual aid societies, quickly realized the critical importance of providing educational opportunities for the children of emancipated slaves. The examples of Richard Allen and Absalom Jones were there to illustrate the truth about education as the key to success in any chosen career. Accordingly, these leaders took the initiative to open schools for black children in several cities. Richard Allen opened a day school for children as well as a night school for adults in Bethel AME Church in Philadelphia. On his part, Prince Hall opened a school for black children in his home in Boston. Other pioneers in this venture included Quakers like Anthony Benezet (in Philadelphia), and the New York Manumission Society which, beginning in November, 1787, organized the famous Free African Schools of New York.

In the light of the struggle for civil rights which seemed to have come to be identified in people's mind with the 1950s and 1960s, it is informative to note that, even as early as the period under consideration in this chapter, black leaders were not content with simply establishing schools for black children. Rather, they vigorously pursued the task of providing quality education for black and white children at the same time. This goal apparently could only be achieved where there was equal opportunities for black and white children to receive the same type of education. In other words, institutionalized racial discrimination must be removed from the educational system of the country. Accordingly, a strong campaign for equal educational rights was mounted by black leaders of this early national period. This campaign for equal education was led by Prince Hall and a group of Boston blacks who jointly filed a public petition on October 17, 1787, complaining bitterly about racial discrimination in the provision of educational facilities for black children in the State of Massachusetts.

The struggle for civil rights at this time covered other areas of deprivation suffered by black people. Among these was the crucial issue of voting rights. This was the subject of a protest movement led by Paul Cuffe who was barred from the ballot box in Dartmouth, Massachusetts, in 1780. In protest, he refused to pay taxes and preceded to file a petition which, after a long controversy, led to an all important decision that "taxation without representation" was tyranny in America—a clear echo of the revolutionary slogan which preceded the American War of Independence.

It is customary these days to associate the African American struggle for civil rights with the much publicized events of the 1950s and 1960s. This tendency among scholars and the general public is inescapable in view of the fact that those events are among the most adequately documented events of black American History. However, one must reiterate at this point that the fact the accomplishments recorded since the 1950s were made possible by the foundation already laid in less dramatic events, some of which have been chronicled in this chapter. Indeed, the accomplishments of African Americans in the eighteenth century are nothing short of heroic. Many blacks convincingly demonstrated their intellectual capabilities at a time when they were written off by the rest of society as biologically incapable of any significant contribution to human progress.

SUGGESTED READINGS

Richard Barksdale & Kenneth Kinnamon (eds.), *Black Writers of America: A Comprehensive Anthology:* NY, 1972.

Lerone Bennett, Jr., *Before the Mayflower.*

W. R. George Carol, *Segregated Sabbaths: Richard Allen and the Rise of Independent Black Churches, 1760–1840*: N Y, 1973.

Martin R. Delany, *The Condition, Elevation, Emigration and Destiny of the Colored People of the United States*: Baltimore, 1852.

Ezekiel Ete, "Onesimus: 'The True Father of Inoculation in America,'" *African News Weekly,* February 25, 1994, p. 19.

Philip S. Foner, *History of Black Americans: From Africa to the Emergence of the Cotton Kingdom*: Westport, 1975.

Gayraud S. Wilmore, *Black Religion and Black Radicalism*: Garden City, NY, 1973.

Study Guide 6

1 What became the name for all existing laws dealing with slavery that were incorporated as a unit after 1705?

2–4 What were some basic rights denied African Americans under the slave codes?

5 While most African Americans were bondsmen (slaves), how were others legally classified?

6 Name the first known black author.

7 Give the title of one of the works of the above (**6**) person.

8 Give the native name of Gustavus Vassa.

9 What is the title of Vassa's autobiography?

10 Who was the first known published black poetess?

11 Name her (**10**) first published work.

12 Who was the black man on the Commission that helped layout Washington, D. C.?

13–14 In what two academic areas did he (**12**) have special talents?

15 Who wrote *Poor Richard's Almanac*?

16 What black man first settled at what became Chicago?

17 What African American helped to introduce smallpox inoculation to the country?

18 Name the first known African American physician.

19–21 What were the locations of three of those early black Baptist churches?

22–23 Name the two black leaders in Philadelphia that helped establish the separate black church in 1794.

24 Expand the abbreviation A. M. E.

25 Who began black Masonry in America?

7

Colonial America to the United States of America

The earliest known African American history was recorded in the south. Initially the Africans arriving in the British North American mainland colonies landed at Jamestown, Virginia in August, 1619. These twenty "Negars" were not characterized as slaves (as they would later be known), but were called indentured servants. Before the English could accept the idea of slavery, a certain mind set had to develop. And that mind set came near the mid-1660s. As long as the English deemed it a sin to own other men, and with their thoughts of the Africans as "men," they could not readily engage in slave holding. First these Africans would have to be cast as sub-human, benefiting from Christianity as slaves. Second, there would have to be an economic necessity for slavery. In colonial America, there was always a shortage of "hands" (labor force), but a staple crop where unskilled "hands" could be used did not occur until the next century.

Virginia and her southern colonial neighbors led the way in making laws that abridged the rights of African imports; marriage laws were among the first items legislated. According to Benjamin Brawley, "slavery" was first mentioned in the codified laws of the various colonies for the first time as indicated in the chart.

Colony	Years of Initial Laws Pertaining to Africans as Slaves*	Colony	Years of Initial Laws Pertaining to Africans as Slaves*
Massachusetts	1641	South Carolina	1682
Connecticut	1650	Pennsylvania	1688
Rhode Island	1652	New Hampshire	1714
Virginia	1661	North Carolina	1715
Maryland	1663–64	Delaware	1721
New Jersey	1664	Georgia	1755
New York	1665		

*Such law might have prohibited or condoned slavery, but the true concept of slavery was mentioned.

Whether the African coming to America was transported to the southern colonies or another area of the colonies really made a difference. For the southern colonies, agriculture became the key element in its economic life. Therefore, a great need for helping hands existed. Also, the religious orientation of the people did not "rail" against slavery. Thus, slavery became an essential part of the southern way of life. In the agricultural regions of other areas, there was a need for additional hands, but religion, especially with Quakers in the middle colonies, tempered the use of Africans as slaves. New England's environment did not support agriculture. But, due to the law prohibiting Africans brought to these colonies from being shipped elsewhere, Africans accumulated in the maritime colonies. Therefore, they might have become domestic servants, laborers in the various New England industries, fishermen, etc.

As early as 1638, there seems to have been Africans in New England. The ship *Desire* landed at least two blacks at Boston Harbor that year. These persons, too, probably became indentured servants. Because of the earlier mentioned law not allowing African chattels brought into the New England colonies to be taken to and sold in other colonies, they accumulated in New England. But laborers were needed in the middle colonies. And, of course, the southern colonies were the real destinations of most of the Africans.

It was during these years that many of the institutions in the African American community began. It was also during these years that the idea of slavery and entrenched racism became a reality. As early as 1640, one can see the beginnings of racial prejudice in Maryland's John Punch case when after jointly running away, the white servant was given only additional years to serve his master, but John Punch, a black man, was sentenced to serve his master for the remainder of his earthly years.

When the Africans were first carried to Catholic Latin American colonies, they were baptized before being taken away from Africa. But initially when Africans were first brought to what became the United States, the church was initially removed from them, especially those held in bondage. At first, there was fear that blacks were subhuman and did not have a soul that Christianity could save. Second, there was the fear that Christians could not be held as slaves. Around 1667, or so, Virginia solved this problem by passing a law which stated that becoming a Christian did not alter the status of an African. The matter was now settled. Plus it was found that Christianity could be used as another means of controlling slaves' behavior. Jesus had taught "Servants obey your masters." So to be a "good" was to be more like Jesus.

Although followers of historian U. B. Phillips love to point out that Africans in the colonies liked, accepted, and tolerated their positions of bondage, early on, one can see foreshadows of Gabriel Prosser, Denmark Vesey, and Nat Turner. On April 7, 1712 in New York a slave uprising occurred. Perhaps not very openly and conspicuously could one show one's disapproval for being held in bondage but in Massachusetts, 1723 and New York, 1741 there were insinuations that Africans were setting the local's property on fire. The danger of having a large African population in the individual settlements seemed to concern the locals, especially after the English gained a domination in the slave trading business in Africa after the Treaty of Utrecht settling the War of the Spanish Succession in 1714. In 1720, Charleston, South Carolina, a slave conspiracy was discovered and the leaders were burned, hanged and banished. In South Carolina, September 9, 1739, Cato led a conspiracy at Stono, west of Charleston, which aroused fear in the hearts of whites.

In the southern colonies, one viewed slavery mainly as a labor source. In the New England colonies, slaves were an article of commerce, since plantation agriculture never developed. In the middle colonies, Africans were viewed as both an article of commerce for the shipping business and a source of labor. Under the Dutch in the middle colonies, slavery did not develop into anything significant. After the English took over in 1664, things took a different turn. By 1684, slavery was recognized in the laws of New York, formerly known under the Dutch as New Amsterdam.

In 1693, black Christians founded the Negro Society of Boston to care for the welfare of the city's black populace. On "the other side of town," the railing against the practice of slavery began early. In Massachusetts, 1701, Judge Samuel Sewall published his antislavery tract, *The Selling of Joseph*. This publication became one of the first antislavery efforts, urging masters to give religious instructions to their slaves. Though the Congregation churches which dominated portions of New England might have urged its members to read the Bible and become somewhat literate, thereby not really fostering some of the real foundations of slavery, southern religions never really taught against slavery.

Perhaps if a system of profit making involving the use of Africans as workers had come about in New England, as had happened in the south, ideas mitigating slavery would not have germinated. But one reason for the maturation of such ideas was that there never developed a massive need for illiterate laborers in northern colonies. Early in the seventeenth century, John Rolfe became an MVP (most valuable person) in Jamestown because of his experiments in making tobacco a mild and acceptable European smoking weed. And one could see the value of this crop from as early as 1621 when the English started to make laws concerning tobacco. Tobacco gave the southern colonialists a commodity to export and tobacco remained an important crop in Virginia, Maryland, and North Carolina until the American Revolution. By 1700 a large percentage of Virginia and Maryland's exports consisted of tobacco. But laborers were needed to produce the export. Africans came to supply much of this labor. Rice and indigo were also dominant crops in the south, especially South Carolina and areas of North Carolina.

The geography of New England played a dominant role in helping to determine the economy of the region. Because the region could not sustain a staple crop, it had turned to fishing, shipping, etc. And in each of these economic areas blacks participated, but in much smaller percentages than in tobacco growing areas.

In the years leading to the American Revolution, one could wonder if the Africans, upon hearing the words of Patrick Henry, gave thought as to whether the words applied to them and their situation—"Give me liberty or Give me death"—or the words that Thomas Jefferson penned in the *Declaration of Independence* that "all men are created equal." John Hope Franklin argues that the colonialists changed their position several times during the Revolutionary Era. Initially, there was acceptance of the institution of slavery. Then there was the stage of blaming. The British were blamed for forcing the colonialists to hold on to slavery, even when the colonialists wanted to rid themselves of the institution. Thomas Jefferson seemed to agree with this position. Then came the position that to fight for colonialists freedom from Britain also meant to fight for black freedom from slavery.

Despite whether or not the words had any meaning for African slaves *en masse*, they did have meaning for certain individuals. On the evening of March 5, 1770 on King St. in Boston, black Crispus Attucks died promoting the view that the colonialists had to fight for freedom from British oppression! During this incident, which later became known as the Boston Massacre, Captain Thomas Preston and his men killed several Boston citizens. Thus, Attucks became one of the first men to die in "the colonialists fight for freedom." The Boston Massacre became celebrated as the first direct attack that led to the American Revolutionary War.

In those early days proceeding July 4, 1776 and the actual hot war, the roll of "black freedom fighters or soldiers" included Alexander Ames, Isiah Barjonah, Primas Black, Epheram Blackman, Pomp Blackman, Caesar Brown, Titus Colburn, Grant Cooper, Samuel Craft, Caesar Dickerson, Pomp Fisk, Prince Hall, Cuff Hayes, Lemuel Haynes, Barzallai Lew, Salem Poor, Job Potomea, Peter Salem, Sampson Talbert, Cato Tufts, Caesar Weatherbee, *et al.* Black men were with the colonialists at Lexington and Concord. And two black men, Salem Poor and Peter Salem, both distinguished themselves at Bunker Hill.

However, it was not just at soldiering that black men distinguished themselves during these years. When colonial Masons would not initiate Prince Hall and other blacks into their fraternity, some British fraternities did admit them, and thus, in 1775, the initiation of these black men laid the foundation for the first African Masonic Lodge, F&AM. Establishment of these Masons helped to enlarge the interstate communication network that came to exist among black people. In this same year, Lord Dunmore of Virginia, the area's high ranking British official, issued an offer of freedom to any black man who would fight for the British. This offer forced George Washington to reverse his earlier November 12, 1775 order barring all black men from joining the Colonial military forces. On December 31, 1775, all free black men were invited to fight in the American ranks. And in 1776, George Washington crossed the Delaware River on Christmas Day with Prince Whipple, a black man, and Oliver Cromwell.

During the war years, there were several feats in the black community: In 1777, Vermont adopted an antislavery constitution. In 1778, Rhode Island offered freedom from slavery as an incentive for black men to join the military. During this same year, a black Rhode Island regiment distinguished itself at the Battle of Rhode Island. In 1779, Pompey Lamb helped Anthony Wayne's troops achieve a significant victory at Stony Point, New York. Also in 1779, Africans petitioned for freedom and an end to slavery in New Hampshire and Connecticut.

In October, 1781, the military phase of the Revolutionary War came to a close with the defeat of the British with the Yorktown, Virginia campaign.

Not only were black Americans involved, but Haitians in the Legion Fontages under French command also participated. Not until 1783, after long negotiations would the war officially end in the Treaty of Paris, 1783. In the meantime, in 1781, over half of the settlers of the land then held under the Spanish, now known as Los Angeles, California were persons of African descent.

In 1783, in the Treaty of Paris, the independence of the United States was finally recognized. Unfortunately, this freedom for white Americans did not simultaneously mean freedom for black Americans. Also in 1783, the Massachusetts Constitution was interpreted by the state courts as having freed all blacks held in bondage in that state. The Massachusetts government even granted the franchise to certain black people. In Maryland, the further importation of slaves was prohibited. And in Virginia, all slaves who had fought in the Continental Army during the Revolutionary War were freed.

Under the Ordinance of 1787 that governed the American Northwest Territory, Congress prohibited slavery. That year New York City came to witness its first free African School; but in Boston, African Americans petitioned unsuccessfully for a public school.

In 1789, Americans got their second Constitution, the Constitution of the United States. Although there are three references in the body of the Constitution to black people, it never points directly to them. In Article I, Section 2, there is the famous Three-fifth Compromise outlines where African Americans were counted for the purpose of taxation and representation as three-fifths of a white person. Then, in Article I, Section 9, in the "Forbidden Powers," slave importation could not be forbidden prior to 1808. Finally, Article IV, Section 2, detailing the relation of the states to one another, rendition of escaped bondsmen is covered.

So this new country, whose Constitution was created to establish justice and promote the belief that all men were created equal, would eventually become an international power by establishing itself as a nation divided by two groups of men—separate and unequal.

Suggested Readings

Lerone Bennett Jr., *Before The Mayflower.*

Benjamin Brawley, *A Short History Of The American Negro.*

John P. Davis, *The American Negro Reference Book.*

John Hope Franklin, *From Slavery to Freedom.*

Greene, Lorenzo J., *The Negro in Colonial New England.*

Benjamin Quarles, *The Negro In The Making of America.*

Saunders Redding, *Americans from Africa: They Came In Chains.*

STUDY GUIDE 7

1–20 Name at least twenty (20) of the black men who militarily distinguished themselves for the colonialists' cause prior to July 4th, 1776.

21–22 Name the two black men who distinguished themselves at the Battle of Bunker Hill.

23 Who became the first black man of note that was initiated into the Masons?

24 *True or False*? Black men were always welcome to fight in the colonialists army.

25–26 Who were the noted black men with George Washington when he crossed the Delaware River on Christmas Day in 1776?

27 What was the last military campaign in the Revolutionary War?

28 From what country came the Legion Fontages?

29 What is the common terminology for that portion of the Constitution that originally counted black and white Americans for both representation and taxation?

30 What became the last year when slaves were legally imported into the United States?

8

Nineteenth Century Antebellum African American Accomplishments

So far as the majority of those of African descent in America were concerned, the beginning of the nineteenth century looked bleak. The invention of the cotton gin, led by Eli Whitney, gave new life to slavery. Added to this mechanical development was the territorial expansion of the United States through the purchase of Louisiana in 1803. Thus, what had appeared to be slavery's dying days following the Revolutionary War, in the early nineteenth century were reversed. The "peculiar institution" [slavery] was resuscitated by the advent of "King Cotton" [dominant staple crop] in the deep South.

Despite this opening scene of the nineteenth century, antebellum America witnessed numerous accomplishments by the children of the African diaspora. They made contributions to human rights, education, science and technology, economics, and religion. Thus, in spite of a climate of prolonged bondage, the antebellum nineteenth century African American carved out a place for himself by being productive and creative in the face of oppression.

During the years immediately following the Revolutionary War, private manumission increased dramatically. Many slave owners influenced by the climate of freedom from the independence era freed their bondsmen. In Virginia, Robert Carter of Nomini Hall emancipated all of his slaves in 1791. It was reported to be the largest private freeing of slaves prior to the Civil War. Likewise, John Randolph manumitted all of his slaves upon his death in 1833.

So many slaves were freed in Virginia that the state passed a law in 1806 that required slaves manumitted from that date forward to leave the state within twelve months. In a similar fashion, Georgia and South Carolina had passed restrictive manumission laws after 1800. Throughout the South similar laws were enacted as the free black population increased.

By 1804 all states north of the Mason-Dixon Line had laws forbidding slavery or providing for gradual emancipation. The latter kept some vestige of the peculiar institution with the region that most readily came to be identified with abolitionists [persons interested in ridding the area of slavery]. For example, New Jersey had some slaves even until the Civil War.

Unwanted in the South, many of these former bondsmen went North only to find an equally unreceptive citizenry. Thus, black people seemed to be in an impossible situation as to where they would live after freedom. This stimulated sympathetic whites and determined blacks to action. The former attracted others who had a less noble motivation. As a result, when the American Colonization Society was organized in Washington, D. C. in 1816 it had members who wished blacks well along with those who saw them as unwanted persons who should be exported beyond the borders of the United States.

As early as 1814, Paul Cuffe, a free man of African and Native American ancestry, petitioned the United States Congress for a vessel and supplies to carry a few freed families to Sierra Leone for settlement. Despite some endorsements from various members for the plan, it was denied. Primarily this resulted from the strong anti-British mood generated by the War of 1812. At this time, Sierra Leone was a British colony and therefore unfavorably viewed because of association. Eventually Cuffe, who became a wealthy shipper, transported thirty-eight former slaves at his own expense in his own vessel.

Later, the American Colonization Society became the catalyst for the founding of the nation of Liberia on the West coast of Africa in 1822. The first settlers from America set sail in 1820 from New York. This initial voyage was composed of eighty-six blacks. One year later, this homeland for freed American slaves attracted America's first black missionaries. On January 23, 1821, Lott Carey, Collin Teague, their families, and Joseph Langford departed for Liberia as Christian laborers.

On the American domestic scene, the cause for human rights expanded as the United States outlawed the African slave trade on January 1, 1808. With the realization of this goal, anti-slavery sentiment was turned toward a call for the end of the peculiar institution. Quakers particularly became consistently active in presenting before Congress petitions and memorials calling for the abolition of slavery. Throughout the years between 1812 and 1819, Quakers from such southern citadels of slavery as North Carolina, Virginia, and Tennessee joined the Society of Friends [Quakers] in the North calling for the dismantling of human bondage. Thus, at this early juncture of the nineteenth century, slavery had become a moral issue. Probably as illustrative as anything on this note was the black Presbyterian clergyman Henry Highland Garnet's declaration that it was wicked to submit to slavery.

A vital component in the abolitionist strategy was the Underground Railroad. This was a covert network that assisted runaway slaves. This operation brought together both blacks and whites as conductors and supporters of the railroad. The most famous conductor was Harriet Tubman, who escaped from slavery in Maryland in 1849. Her bold exploits resulted in the liberation of over three hundred slaves. At least nineteen times she returned to the South to spirit away those held in bondage. Huge bounties placed upon her head did not deter her efforts in bringing about freedom for her fellow enslaved brothers and sisters of the African diaspora.

Another African American who rose to prominence in the human rights struggle in antebellum nineteenth century America was Frederick Douglass. After having escaped slavery, Douglass became a spokesman for the Massachusetts Anti-Slavery Society in 1841. Initially, Douglass was used by the abolitionists as an exhibit of wretchedness. He was portrayed as a demonstration of what slavery had done to a human being. However, through his resourcefulness and personal initiative, Douglass became an articulate orator of the abolitionist position. His protestations were not confined to oral communication. He went on to found his own newspaper the *North Star* in 1847. In 1850, he changed the name of it to *Frederick Douglass' Paper.*

An even earlier African American journalist who spoke out against slavery was David Walker. In 1829 in Boston, he first published his militant anti-slavery pamphlet, *An Appeal to the Colored People of the World.* Its national distribution led to the publication of his newspaper, *Appeal.* Its militant call for action against slavery gave many southerners the mistaken notion that this paper was what stirred Nat Turner's violent insurrection in 1831 in Southampton County, Virginia. Although it is doubtful there was a connection between Walker's Appeal and Nat Turner's rebellion, both did suggest that the human rights struggle against slavery by 1831 had taken a militant, violent turn.

The African American's call for reform in human relations was centered around abolition, but was not confined to it. A prime example of the wider call for reform was seen in the career of Sojourner Truth. In addition to an end to slavery, she espoused the need for women's rights, penal and asylum reform. In 1852 in Akron, Ohio she addressed the National Women's Suffrage Convention. She and Frederick Douglass became the African American community's two best known advocates of general human rights in antebellum America.

As was the case throughout most of the African American experience, many black leaders during the War of 1812 believed that participation would win concessions for blacks. Consequently, not only did the African American serve in the war, but served ably as well. In 1813 on Lake Erie, blacks composed ten to twenty-five percent of Commodore Oliver H. Perry's victorious force. Blacks' participations in 1814 at Plattsburg and Lake Champlain were so commendable that Andrew Jackson praised their bravery. Then in 1815 in New Orleans, six hundred African Americans, many of whom were led by black officers, especially in the Corp d'Afrique, fought with Jackson in the successful defense of New Orleans. Despite an exemplary record in the War of 1812, African Americans in many cases had promises of freedom betrayed by both sides. On the other hand, many did secure their freedom as a result of their military service. More importantly, soldiers and sailors had an opportunity to see Canada and the freedom with which people of African descent had there.

Although education for the black masses was unavailable in antebellum America, the nineteenth century saw many gains in this area. In the North, this period was one of increased educational opportunity for the African American. Even though public education was provided for African American children in many northern communities, segregated schools were the norm. It was not until the decade preceding the Civil War that segregation in education relaxed because of abolitionist pressure.

Generally throughout the South it was illegal for anyone to teach a slave to read. After the free black, Denmark Vesey, led a slave uprising in South Carolina in 1822, southern states moved on an individual basis to outlaw education for any African American, regardless of his condition.

Black educational progress reached a milestone in 1833 with the founding of Oberlin College. From its inception, the Ohio institution admitted both African Americans and females. It became America's first college to have such a policy. By the beginning of the Civil War, one third of Oberlin's student body was African American.

Despite this antebellum effort at a desegregated higher education, the pre-Civil War nineteenth century saw the germination of the historically black college. Two privately owned schools of this mold began at that time. Lincoln University in Pennsylvania began in 1853 as Ashmum Institute. Later in 1856 Wilberforce University in Ohio was founded by the Methodist Episcopal Church. During this antebellum venture the school was primarily charged with serving the mulatto offspring of southerners. At the beginning of the war between the states, Wilberforce's operation ceased. It was later reopened and henceforth sponsored by the African Methodist Episcopal Church.

In 1826 the first two African Americans to finish college were graduated. Edward Jones took his degree from Amherst College [Massachusetts], while John Russwurm matriculated at Bowdoin College [Maine]. One year after his graduation, Russwurm set a precedent for the educated African American as he rendered public service by joining Samuel Cornish in founding, *Freedom's Journal,* the first African American newspaper.

The expansion of educational opportunities for antebellum African Americans opened other doors for the race. In 1845 in Worchester, Massachusetts, Macon B. Allen became the first African American formally admitted to the bar [lawyer]. Both John Sweat Rock and James McCune Smith were practicing physicians in antebellum America. The latter brought his talents back to the United States even though he was educated in Scotland at the University of Glasgow.

Literary works came forth from the educated ranks of the black intelligentsia. In 1853 William Wells Brown published the first novel written by an African American. However, his *Clotel* was published in London. Five years later, when *The Escape* was released, he became the first African American to author a play. Important pioneering histories, *Textbook of the Origin* and *History of the Colored People* (1841) and *Services of Colored Americans in the Wars of 1776 and 1812* (1852) were authored by J. W. C. Pennington and William C. Nell, respectively. Martin R. Delany, a Harvard Medical School product, in 1852 penned *The Condition, Elevation, Emigration, and Destiny of the Colored People of the United States.*

These were only a few examples of the literary productions by antebellum African Americans. In addition to the aforementioned volumes, many other pieces of literature appeared as slave narratives. Abolitionists particularly encouraged and supported autobiographies and biographies that portrayed the horrors of the peculiar institution. Frederick Douglass for example, wrote two autobiographies prior to the Civil War. In 1843 he published *Narrative of the Life of Frederick Douglass, An American Slave* and in 1855 his *My Bondage and My Freedom* appeared.

Education likewise manifested itself through scientific and technological advances by the antebellum black American. Of course, the Industrial Revolution came to its fullest development after the War Between the States. Yet, prior to the conflict, the earliest stages of modernity's inventions were being produced. The African American took his place alongside other inventors from the outset.

The first known patent granted to an African American took place on October 14, 1834. On that date Henry Blair, a former Maryland slave, had his corn planter patented. This was only forty four years after the United States Patent Office had been established. Two years later, Blair obtained a second patent on August 31, 1836 for his cotton planter.

In 1845 Norbert Rillieux invented a new method of refining sugar [the "Jamaica Train"]. This innovation not only improved the grade of sugar, but reduced the manufacturing cost by half. His multiple-effect vacuum evaporation process was so successful that not only was it used on plantations within the United States, but was adopted by sugar producers in Cuba and Mexico as well. The principle behind the "Rillieux Process" is also used in the production of such later commodities such as condensed milk, glue, and gelatin.

As a free black born in the slave state of Virginia in 1800, Lewis Temple grew up in an hostile environment that afforded him no formal education and few economic prospects. As a result, Temple, as a young man decided to cast his lot in New England. There, he settled in the whaling port of New Bedford, Massachusetts, where he secured employment as a metal smith. This occupation enabled him to meet the industry's need to improve its catch. His "Temple Toggle Harpoon" not only inflicted a wound upon the prey, but had lines attached to it, which prevented the animal's escape. His invention, which was patented in 1848, was credited with doubling New England's whaling catch.

Another inventor, James Forten combined his entrepreneurial spirit with his mechanical aptitude. In 1798 he bought a sailmaking shop in Philadelphia—at one time he had served as an apprentice to a white sailmaker in the shop. After his purchase of the business he became the employer of more than forty laborers, black and white. While in this business venture, Forten invented the "Forten Sail Control," which made sailing a more manageable enterprise for sailors.

The aforementioned inventors only represent a sample of the numerous antebellum African American technological developers. For the masses, the period excluded the possibility of obtaining a patent. It was illegal for a slave to get a patent. Yet, there is proof that they too provided mechanical innovations. In 1858 Jefferson Davis was denied a patent for a boat propeller that had been invented by his slave, Benjamin Montgomery. By that date not only was it illegal for slaves to obtain patents, but neither could they assign their inventions to their owners.

As to economic developments, James Forten was only one of many success stories among antebellum blacks. Forten's personal fortune was estimated at about $100,000. In fact, it was Forten, who in 1833 supplied funds for the famed white abolitionist, William Lloyd Garrison to start his newspaper, *The Liberator*. In the process, Forten influenced Garrison to abandon the American Colonization Society's transportation efforts to Africa in favor of a call for complete emancipation.

While James Forten and Paul Cuffe prospered from the maritime industry, Samuel R. Ward led a union of skilled black workers. In New York in 1850 he became president of the American League of Colored Laborers. His efforts not only were generated at developing black craftsmen, but he also encouraged black entrepreneurship as well.

Despite racial strife there is evidence that black economic development still made remarkable gains. For example, in the aftermath of violent confrontations with whites in Cincinnati, it was reported in 1852 that 200 of the city's 3,500 black residents had acquired real estate that had an aggregate worth of $500,000.

Economically, New Orleans was one of the best antebellum cities for blacks. In 1850, there were 650 blacks who owned property valued at $2,354,640. Undoubtedly, the explanation behind New Orleans' phenomenal success was found in its large mulatto population, many of whom had inherited estates from their white fathers. Among New Orleans' well known antebellum blacks was Thomy Lafon, who possibly was the wealthiest pre-Civil War African American. He became well known for his generous gifts that benefited such causes as black education and orphanages. In fact, Lafon had been so philanthropic that upon his death, the Louisiana state legislature ordered that a bust of him should be on public display.

As wealth grew among African Americans, philanthropy was displayed by others who did not have as large holdings, but a similar spirit of sharing. A favorite beneficiary of African American gifts were educational institutions whose doors were open to the race.

Antebellum African American nineteenth century strides had their greatest impact in the area of religion. Although individual congregations had been founded in the eighteenth century by both-black Baptists and Methodists, in the nineteenth century, these spread and became interstate institutions. In 1816 in Philadelphia, the African Methodist Episcopal [A.M.E.] Church was organized. Five year later in New York, the African Methodist Episcopal Zion [A.M.E.Z.] Church became the second national black church.

The founding of both of these black controlled religious bodies provided valuable training for African Americans. In addition to the Christian catechism, the parishioners learned organizational skills that aided them in business and later in politics. The nurturing that the black church gave to the African American community was so extensive that C. Eric Lincoln referred to it as "the womb of black culture."

Hence, from its inception, the church provided a multi-faceted ministry to its members. The African American Church began as being an organ for liberation and racial improvement. In 1830 in Philadelphia, Richard Allen, bishop of the African Methodist Episcopal Church, chaired the first national African American convention. It convened at the Bethel Church from September 20 to 24. Its purpose was to launch a church affiliated program to socially improve the African American's position. One year later, at the Wesleyan Church in Philadelphia, the first annual Convention of the People of Color convened. Delegates from five states met to study black conditions, explore the feasibility of black Canadian settlements, and raise money for an industrial college in New Haven. Prior to its adjournment, the convention went on record as opposing the American Colonization Society and recommending an annual meeting.These early gatherings in churches set a precedent for the African American's struggle for human rights to be closely identified with religion. Thus, this period on a national level set in motion an inextricable alliance between social activists and the church. This partnership has continued ever since.

Indeed, the antebellum nineteenth century did open on a gloomy scene. It appeared that the advent of "King Cotton" would forever keep black people in shackles and chains. Yet, despite the hardships and disappointments, the pre-Civil War African Americans claimed victories. Through the race's own efforts and the kindness shown by others, the antebellum nineteenth century African American made historical contributions in human rights, education, science and technology, economics, and religion. It was a time when human effort did bring some triumphs to an otherwise downcast scene.

Suggested Readings

The Annals of Congress. 14th Congress, 1st Session, House of Representatives, January, 1816.

The Annals of Congress. 15th Congress, 1st Session, Senate, January, 1818.

Lerone Bennett Jr. *Before The Mayflower.*

Amos J. Beyan. *The American Colonization Society and the Creation of the Liberian State: A Historical Perspective, 1822–1900.* 1991.

McKinley Burt Jr. *Black Inventors of America.* 1989.

John Hope Franklin and Alfred A. Moss Jr. *From Slavery to Freedom.*

Vincent Harding. *There Is A River: The Black Struggle For Freedom In America.* 1981.

Winthrop Jordan and Leon Litwack. *The United States, Brief Edition.* 3rd ed., 1990.

Glover Moore. *The Missouri Controversy, 1819–1821.* 1953.

Benjamin Quarles. *The Negro In The Making of America.*

Saunders Redding. *They Came In Chains: Americans From Africa.*

The Schomburg Library of Nineteenth Century Black Women Writers. *Six Women's Slave Narratives,* 1988.

Kenneth Stampp. *The Peculiar Institution: Slavery In The Antebellum South* 1956.

George Brown Tindall. *A Narrative History,* vol. I., 1984.

STUDY GUIDE 8

1	Who invented the cotton gin?
2	When was the "Louisiana Purchase" made?
3	Give another name for the "peculiar institution."
4	What was the dominant staple crop of the antebellum deep south?
5–10	What were some general areas in which African Americans made significant contributions in antebellum nineteenth century America?
11	What common name was given to persons interested in ridding areas of slavery?
12	When was the American Colonization Society organized?
13	Who was the African American that transported freed black Americans to Sierra Leone with his own funds?
14	What African nation did the American Colonization Society help to begin?
15	Give another name for the Quakers.
16	Who became the most prominent "Conductor" on the "Underground Railroad?"
17	Who edited the *North Star*?
18	Who edited the *Appeal*?
19–20	When and where was Nat Turner's revolt staged?
21	Other than Frederick Douglass, who, in the antebellum years, became a leading black spokesperson for human reform?
22	In what war did the Corp d'Afrique fight?
23–24	When and where did Denmark Vesey's uprising occur?
25	In what state is Oberlin College located?
26	Name the first HBCU.
27–28	When and where (what state) was **26** founded?
29	Name the second oldest HBCU.
30	Where (what state) was **29** founded?
31–32	Name two of the first African Americans graduates from American colleges.
33	In what state is Amherst College located?
34	In what state is Bowdoin College located?
35	What was the first black American newspaper?
36–37	Name the co-editors of the newspaper referred to in question **35**.
38	Name the first known black American lawyer.
39	Name the first known African American novelist.
40	Name the first novel written by an African American.
41	Give the first known African American playwright.
42	Name the first play written by a black American.

43 Who was America's first known black to receive a patent?

44 Who produced/invented the "Jamaica Train?"

45 Who invented the "Temple Toggle Harpoon?"

46 What newspaper did white William Lloyd Garrison edit?

47 In 1850, who became President of the American League of Colored Laborers in New York?

48 Who was probably antebellum America's wealthiest African American?

49 What city served as the site of the first Annual Convention of People of Color in 1831?

50 Expand the church related abbreviation A.M.E.Z.

9

The Coming of the Civil War, 1820–1860

The forty year epoch between 1820–1860, commonly referred to as the antebellum era, shaped and colored the lives of all Americans at the time. It was, in fact, a defining period in the American historical experience when the nation had to come to terms with the meaning of its creed and whether the Union was indeed indivisible.

For African Americans, the significance of this era and its attending developments is that people began to accept, rather than deny, the central contradiction of American life—the continued existence of slavery in a society purportedly rooted in the sanctity of human liberty and freedom, both physical and spiritual. Yet more than 130 years later, there is still an absence of consensus among historians and laymen on a common list of developments and causes regarding the coming of the Civil War. It is obvious, nevertheless, that a divisive sectional conflict was at the core of America's drift toward disunion in the decades preceding 1860. And it is equally obvious that slavery was exceedingly consequential, if not the primary contributor, in the historical process that led to a "house divided" in 1860.

The onset of this historical process began with the Missouri Compromise, a development which was intended to avert the very end result it helped to eventuate. The compromise as adopted provided that Missouri and Maine would enter the Union as a slave and a free state respectively. It was further mandated that slavery be "forever prohibited" in all the remaining parts of the Louisiana Purchase north of the 36 30′ parallel. In a final stipulation worked out by Senator Henry Clay to insure Congress' acceptance of the Missouri constitution, it was agreed that the state would pass no law construed as contravening Article IV Section Two of the United States Constitution. Under Article IV Section Two "the citizens of each state shall be entitled to all privileges and immunities of citizens in the several states." In its proposed constitution, Missouri intended to require the state legislature to enact a law barring free blacks and mulattos from entering the state "under any pretext whatever."

Many northern congressmen voiced strong objections to Missouri's intent, even though a number of states east of Missouri routinely barred free blacks in violation of the Constitution. Enough of these same congressmen refused to vote to accept the Missouri constitution, necessitating the demurrer worked out by Henry Clay. Even more ironic, perhaps even perversely so, was that almost the entire debate in the Missouri controversy occurred without any serious discussion of the moral ramifications of slavery. Slaves, except to the extent that they figured into congressional representation and taxation, were left out of the debate. Instead, slavery was discussed in abstract, amoral terms, leaving as a consequence the relative status and immediate future of nearly two million slaves unchanged and unbroached. And, while the Missouri Compromise provided the nation with a "quick fix" in its struggle over slavery, many contemporary observers realize that there was more reason for concern with the solution than jubilation.

Writing a month after Missouri entered the Union, Thomas Jefferson commented with apparent despair that "we have the wolf by the ears, and we can neither safely hold him nor safely let him go." Jefferson compared the Missouri debates to "a fire bell in the night . . . [that] awakened and filled . . . [him] with terror." Even more pointed were the comments of John Quincy Adams who referred to the compromise as "a reprieve only" and possibly the "title page to a great tragic volume." Notwithstanding these less than rave reviews, the compromise did cause tempers to subside and settled temporarily and peaceably, if ignobly, the issue of slavery.

In the decade following the Missouri Compromise, slavery, while remaining a primary source of inter-sectional conflict, was for a time at least eclipsed by several other issues. The most significant of these issues were: Indian removal, obtaining a protective tariff, and internal improvements. Although seldom discussed in connection with the coming of the Civil War, the removal and relocation of five southeastern groups of Native Americans between 1831 and 1837 constituted part of the overall mix of historical developments that paved the way for secession and disunion. Initially, of course, the importance of Indian removal lay in the horrendous suffering and travail visited upon thousands of indigenous Americans, but also critical is the role this development played in freeing-up hundreds of thousands of acres in the old southwest—*i.e.*, Alabama, Mississippi and Arkansas—for expansion of the plantation economy. With this expansion came new and fertile land to insure the continued territorial viability of slavery as well as the political wherewithal of Congress to protect the South from any real or imagined threat to its sectional interest.

President Andrew Jackson was prominently figured in Indian Removal and the subsequent "trail of tears." He openly opposed and refused to enforce the U.S. Supreme Court decision in the *Worcester v. Georgia* case. In that case, the court ruled that the Cherokees and their territory were autonomous and not subject to the control of the state of Georgia. Jackson's willingness to back Georgia in its effort to ignore the court decision no doubt emboldened many supporting southern state's rights; perhaps Jackson's support even convinced some that he would not oppose nullification if and when the doctrine was applied to acts of Congress. Many northerners, not suprisingly, opposed Indian removal. Their opposition was inspired not so much by humanitarian concern as by the potential territorial and political windfall such a development would wrought in favor of the South. Nor were northern apprehensions completely unfounded as settlement and development in the Alabama Black Belt and Mississippi Delta during the 1830s serve to illustrate.

The singular event most often associated with the nation's move toward Civil War in the decade following the Missouri Compromise, however, was the Nullification Crisis of 1833. The origins of the crisis date back to 1828 when Congress over the vehement objections of southerners passed a protective tariff. The Tariff of Abominations, as it was often refered to, provided for the highest duties up to that time to be charged on a myriad of imported goods including wool, hemp, flax, fur and liquor. The tariff was subsequently lowered in 1832, but southerners remained unalterably opposed to it. South Carolina quickly emerged as the southern state most ardent in its opposition to the tariff. In formulating their arguments against the tariff, leaders in South Carolina drew liberally on the views of the state's native son, John C. Calhoun. Particularly useful for their purposes was Calhoun's 1828 essay, the "South Carolina Exposition and Protest," where he repudiated the nationalist philosophy he earlier championed and outlined a defense for the right of a state to reject an act of Congress.

President Andrew Jackson, who at the time was serving his second term following reelection in 1832, was incensed by South Carolina's posturing. He responded by informing South Carolina nullifiers through a member of the state's congressional delegation that "they can talk and write resolutions and print threats to their hearts' content, but if one drop of blood," Jackson warned, "be shed there [South Carolina] in defiance of the laws of the United States, I will hang the first man of them I can get my hands on to the first tree I can find." Despite Jackson's stern warning, the South Carolina legislature authorized the convening of a special convention. When it met on November 24, 1832, the convention passed an Ordinance of Nullification that prohibited the collection of tariff duties in the state after February 1, 1833. The state legislature followed suit by authorizing the raising of an army and appropriating the necessary funds to outfit and equip the troops.

Developments in South Carolina prompted Jackson to mobilize a military with a target of 50,000 men in uniform by early January, 1833. But at the same time, Jackson was working to resolve the crisis without military confrontation. Jackson's efforts include encouraging Congress to reduce the tariff as well as issuing a Proclamation to the People of South Carolina. In that Proclamation, Jackson maintained, "nullification could only lead to the destruction of the Union." "The laws of the United States," he continued, "must be executed. I have no discretionary power on the subject . . . Those who told you that you might peacably prevent their execution deceived you." Nor should it be forgotten, Jackson reminded South Carolinians, that "disunion by armed force is treason." Jackson went on to inquire, perhaps rhetorically, "are you [South Carolinians] really ready to incur . . . [that] guilt."

Jackson did not want to broach the extent to which his refusal to enforce the U. S. Supreme Court decision in the *Worcester v. Georgia* case contributed to developments in South Carolina. Nor did leaders in South Carolina attempt to use, at least not publicly, Jackson's reversal of positions to their advantage. Instead, attention during the months preceding the February first deadline was riveted on Congress. Administration leaders introduced a new tariff bill and a Force Bill that granted President Jackson additional authority to execute revenue laws. Meanwhile, Jackson continued to express a determined resolve to preserve the Union by force of arms if necessary, which purportedly included hanging John C. Calhoun "as high as Haman" in the event that nullification were attempted. Anxious obviously to avoid a showdown with Jackson, Calhoun convinced leaders in South Carolina to postpone nullification pending Congressional action on the tariff. A compromise tariff was pushed through Congress by early March, 1833 due largely to the joint efforts of Calhoun and Henry Clay.

In response, South Carolina nullifiers professed satisfaction with the new legislation and proceeded to repeal the Nullification Ordinance. But as written, the new tariff made few immediate reductions and provided only for a gradual scaling back of rates over a ten year period. So while the crisis only resulted in sable rattling, and the nation averted a possible violent confrontation between a state and the federal government, the incident, nevertheless, spoke volumes about the depth of the sectional conflict. It clearly demonstrated that there were searing sociocultural and economic differences within American society which militated against a common national identity. Generally Americans of the period felt and evidenced a greater affinity to and for their individual state and region of residence. This was especially true in the south—the 1833 crisis only served to increase the southern feelings of isolation from the rest of the country as its institutions, particularly slavery, came under mounting criticism and attack.

Unlike either slavery or the tariff, the concern over internal improvements proved decidedly less controversial and volatile as a sectional issue. During the 1820s, federal funding for infrastructure projects began to emerge as an issue that divided Americans along regional lines. In the early 1830s the issue was still a source for some conflict, mostly between northeasterners who opposed it and westerners who were strong advocates. By the latter 1830s, opposition to internal improvements was waning as the need for government intervention became more generally accepted within the American body politic. The 1830s, then, which began so acrimoniously ended more tranquil, but with many hugely important developments yet to occur as the country meandered its way toward Civil War.

Although starting quite undramatically the ensuing decade of the 1840s soon provided its own set of developments that configured in such a way to reignite smoldering sectional passions. These developments included an expanding and increasingly demonstrative anti-slavery movement along with an emerging national spirit of manifest destiny and the Mexican war. Organized opposition to slavery in the nineteenth century was initially more of a southern than northern phenomenon. Prior to 1830, over half of all abolition societies were found in the South. A reversal of that trend began in the 1830s when northerners started banding together in an unprecedented number of anti-slavery organizations. Already alarmed by earlier attacks on its peculiar institution, the South in the 1840s felt compelled to mount a defense of the southern way of life and institutions. Those individuals and groups in the South voicing opposition to slavery were silenced, abolition literature coming into the South was seized and efforts were made to limit debate in Congress on the peculiar institution. The 1840s also occasioned discussions aimed at reviving the Atlantic slave trade and creating a slavery-driven Caribbean Empire. Indeed, Southerners by the 1840s were well on their way to assuming an embattled mind-set. Such a perspective led in turn to a closing of southern ranks and a counterassault posture against all who spoke disapprovingly, uncharitably or ill of the South. Gone were the days when the South spoke almost apologetically of slavery as a regrettable though "necessary evil." In its new and more strident defense of slavery, the South now characterized the institution as a "positive good."

Abolitionist crusaders responded with vigor and resolve. They, too, escalated the dialogue and caricatured both the institution of slavery and its victims in the most pejorative of terms. Blacks who were ex-slaves, Frederick Douglass, Sojourner Truth, Harriet Tubman and William "Box" Brown among others were often utilized to provide gripping first hand accounts of life under slavery. Such testimonials had by the mid 1840s become a staple in abolitionist oratory. A whole cadre of African Americans however, emerged as abolitionists in their own right. Frederick Douglass being among those who made the transition from white sponsorship to independent abolitionist crusader. Sojourner Truth followed a similar path as did William Brown. Many other black abolitionists who were born free gave generously of their time and resources to promote the anti-slavery cause. Still abolitionists were not a monolithic group. They differed in their advocacy of means and ends. The most apparent division within the movement was between the Garrisonian wing which advocated immediate abolition and the Theodore Weld faction which proposed a more gradualistic approach. Southerners generally saw no qualitative difference between the two. Each was viewed as equally abhorrent. Furthermore abolitionist agitation did little at the time to ameliorate the circumstances under which those in the slave community lived and toiled. Southern states blamed abolitionist agitation for endangering the lives of whites in the region; possibly even contributing to the deaths of whites in the Nat Turner Rebellion of 1831 in Virginia. The abolitionist crusade, to be sure, led to legislation across the South that virtually eliminated the practice of manumission by individual slaveowners and made the already precarious status of free blacks even more tenuous.

It was against this historical backdrop that the nation took on the Texas question and the war with Mexico all in the name of manifest destiny [belief that God had ordained that the United States should stretch from 'sea' to 'sea']. America's ability to push back the frontiers east of the Mississippi during the first half century after its founding tended to foster a vision of unlimited continental expansion. The settlement of Americans in Texas, which was then Mexican Territory, and their subsequent war for independence and application for admission to the Union did much to fuel the nation's growing preoccupation with manifest destiny. Many Americans viewed the admissions of Texas as precisely what was needed to insure expansion west of the Mississippi. Even Northerners were generally in support of annexation. Still some northerners saw in this expansion the potential for upsetting the delicate free/slave state congressional balance in a way redounding to the advantage of the South. In December 1845, following years of annexation efforts dating back to the Jackson administration, Texas was finally admitted to the Union. The most intense lobbying for the admission of Texas occurred during the administration of John Tyler, who succeeded President William Henry Harrison after his death in 1841. Tyler's efforts paid off as Texas became a state only weeks before he left office.

Tyler's successor, James Polk, was also an expansionist at heart. He would lead the nation to victory in the Mexican war, which officially began in May 1846. Nine months into the war. Mexico was already thoroughly beaten, but refused to agree to terms. A peace treaty was eventually negotiated in February 1848. In the Treaty of Guadalupe Hidalgo, Mexico accepted the Rio Grande as the boundary of Texas and ceded New Mexico and Upper California to the United States. In return the United States agreed to pay Mexico $15 million and assume $3.25 million in claims against it by American citizens against Mexico. With its victory over Mexico, America made huge territorial gains that included the entire Pacific Coast from south of San Diego to the 49th parallel and all the land between the coast and the Continental Divide. As many predicted continental prosperity quickly gave rise to disharmony, bringing the country once again face to face with the disquieting issue of slavery. Fearing the other side might gain advantage from continental-expansion, the pro and anti-slavery forces moved to checkmate, if not, outmaneuver each other. The urgency of the issue became more pronounced in the wake of gold discoveries in California and the resulting population growth. California would soon organize and apply for statehood. But whether it entered as a slave or a free state was the question. The South, of course, preferred to enter as a slave state. It was argued that the South's sectional interest was apt to be seriously compromised. The North likewise pointed to irreparable damage to its sectional interest, if California became a slave state. Consequently, the 1840s ended with the nation mired in controversy yet again.

Responsibility for extricating the country from the throes of this latest controversy fell to Congress. Work began early in 1850, but attempts at resolution remained stalemated until after the death of President Zachary Taylor who repeatedly threatened to veto any compromise presented to him because of his determination to admit California as a free state without concessions to the South. When adopted, the Compromise of 1850 stipulated that California be admitted as a free state. The remainder of the Mexican Cession was slated to become two territories, New Mexico and Utah. Each could be admitted to the Union when two-thirds of the residents vote to enter as either a slave or free state. Other features of the compromise included a $10 million compensation to Texas for agreeing to a narrower Western boundary, the abolition of the slave trade in the District of Columbia beginning January 1, 1851, and a vastly expanded Fugitive Slave Law. The enlarged Fugitive Slave statute provided for the appointment of federal commissioners with authority to issue warrants, summon posses and require citizens under threat of fine or imprisonment to aid in the capture of runaway slaves. Fugitives could also be returned to their alleged owners without a jury trial upon submission of an affidavit. Southerners were naturally elated over the Fugitive Slave provisions while northerners indicated their indignation and repugnance for them. The new provisions, if enforced, meant that the free states were no longer safe heavens and fugitives would have to continue on to Canada. But the law proved unenforceable, much to the dismay of southerners. In numerous localities throughout the North local citizens risked fine and imprisonment to prevent the return of fugitive slaves. In early 1851, for example, Frederick Jenkins, an alleged runaway, was captured in Boston where he worked as a waiter in a coffee house. While Jenkins was detained for extradition, local blacks broke into the courthouse and freed him. Similarly, in October 1851 a slave named Jerry, who had escaped from Missouri, was arrested in Syracuse, New York. After dark, a crowd formed which later stormed the building where Jerry was held, freeing and spiriting him away.

As compromises go, the 1850 edition was actually a misnomer. In fact, the legislation was born of very little of the give and take normally associated with compromises. Nor for that matter did compromise provide the nation with much of a respite from its impending crisis, the Civil War. Within a year after the Compromise of 1850, the country was once more propelled into dramatic controversy. This would be the first in a successive wave of controversies after 1850 that nudged America ever closer to the widening abyss of sectional disunity. The initial incident in this sequence of controversies was triggered by the publication of Harriet Beecher Stowe's *Uncle Tom's Cabin*. Though its literary merits were often questioned, the book's story line was powerful and provocative. It was fraught with heartrending scenes of pain, self-sacrifice, and heroism. The book also represented the first time a white American writer depicted blacks, slaves in particular, as possessing normal human qualities. More specifically, the work delineated a tale of Uncle Tom the pious and patient slave, Eva the saintly white child and Simon Legree the nefarious slave driver. The on-stage presentation of the story proved particularly effective, leaving many audiences in tears. The impact of the book on the nation's psyche was indeed profound. The book sold almost 10,000 copies immediately and 300,000 within the first year. The popularity of the book was nothing short of a propaganda windfall for abolitionists, contributing, accordingly, to a deepening of northern apprehensions about slavery and southern fears of possible attacks against its "peculiar institution."

It was in this already highly charged atmosphere of sectional recriminations that the Kansas-Nebraska controversy emerged. The controversy was sparked by congressional consideration of the Kansas-Nebraska Act. Northerners after learning of the legislation's implications were livid and immediately began campaigns of letter writing, petitions and public meetings. Even so, together with President

Franklin Pierce's backing and strong southern support the bill's sponsor, Senator Stephen Douglas of Illinois, was able to engineer its passage. The legislation had the practical effect of reversing the Missouri Compromise's prohibition of slavery beyond the 36° 30' parallel. It also introduced the doctrine of popular sovereignty. Under popular sovereignty the actual settlers within a given territory would decide by virtue of a referendum whether to join the Union as a slave or free state. The repeal of the Missouri Compromise was especially difficult for most northerners to accept considering the territories in question had for thirty-four years been off limits to slavery. Indeed no matter what the rationale, northerners found the prospect of reopening territories beyond the 36° 30' parallel to the "peculiar institution" as simply untenable. As a result, northerners tried desperately to flood these territories, particularly Kansas, with settlers of anti-slavery persuasion just as southerners sought to do precisely the opposite. The repercussions from these conflicting efforts took many forms including confrontations, mayhem, bloodshed and even massacres. Between 1854 and 1856 some 200 lives were lost, leading many northern newspapers to dub the situation "Bleeding Kansas." Northern voters in the wake of the Kansas-Nebraska Act vented their anger at the polls. In the 1854 congressional elections only twenty-five of the ninety-one incumbent free state Democrats won reelection. The Americans or Know-Nothing Party and the newly formed Republican Party were the big winners. The Know-Nothings won a string of local victories and elected more than forty congressman. The Republicans whose ranks consisted of Free Soilers, Conscience Whigs and Anti-Nebraska Democrats were at the time of the 1854 election a purely sectional party. They, nevertheless, won over a hundred seats in the U.S. House of Representatives and control of a number of state governments.

From its sectional beginnings, the Republican Party had become by 1856 a bona fide national political entity. Republicans proudly touted themselves as the party of freedom, though not of abolition. They insisted slavery be kept out of territories beyond the 36° 30' parallel, reasoning that if America was to remain a land of opportunity, free white labor must have unrestricted access to settlement in the West. The Republicans in 1856 chose as their presidential standard bearer John C. Fremont who was a hero in the conquest of California where he earned the nickname "the Pathfinder." He brought to the campaign virtually no political experience, but was emphatic and articulate on the issue of slavery. The Republicans' objectives were clear and succinct: "Free soil, free speech, and Fremont."

Disturbed by developments during the Pierce administration and the possible political fall out, Democrats opted not to renominate the president, choosing instead James Buchanan, United States Minister to Great Britain. Candidate Buchanan and the Democrats spent most of their time painting the Republicans as a sectional party bent on destroying the Union. This campaign strategy worked as Buchanan won both the popular and electoral vote. His election was expected to place the ship of state back in capable hands and signal the beginning of an inter-sectional rapprochement. Such expectations, however, were seemingly dashed two days into Buchanan's administration when the U. S. Supreme Court issued its Dred Scott ruling. The case grew out of a petition filed on behalf of Dred Scott, a slave owned by Dr. John Emerson. Between 1834 and 1838 Scott accompanied his army-officer owner from Missouri to Illinois to the Wisconsin Territory and back to Missouri. Following Emerson's death in 1846 a lawyer agreed to bring suit in Missouri to obtain Scott's freedom. It was argued that Scott's residence in Illinois, where the Northwest Ordinance prohibited slavery, and in the Wisconsin Territory where it was similarly outlawed by the Missouri Compromise, made him in effect a free man. In its March 6, 1857 decision, the Supreme Court ruled that Scott, because of his slave status, was chattel and not a citizen—therefore, he could not sue in federal court. Furthermore, the court reasoned that under the Fifth Amendment of the Bill of Rights the federal government was prevented from depriving any person of life, liberty or property without due process of law.

Dred Scott's status no doubt mattered little to most white Americans. Though for African Americans in slavery the decision left no question as to their legal status. The court had unequivocally decreed that under the Constitution slaves were property and without rights of any kind. The larger and consequential question for whites was whether Congress or local legislatures had the power to outlaw slavery in the territories. Chief Justice Roger Taney and a majority of the court held that neither Congress nor local legislatures had that power. In so doing, the Supreme Court rendered the Missouri

Compromise unconstitutional, threatened the principle of popular sovereignty and by implication transformed slavery from merely a local to a national institution. In short, slaveowners could travel into any territory without fear of having the status of their chattel altered. The exceptions were the states which specifically prohibited slavery.

In the wake of the Dred Scott decision more and more northerners became convinced that the South was engaged in an aggressive attempt, a conspiracy even, to extend the peculiar institution as far as possible. So the hope of an inter-sectional reconciliation prompted by the election of James Buchanan never materialized. Furthermore, the nation's gloomy state of affairs was further exacerbated by the New York Stock Market panic during the summer of 1857. While perhaps unavoidable, considering the feverish expansion and speculation of the past decade, the panic caused a sharp and immediate downturn in the economy. Northerners blamed the southern-dominated Congress, emphasizing in particular the reduction of tariff duties to their lowest levels in almost fifty years. These reduction, northerners maintained, led to increased foreign competition, rising unemployment and plummeting prices. The South, it was alleged, sacrificed the nation to realize its own prosperity. Conversely, the South saw in the panic proof of the superiority of the plantation economy. Indeed the southern economy, leaders in the South proudly pointed out, was little affected by the panic. This was true because, as southerners even admitted, the world price of cotton remained consistently high.

In the final years of the decade two other events occurred, the Lincoln-Douglas Debates and the Raid on Harpers Ferry, both serving to additionally aggravate already frayed sectional sensibilities. In the U.S. senatorial race of 1858 in Illinois, Abraham Lincoln challenged his opponent Stephen Douglas to a series of seven debates. The challenge was accepted and the debates followed. The debates are noteworthy because they kept the issue of slavery alive and at the center of a national public debate. In the senate race Douglas won by a close vote in the Illinois legislature over Lincoln, but Republicans piled up huge congressional victories throughout the North. Even moderate southerners found these victories disturbing, so much so that they became increasingly uneasy about the future. The escalating rhetoric of some national Republican leaders like Senator William Seward of New York who spoke of an "irrepressible conflict" between freedom and slavery caused southerners still further anxiety and alarm.

Undoubtedly, though, John Brown's raid on Harpers Ferry, Virginia, a town on the Potomac upstream from Washington, occasioned the greatest alarm, horror and trepidation on the part of southerners. Brown previous exploits had been confined to Kansas where he was alleged to have masterminded the Pottawatomie Massacre. At Harpers Ferry Brown planned to seize the local federal arsenal and to arm nearby slaves whom he expected to rally around him. A black republic would then be created in the mountains of Virginia from where Brown expected to wage war against the South to end slavery. Brown's efforts ended in defeat and he was convicted of treason and hanged. Many northerners, especially abolitionists, viewed his actions as heroic and in death revered him as a martyr. Frederick Douglass and Harriet Tubman were among those insisting on martyrdom for John Brown.

Brown's raid was the last major development to impact the coming of the Civil War prior to the presidential election of 1860. No doubt most American at the time realized the election was to be a crucial one. The nation was clearly at a crossroads with the future of the Union, inextricably tied to the outcome of the election. The candidates in the election included four men, two of whom represented rival wings of the Democratic Party. John Breckinridge and Stephen Douglas were the nominees of the southern and northern wings of the Democratic Party respectively. A third candidate, John Bell, ran on the Constitutional union Party ticket and the fourth standard bearer was the Republican Party nominee, Abraham Lincoln. Neither aspirants, it was thought, would amass a majority of the popular vote. The election would turn on winning the lion share of the electoral vote in the populous northern and western states. Lincoln and the Republicans were considered to have the best chance to do so given their economic program and strong stand against slavery in the territories. As the election approached, Douglas, Lincoln's only serious rival for northern and western votes, almost conceded defeat and spent the remainder of the campaign in the South urging voters not to forsake the Union no matter who won the presidency. Lincoln's popular vote totalled nearly 1.9 million to Douglas' almost million. Breckinridge and Bell polled 848,000 and 593,000 popular votes respectively. In the electoral count Lincoln won by a huge margin, 180 to Breckinridge's 72, his closest opponent.

Southerners who were poised for Lincoln's victory began almost immediately to set the wheels of secession in motion. South Carolina led the way, calling for an election of delegates to a convention to chart the state's future. By December 20, 1860 the convention had voted unanimously to secede, using Calhoun's logic to justify its action. "South Carolina," the delegates declared, "has resumed her position among the nations of the world." Other states of the Lower South soon issued their own notices of secession. By early February 1861 a provisional government of the Confederate States of America had been created. Only Virginia, Tennessee, North Carolina and Arkansas were not in the fold by mid-February. All four would be by mid-April. Even so, Senator John Crittenden of Kentucky and other moderates endeavored to preserve the Union through compromise. Crittenden proposed a constitutional amendment in which slavery would be "recognized as existing" in all territories south of latitude 36° 30'. The amendment also guaranteed no future tampering with slavery in the southern states through the amendment process. A number of other promises were thrown in as well to win over the South. But Lincoln showed no inclination to make any deal to open new territories to slavery. Simply put he was "inflexible on the territorial question. . ." As a result, the Crittenden Compromise never moved beyond the proposal stage.

Lincoln's inflexibility, however, must not be viewed in isolation from the larger context of developments at the time. The South, for instance, had given every indication of casting its collective lot with secession. Southerners seemed hardly disposed to embrace a compromise, be it the Crittenden proposal or any other. Based on its rhetoric and seizure of federal arsenals along with other actions, the South was obviously placing itself on a war footing. The likelihood, therefore, of a scenario, different from the historical one, in which secession was preempted, a mutually acceptable compromise negotiated and war averted had become quite improbable by early 1861. At that juncture, very probably, as William Seward insisted, the nation was confronted with an "irrepressible conflict." To be sure on April 12, 1861 with the South's firing on Fort Sumter the country was plunged into Civil War.

Finally, African Americans although generally depicted as non-factors and inconsequential in the gathering storm that precipitated the Civil War, were in actuality quite consequential. After all, slaves were the very life force of the South's peculiar institution. Moreover, it was the perceived threat of slaves to white free laborers that help generate and sustain the abolition movement. Then, too, it was the plight of African American slaves that provided much of the heartrenching degradation of abolitionist rhetoric. Indeed by acknowledging only the institution and not its victims America compounded an already profoundly difficult crisis. In the end, the nation was swept up into the most unthinkable of national tragedies, Civil War—but within that "calamity" were sown the seeds of both African American emancipation and a new psycho-socio millennium.

SUGGESTED READINGS

Thomas Bailey and David Kennedy, *The American Pageant: A History of the Republic.*

Paul Bergeron, "The Nullification Controversy Revisited," *Tennessee Historical Quarterly* vol. 35 (1976).

Stanley Campbell, *The Slave Catchers: Enforcement of the Fugitive Slave Law,* 1850–1860.

Joseph Conlin, *The American Past: A Survey of American History.*

William Cooper, *Liberty and Slavery: Southern Politics to 1860.*

Walter Ehrlich, "The Origins of the Dred Scott Case," *Journal of Negro History.*

Richard Ellis, *The Union at Risk: Jacksonian Democracy, States and Nullification Crisis.*

Don Fehrenbacher, *The Dred Scott Case.*

Paul Finkelman, *An Imperfect Union: Slavery, Federalism and Comity.*

George Fredrickson, *The Black Image in the White Mind.*

William Freehling, *Prelude to Civil War: The Nullification Controversy in South Carolina, 1816–1836.*

The Road to Disunion: Secessionists at Bay, 1776–1854.

Carter Goodrich, "Internal Improvements Reconsidered," *Journal of Economic History* vol. 30 (June 1970).

Norman Graebner, *Empire On The Pacific.*

Holman Hamilton, *Prologue to Conflict: The Crisis and the Compromise of 1850.*

Nathan Huggins, *Black Odyssey: The Afro-American Ordeal in Slavery.*

Carlton Jackson, "The Internal Improvements Vetoes of Andrew Jackson," *Tennessee Historical Quarterly,* vol. 25 (1966).

Harry Jaffa, *Crisis of the House Divided: An Interpretation of the Issues in the Lincoln-Douglas Debates.*

Robert Johanssen, *Lincoln, The South and Slavery; Stephen Douglas;* and *To The Halls of Montezuma.*

Aileen S. Krachitor, *Means and Ends in American Abolitionism: Garrison and His Critics on Strategy and Tactics,* 1834–1850.

Susan Lee and Peter Passell, *A New Economic View of American History.*

John McCardell, *The Idea of a Southern Nationalists and Southern Nationalism,* 1830–1860.

Eric McKitrick (ed.), *Slavery Defended: The Views of the Old South.*

Glover Moore, *The Missouri Controversy.*

John Niven, *The Coming of the Civil War.*

James Oakes, *The Ruling Race: A History of American Slaveholders.*

J. P. Ochenkowski, "The Origins of Nullification in South Carolina," *South Carolina Historical Magazine* Vol. 83 (1982).

Lewis Perry, *Radical Abolitionism: Anarchy and the Government of God in Anti-slavery Thought.*

Edward Pessen, *Jacksonian America: Society, Personality and Politics.*

Merril Peterson, *The Great Triumvirate: Webster, Clay and Calhoun*; and *Olive Branch and Sword: The Compromise of 1833.*

Benjamin Quarles, *Allies for Freedom: Blacks and John Brown.*

Robert Remini, *The Jacksonian Era.*

Michael Rogin, *Fathers and Children: Andrew Jackson and the Subjugation of the American Indian.*

Ronald Satz, "Indian Policy in the Jacksonian Era" in Leonard Dinnerstein and Kenneth Jackson (eds.), *American Vistas,* 1607–1877.

Richard Sewell, *A House Divided: Sectionalism and the Civil War.*

James Stewart, *Holy Warriors: The Abolitionists and American Slavery.*

Charles Syndor, *Slavery in Mississippi.*

William Taylor, *Cavalier and Yankee: The Old South and American National Character.*

Larry Tise, *Proslavery: A History of the Defense of Slavery in America,* 1701–1840.

Mary Young, "Indian Removal and Land Allotment: The Civilized Tribes and Jacksonian Justice," *American Historical Review,* 64 (Oct., 1958).

STUDY GUIDE 9

1 How might the period in American history from 1820–1860 be referred?

2–3 Under the Missouri Compromise, name what two states were affected?

4 What line was "drawn" in the Missouri Compromise?

5 What group of people were involved in the "trail of tears?"

6 In what court case did the court rule that the Cherokees and their territory were autonomous and not subject to the control of the State of Georgia?

7 Name the American President at the time of *Worcester v. Georgia*.

8 In 1828, who wrote "South Carolina's Exposition and Protest?"

9 What antebellum southern institution was characterized as a "necessary evil?"

10 What antebellum southern institution was characterized as a "positive good?"

11–14 Give the names of four black abolitionist orators who were ex-slaves and who were mentioned in this chapter.

15–16 When and where did the Nat Turner rebellion occur?

17 What name was given to the belief that God had ordained that the United States should stretch from "sea" to "sea"?

18 What peace treaty ended the Mexican War?

19–23 Give a gist of the facets of the Compromise of 1850.

24 Give the author of *Uncle Tom's Cabin*.

25–27 Give three characters from *Uncle Tom's Cabin* mentioned in this chapter.

28 What U.S. Senator sponsored the 1852 Kansas-Nebraska Act?

29 How did northerners dub the violence in Kansas between 1854 and 1856?

30–32 What political groups comprised the Republican coalition of 1854?

33 Give the 1856 Republican Party Presidential standard bearer.

34 What 1857 court case defined the rights of black Americans?

35 Who won the 1858 Illinois U. S. Senatorial race?

36 Name his (**35**) leading opponent.

37 In 1859, who led the raid on Harpers Ferry?

38–45 Name the four major U. S. Presidential candidates of 1860 and in the blank next to each, give the political banner under which he ran.

46 Who won the 1860 U. S. Presidential election?

47 Name the first state to secede from the Union after the election of 1860.

48 Give the date of the secession of (**47**) the above state.

49–50 Give at least two other states that eventually joined (**47**) the above state in secession.

10

The African American and the Civil War

There have been numerous books, articles, and essays, as well as conflicting interpretations written in an effort to explain the cause of the American Civil War. These narratives emanated from the concepts of a diverse group of historians, many of whom were associated with a particular school of thought. Some of these historians blamed the South for the war, while others pointed to the North as the initiator.

A majority of the Northern writers proclaimed that the war started when the North made an attempt to protect the union and the Constitution against the militancy of the South and the slave owners who were committed to an immoral institution. But to the contrary, most of the Southern writers stated that slavery was an opportunity for the war and not its cause. The Southerners charged that the war was caused by the aggression of the North who was bent on destroying the South. Moreover, the South said that the North used its power for political and economic gain.

The late James Ford Rhodes, a member of the nationalist school, called the Civil War an "Irrepressible conflict" between the two sections. He concluded that the South was in the wrong. Some members of the Progressive school viewed the war as a social conflict between Northern capitalists and the planting aristocracy of the South. James G. Randall and Avery Craven, both writing as members of the Revisionists school, interpreted the war as an "avoidable or repressible" conflict. Both writers agreed that the war could have been avoided if both sections had been willing to resolve their differences through political means. Randall blamed the war on what he called a "blundering generation."

Regardless of what caused the Civil War, one fact remains—African Americans played a major role in the war. When the Republican party elected Abraham Lincoln in November of 1860, African Americans rejoiced over the election. And Northern African Americans, many of whom were abolitionists and had been pushing for separation, were pleased that the South seceded and had organized the Confederacy in February of 1861.

On April 12, 1861, the Confederate forces fired on Fort Sumter in South Carolina. Shortly after the Confederacy took over the fort, Lincoln called for 75,000 militia to serve over a ninety day period to end the rebellion. Numerous offers by Northern African Americans were made to enlist in the union army. In Pittsburgh, Pennsylvania; Detroit, Michigan; Albany, Ohio; and many other Northern cities, African American military units were organized with intentions of serving the union.

Although African Americans were willing to fight for the union, the white population and the Lincoln administration were opposed to recruiting African Americans. The attitude of the North was that the war was a white man's battle to preserve the Union rather than to end slavery. Having a different strategy going into the war, the North planned for a short war, while the South sought the support of the non-slaveholding population to fight. Neither the South nor the North recognized African Americans as possible fighters at the beginning of the war.

According to the United States Census of 1860, there were 4,441,830 African Americans in both the North and South. This total population was composed of 488,070 free African Americans and 3,953,760 slaves. Approximately 430,000 slaves were located in the Union border states of Delaware, Kentucky, Maryland and Missouri. The Confederate states: Alabama, Arkansas, Florida, Georgia, Louisiana, Mississippi, North Carolina, South Carolina, Tennessee, Texas and Virginia had a total white population of 5,220,000, while the Union had an overall white population of 21,570,000. By employing the slave population as soldiers, the Confederacy could prolong the war.

Even though the North and South would not allow African Americans to enlist at the beginning of the war, both sections would eventually make official and unofficial use of their services. Unofficially, the southern slave population aided the Confederacy at the outset of the war. Slaves, by working as factory laborers, plantation workers, food producers, and general laborers, freed the majority of white men from these tasks, allowing them to fight in the military. As the war progressed, the Confederacy would come to officially allow free African Americans to fight.

In the Spring of 1861, Governor Thomas O. Moore of Louisiana passed an order allowing free African Americans to organize a regiment. The first African American regiment was called the First Native Guards, Louisiana Militia, Confederate states of America. Several other areas in the South accepted the services of free African Americans who volunteered to aid the Confederacy during the first weeks of the war. The free African Americans were utilized to build fortifications, earthworks, and perform other tasks.

The African-American Native Guard regiment of Louisiana was never used by the Southern government. On the other hand, other African American militia units were used in the state. During the early phase of the war, more than 3,000 African Americans volunteered for service in a number of military units. At the outbreak of the war, the majority of free African Americans in Louisiana lived in New Orleans. In addition to serving in the militia to protect the city of New Orleans, many free African Americans joined the Confederate Army.

Supporters gave assistance in the form of money or service. A free African American real estate dealer in New Orleans gave $500 to finance the Confederate Army. The successful free African American neighborhoods in New Orleans announced that they were prepared to fight at any time along with other residents. However, when the Union forces defeated the Confederate forces at New Orleans and took control of the city on May 1, 1862, the African American regiment would not evacuate the city with the Confederate Army. The regiment remained in the city to greet the victorious Union forces and pledge their loyalty to the Union.

The motive leading southern African Americans to support the South was questioned. Some African Americans probably served out of loyalty to the South. Yet, others participated believing that they would receive better treatment. Moreover, some southern African Americans freely offered their service out of fear that the local authorities would force them to serve in the military. When Major General Benjamin F. Butler took control of New Orleans in the Spring of 1862, he met with the leaders of the free African American districts in the city. Butler wanted to know why they would support the Confederacy, which was organized for the purpose of keeping their people in permanent slavery. They answered that "they had not dared to refuse; that they had hoped, by serving the Confederacy, to advance a little nearer to equality with whites . . . " After initially siding with the South, African Americans expressed a desire to serve the Union. Later, they were enlisted in the Union Army and fought well for the duration of the war.

A number of Southern slaves also considered volunteering their service to the Confederacy as countless numbers of African American slaves attempted to join the Union forces by crossing the Southern lines. On one occasion, General Benjamin F. Butler would not return several runaways. He declared them as contraband of war that were being used by the enemy as workers. When a similar situation occurred in Missouri, the outcome was different. General John C. Fremont of the Union Army declared a martial law in Missouri that freed all slaves. But Lincoln continued to insist that the war was to keep the Union together and not to interfere with slavery. He rescinded Fremont's order and advised him to follow the common law regarding slavery. Being disappointed with the Union's refusal to accept their service, some of the Southern slaves returned to the South, indicating that they anticipated fighting for the South hoping that it would lead to their freedom. In addition to reemphasizing that the war was being fought to perserve the Union, the North gave other reasons for not allowing African Americans to fight during the early stages of the war. Some felt that African Americans were not eager to fight against southern whites. Others felt that African Americans would launch an attack to abolish slavery in the South. It was finally stated that if African Americans were allowed to fight, they would massacre the slave owners. While the North returned runaways to the South and refused to officially allow them to fight, the South at this time in the war had gone all out to recruit both free and enslaved African Americans. In South Carolina, Virginia, Tennessee, and other Southern states, laws were passed drafting African Americans into Confederacy service. Although most African American soldiers worked as fortification workers, some were later used as fighting soldiers. These African Americans played a vital role in numerous Confederate victories.

Not only did black Americans contribute to the Confederacy in regiments and battalions, but many were recognized for their individual performance. For example, African American Preston Roberts was the quartermaster for General Nathan B. Forrest as well as an outstanding Confederate leader. Roberts was in charge of seventy-five black cooks; he was allowed to handle the finances for purchasing food, and he occasionally worked as a spy. For his service, Roberts received the Cross of Honor, the highest Confederate award.

Two other African Americans were cited for gallant service to the Confederacy. Ol' Dick was a drummer for the eighteenth Virginia Regiment. He was noted for his skill with a bowie knife in cutting out Northern soldiers' intestines. Ol' Dick was described as "a gentleman and a true patriot." John Tinsley, a free man of color, was a prominent telegraph engineer for the Confederate Army who, working with a group of African Americans and whites, repaired telegraph lines.

Some African Americans supported the Confederacy out of loyalty to their owners who had been sympathetic toward them. The majority of the slaves, however, did not support the South. As the war intensified, thousands of slaves fled from the South to join the Union Army. When Federal troops marched into Virginia, some 5,000 slaves were waiting to meet them. Approximately 9,000 slaves flocked to South Carolina when the Union army arrived. Despite Lincoln's ban against using Negroes in the war, some Union generals disregarded the law and utilized thousands of slaves as soldiers.

Having lost battles at First Bull Run, Ball's Bluff, Wilson's Creek, and second Bull Run or Manassas, Lincoln considered taking more drastic action toward the war. Realizing that the key to victory rested with the 4,000,000 slaves in the South, he contemplated a plan to gaining the Union slaves' loyalty by offering them freedom. When Lincoln discussed the plan with his Cabinet, he was advised to postpone the idea until a later date. To announce such a plan at a time when the Union was losing the war would be viewed by the public as a retreat from the war. Meanwhile, Congress continued to pass legislation that would help weaken the South. Congress had already passed a law on June 19, 1862 abolishing slavery in all the territories. On July 17, 1862, the Second Confiscation Act was passed. This law proclaimed that anyone supporting the South would be punished by having their slaves freed. In the same month, Congress enacted legislation stating that runaway slaves were not to be returned to their owners unless the owners were supporters of the North. The Militia Act passed by Congress in the following months of 1862 gave freedom to soldiers who were slaves and their families who belong to the enemy. These measures were still not enough to curb the South's momentum in the war.

As previously stated, when Lincoln first discussed the proclamation issue with his Cabinet in August of 1862, Secretary of State, William H. Seward, favored the idea, but was opposed to issuing it at the time. Seward felt that it was not politically expedient to announce the proclamation while the morale of the public was so low. Finally, Seward lamented that if we held out our hands to "Ethiopia," rather than "Ethiopia" stretching out her hands to the government, it may be looked upon as the final act of an "exhausted government." Therefore, Lincoln decided to delay the issue.

Lincoln patiently waited for a more convenient time to publicly announce his proclamation plan. That opportunity presented itself in September of 1862. In that month, General Robert E. Lee, Commander of the Confederate Army, led an attack against the Union at Antietam in Maryland. The Union forces, who were under the command of General George B. McClellan, forced Lee to retreat to Virginia. The battle was actually a stalemate, yet it has been described as the most decisive conflict of the war.

Lincoln used Antietam as a catalyst to announce his Emancipation Proclamation Plan. Even though the Union did not win the battle, Lincoln, nevertheless, interpreted Lee's retreat as a victory. Having delayed the issuance of the proclamation because of a number of defeats, Lincoln realized that the plan would be more acceptable following a victory. He, therefore, disguised Antietam as a victory for the North and announced the Emancipation Proclamation on September 22, 1862.

The fact that the Emancipation Proclaimation was issued in September of 1862 does not mean that it took immediate effect. In fact, the proclamation issued in 1862 was the first of two proclamations. The first proclaimation was only a warning to the rebellious states. It announced Lincoln's plan for a second proclaimation to end slavery. The proclaimation stated that on January 1, 1863, another proclaimation would be passed. Moreover it proclaimed that all of those slaves that were in the states still in rebellion against the Union would be freed. In addition, it stated that if a rebellious state should rejoin the Union prior to January 1, 1863, it would no longer be a seceded state, and the proclamation would not apply to its slaves.

When the rebellious states refused to accept Lincoln's first proclaimation, he passed his second proclamation on January 1, 1863, freeing those slaves in states that were still in rebellion against the Union. Lincoln realized that he had no other option left. He had been advised by his own diplomats that a strong emancipation policy would remove the "pro-Confederate sympathies of England and France." Some of the governors in the North told Lincoln that a number of the young men were hesitant about joining an army that was fighting to preserve slavery. These and other pressures weighed heavily on his decision to issue the proclamation.

As strange as it may sound, the Emancipation Proclamation did not free a singe slave. The proclamation had a number of motives. The primary objective was to replace hesitant white Northern soldiers with African American soldiers. The North did not have enough white soldiers to defeat the South. A second reason for the proclamation was to provide a new boost toward victory in the North by selling the idea of emancipation as a moral issue. The third motive was to win international sympathy for the Union by keeping foreign nations, especially England who was anticipating entering on the side of the South, out of the war.

All of these motives were accomplished. England decided not to intervene following the announcement of the first proclamation. Thousands of African Americans flocked to join the Union, and eventually, the North defeated the South. Though the Emancipation Proclamation did not apply to the Border States where some 800,000 African Americans were still enslaved, Lincoln maintained an end to slavery where he could enforce it, and passed a law where he could not enforce it.

Nevertheless, African Americans understood that they had an opportunity to free themselves by enlisting in the Union Army. Eager for the opportunity to fight for their freedom, thousands of African Americans from both the North and South were officially enlisted by the War Department. There was strong opposition towards allowing African Americans to enlist. This opposition was almost as strong in the North as in the South, and appeared in both the military and the civilian society.

In the North, the Northern Democrats (called copperheads) stated that the war was being fought to free "niggers." General Butler stated that the prejudice against African American soldiers by white officers was fearful. The aristocratic females in Boston "hooted" the Massachusetts 54th African American Regiment. The Northern Democratic newspapers such as the Chicago Times wrote "Niggers . . . big black stinking buck niggers." In Boston, the State Senate passed a law stating that "no one of African descent should be commissioned or hold office in the Army of the United States."

Perhaps the most atrocious opposition was the race riots that took place in a number of Northern cities. When whites were no longer volunteering, Congress passed the National Conscription Act on March 3, 1863. The Democratic papers called it an extreme form of tyranny. In addition, the papers stated that white men were being forced to free "niggers . . . " One New York politician proclaimed that the war was an oppressive act against White Southerners designed to liberate the "niggers!" "Free Niggers—the black savages lusting for our women will roam the streets . . . " "Do you want to spill your blood so niggers can be free?"

Riots occurred in a number of big cities such as Chicago, Philadelphia, and New York. The most vicious of all the riots broke out in New York. The incident was sparked by Irish workers who were competing for jobs. The incident lasted for three days during the month of July. The number of fatalities and injuries numbered more than a thousand. On one occasion, a small girl from an orphan asylum was beaten to death. Some African Americans were hung on lamp posts; one African American who was reportedly hung from a post, had his flesh cut into small pieces and thrown to the mob. Troops were called in to restore order.

These atrocities did not dampen the spirit of African Americans toward the war. They continued to enlist. When Lincoln was criticized for allowing African Americans to serve, Lincoln explained his act as an expedient one. He stated that the South could not be defeated through the Democratic process, which would sacrifice the total population of white men in the North. Moreover, he said that if all the African Americans fighting for the North were allowed to fight for the South, the North would have to give up the war within three weeks. Lincoln told his critics that as long as he was President, the primary purpose for the war would be to restore the Union. However, he closed by saying that the South could not be defeated without the emancipation policy.

As the war continued, some of the criticism and hatred subsided to a minimal level. But African Americans were still discriminated against as soldiers: A white soldier received $13 per month; African American soldiers were paid $10 per month, and $3 per month was deducted for clothing. One African American regiment from Massachusetts went without pay for a full year until they were paid the same. Furthermore, African Americans were not treated the same in matters concerning assignment of duty, medical treatment, food, and rank. Despite these differences, African Americans went on to serve gallantly. Seven months after they were allowed to enlist, the tide of war began to turn in favor of the North. African Americans fought in almost all of the major battles such as Gettysburg, Miliken's Bend, Fort Wagner, Nashville, and many others. Ulysses S. Grant, Commander of the Union Army, General George H. Thomas, a Union officer, Edwin M. Stanton, the Union Secretary of War, and Lincoln all gave high praises for African American's performance on the battle field.

The single most worst incident during the war that made African Americans more determined to fight was the massacre at Fort Pillow. Fort Pillow was a Union garrison located in Tennessee. On April 12, 1864, Confederate General Nathan B. Forrest led an attack against the fort. When the Confederates finally entered the fort, they began to butcher the 600 white and African American occupants, including the injured. People who were already dead were mutilated, even children seven and eight years old. A number of African American women were murdered. The dead and injured African Americans were stacked in piles and burned. Three-hundred black Americans were massacred; five were buried alive.

When Forrest made an official report of the encounter, he stated that only a small number of Union officers escaped. The report showed that a total of 500 Unionists had been killed. Forrest said he hoped that those facts would show the North that African American soldiers could not cope with Southerners. The Fort Pillow affair renewed the African American commitment toward the war. They were determined to avenge their brothers massacred at the fort and determined to prevent such an event from ever happening again.

African Americans' eagerness for vengeance was exemplified in a number of battles following the Fort Pillow massacre. Decatur Dorsey, acting as color-sergeant, received a medal from Congress for gallantry at Petersburg, Virginia on July 30, 1864. Four received the Gilmore Medal for courageous action at Fort Wagner, South Carolina. During the battle of Chapin's Farm, on September 29, 1864, Sergeant-Major Christian Fleetwood, Corporal Charles Veal, First Sergeant James E. Bronson, and a host of others received awards for valor during the battle. A total of thirteen were awarded the Congressional Medal of Honor.

African Americans did not serve just in the Union Army; a substantial number also enlisted in the navy. The most noted African American sailor was William Tillman, a cook on the Union vessel, the *S. J. Waring*. When the Confederate ship, *Jefferson Davis*, captured the *S. J. Waring*, Tiliman rescued the vessel.

The Confederates held the ship for seven nights. While the officers of the *Jefferson Davis* were asleep, Tillman snuck into the cabin and killed them. He took over the ship and sailed it to New York. Tillman was greeted as a hero and given a $6,000 reward. African Americans made major contributions to the Union's Navy victories. Of the 118,044 men that served in the Union Navy 29,511 were African Americans.

The African Americans, who enlisted in the army and navy of the North, not only avenged those massacred at Fort Pillow, but the continuous enlistment of thousands would eventually lead to the defeat of the South. Before the war came to an end, some 200,000 African Americans had fought for the North. About 120,000 came from the South and 80,000 from the North. Approximately 300,000 served the army in other capacities such as spies, cooks, teamsters, nurses, carpenters, and other positions.

African Americans fought about 450 battles. The 154 African American regiments and 140 infantry units made up roughly twenty-one percent of the total number who fought in the army, and more than twenty of these men would be awarded the Congressional Medal of Honor. The mortality rate for African American soldiers was nearly forty percent higher than that of white soldiers. More than 38,000 black men were killed during the war.

Realizing that the use of African Americans by the North as soldiers would eventually result in victory for the North, the South made a last desperate attempt to stem the tide of a Northern victory. On March 13, 1865 Jefferson Davis, President of the Confederacy, signed a bill known as the "Negro Soldier Law." The legislation allowed the enlistment of slaves as soldiers in the Southern Army. In slave states, slave who wanted to fight could not be freed without the consent of their owners. Several companies of slaves were recruited. However, before any companies could be organized, the Southern capital at Richmond, Virginia was captured. On April 9, 1865, Gen. Robert E. Lee surrendered to Gen. Ulysses S. Grant at Appomattox Courthouse, Virginia , ending the Civil War.

When the South fired on Fort Sumter, South Carolina on April 12, 1861, Lincoln called for 75,000 militia to put an end to the rise-up. African Americans immediately offered their service as soldiers, but Lincoln refused their offer, saying that he was taking action to preserve the Union, which involved neither African Americans nor slavery.

During the early stages of the war, the North found itself militarily incapable of coping with the South. Much of the success of the South during the early phase of the conflict resulted from the large numbers of African Americans who supported the Southern war effort.

When it became evident that the North could not defeat the South under the existing circumstances, Lincoln signed the Emancipation Proclamation. This act would eventually allow thousands of African Americans to enlist as soldiers in the Union Army. The enlistment of African Americans in the army and navy would eventually turn the tide of the war in favor of the North.

In an effort to prevent a Northern victory, the South passed a law allowing slaves to fight for the Confederacy. Though some slaves were recruited, it was too late. Lee surrendered to Grant on April 9, 1865, ending the Civil War. Thus, African Americans had made their own freedom possible. But, their freedom would not occur until the adoption of the thirteenth Amendment during the Reconstruction period following the war.

Suggested Readings

Thomas A. Bailey, *Probing America's Past: A Critical Examination of Major Myths And Misconceptions,* Vol. 1.

Peter M. Bargrnan, *The Chronological History Of The Negro In America.*

Ebony eds. *Ebony Pictorial History Of Black America: African Past To The Civil War,* Vol.1.

Leroy H. Fischer, guest ed.-in-chief. "The Western States In the Civil War: Six for the Union; Three for the Confederacy." *Journal of the West* (January, 1975), Vol. XIV, No.1.

John Hope Franklin and Alfred Moss Jr. *From Slavery To Freedom.*

Rhoda L. Goldstein, ed. *Black Life and Culture in the United States.*

Gerald N. Grob and George Athan Billias, *Interpretations of American History: Patterns and Perspectives,* Vol.1.

Rayford W. Logan and Irving S. Cohen, *The American Negro: Old World Background And New World Experience.*

James M. McPherson, *The Negro's Civil War: How American Negroes Felt and Acted During the War for the Union; Ordeal By Fire: The Coming of the War,* Vols. I and II.

Robert W. Mullen, *Blacks in America's Wars: The Shift in Attitudes from the Revolutionary War to Vietnam.*

Fletcher Fletcher, *Civil War In Pictures.*

J. A. Rogers, *Africa's Gift to America: The Afro American in the Making and Saving of the United States with New Supplement and Its Potentialities.*

Study Guide 10

1 What historian called the Civil War the "Irrepressible Conflict"?

2 In what state is Fort Sumter?

3–6 Name the border states during the Civil War.

7–17 Name the eleven C.S.A. Member states.

18 Who served as United States President during the Civil War?

19 Name the President of the C.S.A.

20 The 54th black regiment was associated with what state?

21–23 Give at least three (3) places where race riots occurred in the north following the passage of the National Conscription Act on March 3, 1863.

24 In what state was the Civil War massacre at Fort Pillow?

25 By the Negro Soldier Law of March, 1865, what Civil War side had decided to use blacks as troops?

26 What city served as the permanent capital of the C.S.A.?

27 Where did the Civil War officially end?

28 When did the Civil War officially end?

29–30 Who surrendered to whom, officially ending the Civil War?

31 When had the military phase of the Civil War begun?

For each person below, indicate whether he was a Union or Confederate soldier:

32 James E. Bronson

33 Benjamin F. Butler

34 Christian Fleetwood

35 Nathan B. Forrest

36 John C. Fremont

37 Ulysses S. Grant

38 Robert E. Lee

39 George B. McClellam

40 Charles Veal

11

Reconstruction

The day of the "jubilo" had finally come. With the closing of the Civil War, slavery as a dejure institution was a thing of the past. African Americans were fixing to enter a new day. This era would become known as Reconstruction. By its simplest definition, Reconstruction was the period in American History emphasizing the rebuilding of the nation following the American Civil War. It is usually dated 1865–1877. Now, if these "facts" are examined, it is shown that neither 1865 or 1877 is hard-and-fast. The same kind of significant activities that occurred after 1865 had gotten started in 1862 when the groundworks were laid in Virginia for the establishment of Hampton Institute (University). Political activities were other dominants aspects of Reconstruction. Therefore, not until George H. White of North Carolina left the U.S. Congress, as a Representative in 1902, bringing down the curtain on black men physically representing states in the deep south in the U.S. Congress, until the "second Reconstruction," can it be concluded that Reconstruction fell.

There were two major problems of Reconstruction. First, there was the problem of restoration of the Union. And the other "problem" was what to do about the freedmen. There were three plans of Reconstruction: Lincoln Plan or 10% Plan; Johnson's Plan; and the Radical Plan (initial part presented in the Wade-Davis Bill). The first two plans took the names of their leading backers. The Lincoln plan received its name from President Abraham Lincoln. Unfortunately, President Lincoln was assassinated the evening of April 14, 1865. His Vice President, Andrew Johnson, then became President. The three **Plans of Reconstruction** were based upon three **Theories of Reconstruction**. Lincoln's theory held that the South had never been out of the union but was simply in a state of **Rebellion** and therefore the President, under Article Four of the Constitution had a right to Reconstruct the Union. U. S. Senator Charles Sumner of Massachusetts had the State Suicide Theory. That is, the states had committed political suicide as member states of the United States' union of states when they seceded from the Union. Congressman Thaddeus Stevens of Pennsylvania had the Conquered Province theory. Once the states had withdrawn from the Union and were defeated in battle, then the said states were to be treated simply as any other territory that had been defeated in war. Both of the latter theories justified Congressional Reconstruction. In the 1869 case of *Texas v. White* the U.S. Supreme Court, threw its weight behind the theory of Lincoln stating that the south had never been out of the Union.

Lincoln's Plan of Reconstruction would have granted amnesty for all who would take an oath for future loyalty to the United States. When ten percent of the number of persons who had voted in the Election of 1860 took a loyalty oath, then that state might elect a slate of state government officials. Louisiana, Arkansas and Tennessee were "Reconstructed" under the Lincoln Plan. When their new U.S. Senators and Representatives arrived in Washington, D.C., the U.S. Congress refused to seat them. Therefore technically, the President's version of Reconstruction had failed. But, in that the new President's home state was Tennessee and the Constitution stating that the President MUST be a citizen of a state of the Union, Tennessee was Reconstructed and never really underwent "Radical Reconstruction."

Next came the Johnson Plan. This Plan would have granted pardon to all who would take a test oath for future loyalty. However, exempted from taking this oath, until granted pardon, were two categories of persons—(1) high ranking Confederate officials and military officers; (2) those southerners [former Confederate, (Confederate States of America)] citizens who had been worth more than $20,000 before the Civil War. The Johnson Plan also called for a Provisional Governor for each state to be appointed by the President; the election of delegates to a constitutional convention; implied, but not stated as a fact, that Johnson required a larger percentage than 10% to take a loyalty oath in order that a state be reconstructed; secession ordinances be repudiated; Confederate war debts and slavery be abolished; finally, there was an implication that Johnson would like to see suffrage extended to a limited number of Negroes. Johnson's Plan, like Lincoln's, was doomed for failure. That left only the "Radical" Plan.

This brings one to ask, and answer, the question why radicals and their plan succeeded? The first big item is who were the "Radicals"? One view is that the label "Radical" came into vogue because these were men who simply wanted to incorporate African Americans into the American mainstream. The so called Radicals were Republicans. And of these, there were three divisions. There were the "Carpetbaggers," "Scalawags" and the largest group were the blacks. The so called Radicals had come into being for several reasons. One, these men did not want to leave the freedmen in the hands of southerners. Two, some radicals wanted to punish the south. Three, some wanted to protect Republican economic policies of a protective tariff and hard money. Four, some detested the Presidents ignoring Congressional leadership. And five, some Republican Radicals wanted to insure the leadership of the nation of the Republican Party. There were a series of acts precipitated by southerners that caused some "Radicals" to react. Southern arrogance was seen in the election of high Confederate officials to state and national posts. Even the former Vice President of the Confederate States of America, Alexander H. Stephens of Georgia, had been re-elected as a U.S. Senator from Georgia. Southern states rejected the XIVth Amendment. In 1866, on his "swing around the circle," President Johnson had displayed arrogance toward Northerners. All over the south, Black Codes were being enacted. And finally, there were a series of race riots. The most serious were in Memphis and New Orleans. To some Northerners, it seemed that southerners were saying that if they could not have "their" Negroes as slaves, then they would destroy/eradicate them.

The "Radicals" used the Joint Committee of Fifteen to serve as a data bank advising Congress on its Reconstruction policies. This Committee was made up of seven members from the U.S. House, seven members from the U. S. Senate and one member from the Supreme Court. One of the first legislative matters from the "Radicals" was passage of the 1866 Civil Rights Bill. This measure defined citizenship so as to cover blacks and also granted due process of law thereby forbidding certain forms of discrimination. Later, one finds that much of this bill was incorporated in the XIVth Amendment. In February, 1866, there was a Congressional measure to increase the life of the Freedmen's Bureau, a governmental agency which had been created in 1865 (to be discussed later). In 1867, there was the Military Reconstruction Act which created five military districts, in the former Confederate states, and placed a military commander over each. The ten remaining ex-C.S.A. states would be placed in these districts. These commanders were to call a Constitutional Convention in each individual "state" where both black men and white men would be involved. The election to these Conventions would be the first time that African American men voted en masse. The next major "Radical" measure was the Command of the Army Act. It prohibited military orders from being issued through anyone other than the commanding general of the army whose offices, at all times, were to be in Washington, D. C. The last major "Radical" measure was the Tenure of Office Act. According to this measure, the President could not remove from office, without Senate approval, any appointee whose appointment to the same required Senate confirmation. The removal of Edwin Stanton, Secretary of War, under this measure is what led, immediately, to Johnson's downfall.

Reconstruction might be divided into three aspects—Social, Political, and Economic. Looking at the first, one might say, Thaddeus Stevens worked for it! Some people, especially blacks, hoped it would happen, but with hindsight, one realizes that this idea conflicted with Republican Party's principles of "sanctity of property." What idea? **Forty Acres and a Mule** . . . an expression representing the desires of some but the fears of many others. This idea hinged on the belief that on January 1, 1866, Congress would give to each freedman forty acres of land which had been confiscated from the "rebs," and a mule to work that land. Such never happened. The closest thing to this dream was the Southern Homestead Act.

The major national dramatical act involving political Reconstruction was the impeachment of President Johnson. From February to May, 1868, the national government was stalemated with the attempt to impeach and remove from office President Johnson. Johnson, a Constitutional Unionist from Tennessee, had become President Lincoln's choice for Vice President in 1864. Upon Lincoln's assassination, Johnson then became the new President. Normally when one thinks of a President of the United States, one sees him heading two distinct bodies. He is leader of the country—the United States of America. And, he is also head of his political party. Johnson was not looked upon by some Republicans as "head" of the Republican Party. This caused some of Johnson's problems. Johnson also had an "outsider" mentality (Eric McKitrick) and maybe even subconsciously he saw himself as being looked down upon by some "ins," or maybe Johnson just had a "small man's" ego. Congressional Republicans saw a chance to be rid of Johnson when, August, 1867, he removed Secretary of War, Edwin M. Stanton. He tried to get both Ulysses Grant and Lorenzo Thomas to replace Stanton. Eventually Johnson was saved from removal, in the impeachment trial, by one vote.

In the south, one aspect of political Reconstruction were the Carpetbaggers and Scalawags. Carpetbaggers stereotyped northern or "outside" whites who came south after the Civil War, possessing so few material things they could carry them in a valise or carpetbag while "robbing" the south blind. Scalawags were native whites southerners who participated in Reconstruction as Republicans to control blacks and gain power. Never in any state have black men controlled the state's political apparatus. In American government, there are three areas of political domain—Executive, Legislative and Judicial; in each of these areas, blacks were prevented from obtaining political positions. For example, during the Reconstruction Era, South Carolina was the only state in which a black man sat on the State Supreme Court: Jonathan J. Wright was the only black man to become State Justice during this time. On the federal level, no black man was elevated to this position until Thurgood Marshall in 1967. The executive branch also remained strictly white until Virginia elected L. Douglas Wilder as state govonor in 1989. Although Pinkney Benton Stewart Pinchback served as Governor of Louisiana for 39 days during Reconstruction, he was elected as Lieutenant Governor. In Mississippi, one African American, Alexander K. Davis, was elected as Lt. Governor during Reconstruction. Richard Gleaves and Alonzo J. Ransier were black and also served in South-Carolina. Louisiana had three black men that served as Lt. Governor during Reconstruction—Oscar J. Dunn, Pinchback and Ceasar Carpentier Antoine.

In the legislative branch of government, South Carolina and Louisiana probably had the highest percentage of black legislators. No historian has proven beyond a doubt that there was ever a black majority in any state, but if any states had a black majority legislature, it would have been South Carolina or Louisiana.

A number of black national figures were elected during Reconstruction. Two black men from Mississippi served in the United States Senate. Mississippi sent both Hiram R. Revels and Blanche K. Bruce to the U. S. Senate. And Louisiana elected P. B. S. Pinchback, although he never actually served in the U.S. Senate. Pinchback was given a salary by the Senate, but never seated. In the U. S. House of Representatives, a number of states had Congressmen who were African Americans. Of course, there was never any such thing as "Radical" Reconstruction in Tennessee, therefore it never elected a Reconstruction era Congressman who was black. Texas also never elected anyone on the national level who was black. However, Norris Wright Cuny was probably the most prominent black man in Texas in the latter half of the 19th century.

Theft was very common during the Reconstruction period. Some historians have even termed this period as the "Era of Good Stealing." Not just in the south, but throughout America, there was corruption. In New York City alone, the Tammany Hall gang might have absconded with more "loot" than in the whole former Confederacy. But with the Civil War just concluded, how much did the South have left to steal? Perhaps some of the legend of all the corruption in the south during Reconstruction, became no more than a justification by Redeemers (Bourbons) for the "overthrowal" of Reconstruction—re-establishment of "white rule" in a "white man's country." Because of the simple hatred of blacks as people, corruption by a few blacks and their associates, Redemption became an easy "sell." As far as this period being an era dominated by "Radicals," studies on individual black legislators have shown they tended not to be radical, but moderate.

In examining Economic Reconstruction, one becomes introduced to agricultural concepts such as sharecroppers, tenant farmers and crop lien. Sharecropping and tenant farming might be distinguished in terms of race. Sharecroppers tended to be black, whereas tenant farmers tended to be white. Sharecroppers, usually poor, rented plots of land to farm, and paid the owner with a share of the crop. Normally, the deal was made on a sixty:forty basis where the farmer (sharecropper) received sixty percent of the net proceeds from the crop, and the land owner received forty percent. But before the sixty: forty division occured, the sharecropper first had to pay the landowner for upkeep of the plot. Remember that most farmers were illiterate, and had no real comprehension of numbers. Land owners took advantage of this ignorance. And farmers found themselves going deeper and deeper in debt every year. This situation helped to create the "Exodus" movement. For the urban freedmen, it was a time when "Freedmen Towns" sprang up. These were areas in the cities that became the centers of black social life, and to a lesser extent, economic life as well. Churches, banks, funeral homes, cafes, etc. began to spring up. In many cases these were enterprises of freedmen who were descendants or were themselves pre-Civil War f.p.c.s (free persons of color). These persons, often, had a little financial worth before Reconstruction. In other words, they had "old money." Some put their "pennies" together and bought church lands, and even provided social care agencies (welfare agencies).

When viewing Social Reconstruction, one first looks at the individual. No longer were these individuals "slaves" in the conventional sense, but Thaddeus Stevens and others realized that to be granted "freedom" and have no money still left one a slave. One was free from the labor chains, but still one was bound by the economic chains. When the labor chains were removed, one still had to prove to one's self that you really was free. This might have simply meant just changing your residence. One moved from the plantation on which you, your parents, and even your grandparents had resided to the adjoining plantation. Sometimes this meant moving from the rural area to the closest urban area. For others it might have meant just "walking the road" to see where it took you. And, for some others it might have meant going into town and getting knee-buckling "sloppy drunk." This was also a period to reunite relations. One might have searched for the spouse one having had in slavery but from whom you had been separated by slavery. It might have meant searching for your parents sold away during slavery. And, for a large number of persons, it was searching for your children, or your brothers and sisters.

To help the former slaves adjust to freedom, the federal government set up the Bureau of Refugees, Freedmen, and Abandoned Lands in March, 1865. It eventually became known as the Freedmen's Bureau, indicating by the new name that it only existed for the sake of the freedmen. In the same year, 1865, to instill in the freedmen thrift, the government set up the Freedmen's Savings and Trust Association. Eventually, the Savings Association "went south," taking with it trust and the small treasuries of many freedmen. As Frederick Douglas put it, the Saving Association became the "black man's cow"—he fed—that gave all of its milk freely to the white man. Though the Freedmen's Bureau ostensibly worked for freedmen, its agents were, perhaps all, white. Most of the money of this agency went into salaries and black folks were not the recipients. The Freedmen's Bureau was directed by Gen. Oliver Otis Howard. Its activities included protection of freedmen in negotiating contracts; dispersement of clothes and food to both southern whites and blacks, and the building of schools and hospitals.

Private groups also got into the act. Freedmen Aid Societies, church affiliated benevolent groups came into being. The major groups were the American Missionary Association (Congregational), Freedmen's Aid Society of the Methodist Episcopal Church and the American Baptist Home Mission Society. These groups got started in the fall of 1861 in Virginia. They provided food, clothing and shelter for the freedmen. Today, almost all the private H(istorically) B(lack) C(olleges) and U(niversities) can trace their origins to some Freedmen Aid Society.

But "all good things must come to an end." Reconstruction, with all of its negatives, was a positive period in American History for African Americans. This was a time when black folks had the chance of standing on their own and being men. Coming to an end in 1877, Reconstruction "closed" for a number of reasons: The use of force and violence, media attack, political "strong arming," dying of "social idealism," etc. all contributed to the "Fall of Reconstruction." Perhaps the leading terroristic group helping to close Reconstruction was the Ku Klux Klan. The KKK had been founded at Pulaski, Tennessee in the fall of 1866. Nathan Bedford Forrest became its leading figure. Among the tactics of these terrorist groups were the use of force, ostracism in business and society against whites (black men's allies), bribery, arson, flogging, and killing (hanging and burning alive). With the majority group facing economic hard times ever since the Panic of 1873, it did not take much convincing by writers and politicians that African Americans were unfit for political rule because of their being "totally corrupt." Reconstruction had to be overthrown. On the local level this meant reinstatement of the "old guard" whites as political leaders as with the "Redeemers" or "Bourbons." And on the national level, it became one of accepting the political and social climate in the south because, for all intents and purposes, the south was back to being an "economic colony" of the north. That was what was truly important in a capitalistic and basically Caucasoid country. Black men still voted, but, unfortunately, there was no one with physical appearance like them to vote for or against. Black men continued to be able to cast ballots until after the election of 1896. Then, and only then, did there come a "bleaching" of the voting rolls. On the national level, in 1876, it meant Rutherford B. Hayes "making" the Wormley Agreement to ensure the continuance of Republicanism and "forget you" Samuel J. Tilden. The South shall rise again came to have real meaning.

SUGGESTED READINGS

Lerone Bennett Jr, *Before the Mayflower.*

Rodolphe L. Desdunes, *Our People and Our History.*

William A. Dunning, *Reconstruction, Political and Economic, 1865–1877.*

John Hope Franklin, *From Slavery To Freedom.*

Eric L. McKitrick, *Andrew Johnson and Reconstruction.*

Benjamin Quarles, *The Negro In The Making of America.*

Kenneth M. Stampp, *The Era of Reconstruction, 1865–1877.*

Kenneth Stampp and Leon F. Litwack, *Reconstruction: An Anthology.*

C. Vann Woodward, *Origins of the New South.*

STUDY GUIDE 11-A

1 What name was given to the period in American History 1865–1877?

2 What name was given to the rebuilding of the nation following the Civil War?

3 In what state was Hampton University founded?

4 Who was the last black Reconstruction figure to sit in the U. S. Congress?

5 What state did **#4** represent?

6–7 What were the two major problems of Reconstruction?

8–10 What were the three (3) Plans of Reconstruction?

11 When was Abraham Lincoln assasinated?

12 Who became the new U. S. President following the assasination of Lincoln?

13–15 In gist, give the three (3) theories of Reconstruction.

16 What 1869 court case stated that the states had never been out of the Union?

17 Give the alternate name for the "Ten Percent Plan" of Reconstruction.

18–20 What states were "reconstructed" under the plan named in **#17**?

21–22 What categories of person were initially exempted from taking a loyalty oath under the Johnson Plan of Reconstruction?

23 What name was given to the Congressmen during Reconstruction who wanted to involve black persons in the American mainstream?

24–26 Name the three (3) division of "Radicals."

27–30 Give at least four (4) reasons why "Radicals" came into being.

31–32 Who, from what state, served as Vice President of the C.S.A.?

33–34 Where, in 1866, had noted race riots occurred?

35 Whose removal from office prompted Presidential impeachment in 1868?

36 Name the only U. S. President to have actually faced impeachment charges.

37 Name the only black man to hold a state level judicial post during Reconstruction.

38 Who was the first black man to have served on the U. S. Supreme Court?

39–40 Who, and from what state, was the first black man ever elected as Governor of a member state of the United States?

41–43 Name the three (3) black men who served as Reconstruction Era Lieutenant Governors of Louisiana.

44–45 Name the two (2) Reconstruction Era black men who served as Lieutenant Governors of South Carolina.

46 Name the only black man to serve as Lieutenant Governor of Mississippi during Reconstruction.

47–48 What states, perhaps, had a majority of black men in their state legislatures?

49 Who was, probably, the most prominent black man in post Civil War Texas?

50 What African American was elected but never served as U. S. Senator from Louisiana during Reconstruction?

STUDY GUIDE 11-B

1–2 Name the two African American U. S. Senators from Mississippi during Reconstruction.

3 What period in American History was referred to as the "Era of Good Stealing"?

4 Where did Tammany Hall operate?

5 Give an alternate name for post Reconstruction era Redeemers of the south.

6 What name was given to the black landless farmers that worked the land after the Civil War on the basis of earning a "share" of the crop being produced?

7 What name was given to the white farmers that did not own the land but rented it and worked it after the Civil War?

8 Give the formal name of the Freedmen's Bureau.

9 Who became the Director of the Freedmen's Bureau?

10 What general name was given to the private groups that operated on a similar scale to the Freedmen's Bureau?

11–13 Give at least three (3) of the specific private groups of **#10**.

14–15 What were some of the reasons why Reconstruction "closed"?

16 Name the leading terroristic group that helped to bring Reconstruction to a "close."

17 Where had **#16** been founded?

18 Give the most infamous leader of **#16**.

19–20 Who vied for the American Presidency in 1876?

12

"From the 'Fall' of Reconstruction to the Dawn of the 20th Century"

With the inauguration of Republican Rutherford B. Hayes as President in 1877, the American people had reached an agreement to remove the federal troops from the South and to "end" Reconstruction. With the "end" of Reconstruction, the fate of the African American had been settled. Even though the Reconstructionist Congress had passed the Civil Rights Act of 1875, asserting that all citizens "of every race and color" were entitled to equal enjoyment of public accommodations, it was sensitive to racial opinion. The African American, though free, would find himself bound by feelings, behavior, and custom that proved, in many respects, to be much stronger than law. This was evidenced by the ruling of the Supreme Court when it declared the Civil Rights Act of 1875 unconstitutional, asserting that only the state could guarantee the rights of its citizens. The plight of the African American was intensified when "survival of the fittest" assertions were used to justify the denial of blacks to full equality. More than ever before blacks were forced to identify, from within their own ranks, leaders who could effectively guide them out of the legacy that Reconstruction had left them.

President Hayes, one month after his inauguration, withdrew the last federal troops from the South. The South was "Redeemed." The fate of the African American citizen was now virtually in the hands of Southerners, as the North considered its job complete and moved on to "new business." No longer did Northerners consider the moral issues of the Civil War, Reconstruction, and the condition of blacks to be their responsibility. Concluding that slavery had been abolished and that the Constitution recognized all men legally equal, they now embraced Social Darwinism, the scientific theories of Charles Darwin applied to man, as an acceptable doctrine. Northerners were allowed to use "the survival of the fittest" to ignore America's social problems and to relegate African Americans to a position of "invisibility." Except in the South, blacks were, in most instances, ignored, as America became consumed with Big Business and material gain.

At the end of the Civil War, few African Americans opted to migrate to the industrial North and the expanding West. Reasons for their tendency to remain in the South were varied. Most blacks were trained to do agricultural work and were fearful of what they would find outside the South. There were some blacks who desired to relocate, but did not have the funds needed to make the move. A strong resistance to black migration came from the South as well as the North; a resistance to both their leaving and their coming. Communication proved to be an additional obstacle to black migration, as black communities in the North and West failed to establish ties with potential migrants, and as railroad tycoons failed to recruit blacks as a source of cheap labor to help develop the Northwest. An additional barrier to black migration came from among the black leaders themselves, individuals such as Frederick Douglas, who were split on the issue of whether migration would work to the advantage or detriment of black migrants.

By 1879, the level of migration to the North and West had increased, causing Southern planters to devise strategies to preserve the Southern way of life. Because black freedmen had no savings, and because there was little land for sale, too often they found themselves victims of short-term credit arrangements that left them in a constant state of indebtedness. This system of legal-bondage, usually in the forms of sharecropping and tenant farming, allowed for the exploitation of laborers, thus leaving blacks with few alternatives.

Those latter fiscal conditions and lynching caused a few to react. Even though the masses listened to the traditional leaders, some others had just reached the breaking point and became a part of the "Exodus Movement." In 1879, there began a movement spearheaded by Benjamin "Pap" Singleton, out of Tennessee, and Henry Adams, out of Louisiana, to relocate blacks to the midwest ("Kansas Fever") and southwest to try to escape the lynching and Jim Crowism of the south. As mentioned in the previous paragraph, African American sharecroppers found that the harder they worked, the deeper in debt they became. Then, the other terror of the "rope" frightened others. Lynching, like Jim Crowism, became a well known phenomenon in the post bellum South. Lynching was a means of extra legal punishment designed to "keep blacks in their place." It was the extreme facet of Jim Crowism. As C. Vann Woodward and others have pointed out Jim Crowism came into vogue in the south following the destruction of the system of slavery. Prior to the Civil War, Jim Crow, as a phenomenon, had existed in the North, but in the South there was no need for it because slavery defined the positions of the races. But with slavery destroyed, Jim Crowism was born in the South to define and delineate race positions. The name came from an old minstrel where the refrain was "Jump Jim Crow . . . " If African Americans went beyond their bounds they were simply ushered back into their place via lynching. In the analysis of lynchings after 1889 by the National Association for the Advancement of Colored People [NAACP], approximately thirty-nine percent of the lynched colored victims were accused of murder, but nearly six percent of the victims lynched had committed no crime. Were Jim Crowism and lynching effective? If Louisiana is taken as a case in point, it can be shown that in the 1890s, the number of registered voters numbered over 130 thousands, but by the turn of the century there were just one thousand.

The growth of the Populist movement and the Southern Farmers Alliance offered some marginal degree of hope for interracial cooperation. Because of Jim Crowism saying blacks and whites could not be in the same organization, C. W. McCune founded the Colored Alliance in 1886 in Texas. The Alliance movement became closely linked with the idea of cooperatives—farmers taking their commodities directly to the consumers and eliminating the middle man as well as politics. There was a brief period when it appeared that the races could use political cooperation to achieve common goals. These efforts were hampered, however, by racial prejudice and economic competition, as blacks became the scapegoat for any defeat experienced by the Populists at the polls. In probably no election was this made plainer than the Election of 1896. In the pre-1896 presidential vote, no one courted the black vote more than the Democratic/Populist Vice Presidential nominee, Tom Watson of Georgia. Unfortunately for Watson, the Republican Presidential candidate, William McKinley defeated Watson's running mate, William Jennings Bryan. Now the Populist seemingly felt that election should just be fought out among white men only. Therefore you had African Americans being disfranchised in record numbers as with the earlier mentioned Louisiana situation.

African Americans tended to view education as their one chance for improvement. Making tremendous sacrifices, black parents, who bore the severe conditions of poverty, became preoccupied with their children having an opportunity to learn to read and write. For many, this, more than any other factor, would help ease the transition from slavery to freedom. As the Freedmen's Bureau began to relinquish its responsibility for providing educational programs for blacks, several groups from the North began to assume some responsibility for educating blacks at all levels. The church took the leadership role in educating the South, and eventually, every black denomination became involved in education, hoping to train ministers who could improve the plight of the black masses. This theological pattern was used from 1877 to 1890. The aforementioned Freedmen Aid Societies thought in terms of setting up four centers in the south for black education—New Orleans, Louisiana; Nashville, Tennessee; Atlanta, Georgia; and Washington, D. C. Some of the first institutions for black higher education already existed in these places and each of them had more than one denominational institution. After the "fall" of Reconstruction, states began appeasing black demands by setting up separate black state supported H.B.C.U.s [Historically Black College/University]. During the last decade of the nineteenth century, the major focus of education shifted more toward vocational training, with a few institutions remaining true to the theological pattern. An ongoing debate eventually emerged over what direction education should take. Some believed that vocational education was adequate in preparing blacks for meaningful occupations. As African Americans assumed more responsibility for their own education, they saw a need to become more self-reliant. Leadership opportunities became more important to them, and by the turn of the century, black educators were assuming many of the posts that had previously been held by well-meaning white educators. Additionally, as will be discussed more fully in the chapter after next, Booker T. Washington had been elevated, largely by white America, to the position of directing black education. He did however, receive some resistance from the black "academicians" who supported classical education. Those educators, led by W. E. B. DuBois and John Hope, were not in total opposition to vocational education, however, they did not want vocational education to limit the political, social, and cultural opportunities for blacks.

Prior to 1900, many believed that blacks would not benefit from urbanization. Although Jim Crowism created a relatively narrow and closed society, many blacks who migrated to large cities found employment that proved to be relatively secure. Some blacks gained political experience and held positions in city government, while others achieved prominence as businessmen and professionals. In the north, although schools were beginning to desegregate, neighborhood schools became the norm. As black migrants, many of whom were from the south, they were forced to settle in predominantly black neighborhoods. The situation worsened with time. This "involuntary segregation" was in part caused by the color visibility of the black population, which made it virtually impossible for them to obtain housing and schooling in certain areas.

When the U. S. Supreme Court rendered its *Plessy v. Ferguson* decision of 1896, based upon a lawsuit brought by Homer Plessy of New Orleans, it sanctioned the patterns of discrimination in America. With the court's application of the "separate but equal" rule, it disallowed any real equality. Contending that the constitutional requirements of due process and equal protection, the court did not seem concerned that the burden of proving inequality of accommodations was now placed upon the individual who felt the facility unequal. The decision allowed for the creation of two societies in America, as many states imposed Jim Crow laws to bar blacks from full citizenship.

Between 1880 and 1900, changes in industry, particularly in the South, altered the relationships between poor whites and blacks. Wealthy conservatives who were aware that they were losing control of black labor, began to rely more heavily on cheap white labor. In many instances, poor whites were played against blacks. As an economic caste system emerged, blacks were denied their full share of the benefits associated with industrialization. Although men such as Elijah McCoy, Granville Woods, and Jan Matzeliger made significant contributions to American industrialization through their inventions, black men often found themselves with few economic opportunities. They continued to provide a labor force on farms, in mines, and in factories, but they were still faced with obvious discrimination and segregation in labor and business. Many displaced blacks were forced to migrate to the cities where they often found themselves relegated to a condition of economic poverty.

Efforts to organize black labor were marginally successful, if successful at all. Examining the history, along racial lines, of organized labor in the United States, the most successful long running 19th century labor union, the A(merican) F(ederation) of L(abor) was a whites only organization. This proved to have been necessary for survival. Earlier than the A.F.L. though, the fallen Knights of Labor had tried to bring about interracial labor cooperation. By 1898, black leaders recognized the obstacles associated with economic competition. Black leaders warned that labor unions would not provide equal opportunity as long as they were dominated by white management which prevented any effective organization of workers on racial lines. Blacks were encouraged to engage in business, to learn trades, and to establish self-help programs. By 1900, the National Negro Business League was not only encouraging greater numbers of blacks to enter business, but was giving advice on how this could best be done. Although these efforts were noble, blacks were hampered by discrimination. Little capital was available to blacks and loans were difficult to obtain.

So now with so many things working against them, black people sort of turned their attention inward and worked on the already mentioned educational avenues. They worked toward building the black church. Almost all public roads were closed where they could act as men—persons in control. The church was one avenue left. They took it. Another avenue left was all black social clubs and fraternal groups. Again they acted.

By 1900, blacks were ready for social and economic change. They were seeking a means of gaining equality and security.

Suggested Readings

Lerone Bennett, Jr., *Before The Mayflower.*

Michael Heintze, *Private Black Colleges in Texas.*

Alton Hornsby, Jr., *The Black Almanac.*

Howard Jones, *The Red Diary.*

NAACP, *Thirty Years of Lynching in the United States 1889–1918.*

Nell I. Painter, *Exodusters: Black Migration to Kansas After Reconstruction.*

Arnold Rice, *The Ku Klux Klan In American Politics.*

C. Vann Woodward, *Origins of the New South.*

STUDY GUIDE 12

1 Whose U.S. Presidential inauguration signalled the "end" of Reconstruction?

2 What was removed from the south that signalled an "end" to Reconstruction?

3 Name the natural scientist that postulated Darwinism.

4–8 Give five (**5**) reasons why post Civil War African Americans [pre-1879] initially refused to migrate en-masse from the south?

9 What name was given to the post-1879 mass migration of African Americans from the south?

10–11 What were two reasons for **#9**?

12–15 Give the names and states for each of the leaders associated with **#9**?

16 The post-1879 migration of blacks from the south to the midwest is sometimes referred to by what cliche?

17 What was the means of extra legal punishment designed to "keep black in their place"?

18 In what section of antebellum America was Jim Crow a real phenomena?

19 Expand the abbreviation NAACP.

20 Who founded the Colored [Farmers] Alliance?

21 Name the 1896 Democratic/Populist U. S. Vice Presidential candidate.

22 Who was the Republican Party's 1896 Presidential candidate?

23 Name the 1896 Democratic Party's Presidential candidate.

24 Who won the American Presidency in 1896?

25–28 What four (**4**) black educational centers were formulated by Freedmen Aid Societies, *et.al.*?

29 Expand the abbreviation H.B.C.U.

30–31 Who were the main leaders of African American education during and after the 1890s?

32 What 1896 court case validated "separate but equal"?

33–35 Name at least three black inventors mentioned in this chapter.

13

Nineteenth Century Black Nationalism

Black nationalism is the conviction that Blacks share a common ethnic background, cultural identity, worldview, and a historical experience characterized by slavery, segregation, colonialism and exploitation. Throughout human history, nationalist consciousness has inspired great movements that have resulted in the realization of certain ideals (*i.e.* the goals of nationalism). Though the objectives may vary, nationalist movements generally espouse certain universal ideals, the most common being freedom and equality. These ideals are often informed by the historical circumstances, *i.e.*, socio-cultural, economic and political conditions of the particular epoch. At times, the goal of nationalism is institutional reform within an existing polity—education, religion, economic and cultural. More generally, black nationalists seek to create an independent polity, a nation state that would provide a conducive environment for the realization of their human potentialities unimpeded by racism. The shared historical, ethnic and cultural experiences constitute the foundation for initiating and sustaining a movement aimed at achieving the defined goal.

Racial/ethnic solidarity is perhaps the leitmotiv of black nationalism. The forging of this solidarity is often geographically exclusive, confined to a particular environment, *e.g.*, the United States, the Caribbean or Africa. At times, it is inclusive, embracing several geographical regions, wherever peoples of African descent are found—Africa, the United States, Latin America and the Caribbean. In its latter dimension, Black Nationalism seeks the unification of peoples of African descent, irrespective of their places of domicile, on the assumption that what affects blacks in one country, affects blacks all over the world. This trans-Atlantic thrust is itself a reaction to the historical practice of justifying the dehumanization of all blacks on the alleged barbaric, heathenish and uncivilized condition of Africa. The mobilization of African and diasporan strength and resources against enslavement, racism and colonial exploitation represents the highest stage of Black Nationalism.

Black Nationalism is therefore propelled by a combination of values—unity, racial and ethnic identity and solidarity, positive self-conception, and a strong affirmation and defense of cultural and historical heritage. The practice of mobilizing black consciousness of domination, oppression and exploitation, and activating the self in pursuit of change, gives Black Nationalism the character of a resistant phenomenon. It affirms vigorously the unique cultural and historical identity of blacks, and insists upon the intrinsic essence and validation of black heritage. The strategies of Black Nationalism often range from relocation to an external environment deemed conducive to survival and the blooming of the human personality and potentialities, to remaining within the geographical confines of a repressive state, but in relative physical distance or isolation from the material and cultural influences of the oppressor class. This isolation could be spatial, that is, a move is made to settle in a locality away from the oppressor, Or, it could be cultural. In the latter case, though blacks live in relative proximity to the hegemonic class, they construct and mobilize race and ethnically based institutions and values, as means of shielding themselves from the negative and destructive influences of that class, and in the process, ensure cultural survival and elevation. This is the cultural-pluralistic strategy.

Nineteenth century Black Nationalism developed on the foundation laid by earlier nationalists. The earliest manifestation of nationalist consciousness among Blacks has been traced to the institution of slavery. The historian Herbert Aptheker has described slave insurrections, particularly the organized, and ideologically driven plots of Nat Turner, Gabriel Prosser and Denmark Vesey as expressions of militant nationalism. The shared experience of oppression, and the dehumanizing character of slavery, inspired many slaves to mobilize and strike violently for freedom. As Wilson J. Moses poignantly declared, "Slavery was—the cause of Black nationalism." Also linked to slavery were attempts by Northern free Blacks to generate racial, ethnic and cultural awareness in order to build self-help and cooperative associations that would significantly change the condition and experience of the race. Though not an organized and militant movement characteristic of later nationalist schemes, these early reform efforts were, however, induced by deep consciousness of shared racial and cultural experience.

The earliest tradition of organized nationalist efforts by individual African Americans, is often traced to the activities of Paul Cuffe, 1759–1817, a Quaker of mixed Negro and Indian heritage. Cuffe has been called a pioneer black nationalist. He developed interest in Africa very early in life. He thought blacks, irrespective of geographical location, could not hope for meaningful advancement and elevation unless, and until, Africa was developed. The key to this development, according to Cuffe, was the abolition of the slave trade, and its replacement with commerce in legitimate products.

Cuffee visited Africa for the first time in 1811, and spent three months in Sierra Leone. In 1815, he took a few blacks to Sierra Leone at his expense. He helped establish a branch of the Friendly Society of Sierra Leone. Cuffe underlined the economic potentiality of Africa, and believed that developing the economic and industrial base of Africa, and the establishment of a viable commercial link with Britain would render slavery obsolete. He returned to the United States in 1816, and launched a vigorous campaign for emigration. He specifically urged wealthy middle class Blacks to relocate to Sierra Leone and engage in agriculture, and other forms of economic activities. His return coincided with the founding of the American Colonization Society, and the members eagerly sought his opinions and solicited his services. Unfortunately, Cuffe died in 1817 without realizing his goal of returning to Africa. Despite his untimely death, Cuffe had succeeded in laying a solid foundation upon which subsequent nationalists would develop their ideas and programs.

Another pioneer Black nationalist whose ideas set the stage for the future was Lott Cary. A contemporary of Cuffe, Cary was born in 1780 in Charles City county, Virginia. He came from a strong religious background. His father was a pious, and highly regarded member of the Baptist Church. Young Cary himself joined the Baptists and was soon licensed to preach. He began to preach on Colored plantations in Richmond, and helped found the Richmond African Baptist Missionary Society. Like Cuffe, Cary identified early on with Africa, and committed himself to "civilizing" the continent. He also believed that African Americans had a responsibility to contribute to the development of Africa. He equally endorsed colonization. Given the deteriorating condition of African Americans, Cary presented Africa as the new frontier. And like Cuffe, he too saw great promise in the combination of colonization and trade. He joined the Colonization Society, and left for Africa in 1821 in company of about 28 colonists. In Sierra Leone, he established a mission among the natives, and converted many to Christianity. In December of 1821, he moved to Liberia, the infant Colonization state. He organized another mission in Monrovia, the capital, and successfully converted many native Liberians to Christianity. Concerned about the level of ignorance among the natives, Cary began a day school. By 1828, he had been designated vice-agent for the administration of Liberia by the Colonization society. Cary died shortly after.

Both Cuffe and Cary sought to mobilize African-American resources and consciousness toward building a future in Africa. They both stressed the cultural and ethnic links between African Americans and Africa, and insisted that the destinies of the two were intertwined. For African Americans, Africa became both a source of identity (an identity that was denied and denigrated in America), and the palladium of their freedom and ultimate salvation.

Perhaps the individual credited with more effectively and compellingly projecting the socio-economic and cultural dynamics of Black Nationalism in the nineteenth century was David Walker, who is referred to by many as the father of Black Nationalist theory. Walker was born a free African American in 1785 in North Carolina. He inherited his free status from his mother. In those days a child assumed the status of his/her mother. But he soon discovered that freedom meant significantly nothing for free blacks. It did not immune them from the abuses, atrocities and violence of slavery and racism. He travelled widely in the United States, especially in the South, and broadened his perspective on slavery. He was horrified by what he saw, and developed a passionate desire to strike a blow at slavery. He settled in Boston in the 1820s, and immersed himself in abolitionist activities. He became an agent of *Freedom's Journal* (first black newspaper) founded in 1827 by John Ruuswurm. This was the earliest manifestation of a growing determination by blacks to assume direct advocacy of their cause. Walker's home in Boston became a rallying point for black abolitionists. He however strongly opposed colonization and emigration, insisting that blacks were Americans and entitled to all the rights and privileges due to a citizen. He averred that blacks had a much stronger claim to America than whites. To emigrate would amount to a voluntary relinquishing of that right. He was, however, optimistic and strongly believed that freedom and integration would materialize someday.

Walker's ideas are contained in his seminal book, *Appeal to the Colored Citizens of the World, But in Particular, and Very Expressly to Those of the United States.* He divided the book into four articles each focusing on a dimension of the African American predicament. He exhorted blacks to boldly challenge and expose the fallacies and irrationalities of slavery, and assert their claims to freedom. Education would, Walker hoped, expose the evils of slavery, and the fallacies that sustained it, thereby instigating blacks to strike for freedom. His ultimate goal was to expunge from African Americans any consciousness of inferiority by instilling in them a positive self conception, an enhanced self-portrait that would nudge them to strike for freedom. He attacked and rejected colonization. He underscored the nationality of blacks as Americans, and condemned those who embraced colonization. The *Appeal* has been described as the harbinger of militant Black Nationalism. It raised issues and espoused values that subsequent Black Nationalists imbibed—an apocalyptic vision, positive self-assertion, hope and optimism, strong affirmation of the American nationality of blacks, justification of resistance to oppression, and disavowal of Colonization. In essence, it inspired a deep sense of worthiness and a preparedness to initiate change. For example, many have drawn a link between the *Appeal* and the revolt of Nat Turner. Walker has been described as the godfather of revolutionary nationalism, a tradition that advocates violence as an instrument of change. From a critique of the historical and cultural experience, the revolutionary nationalist galvanizes racial and ethnic consciousness in the direction of violent confrontation.

As the nineteenth century progressed, Black Nationalism developed into a strong and organized movement, and assumed different shapes, with a variety of ideologies. The distinctive qualities it exhibited were predicated on the optimism rekindled by the abolitionist crusade. Black abolitionism, represented by the convention movement, was a deeply nationalistic phenomenon. Though blacks had not achieved the promises and aspirations inspired by the eighteenth century revolutionary values, some had gained freedom, giving birth to the free colored class. This class was more determined to use the limited freedom gained, and the relatively liberal atmosphere of the North, (where many of them had migrated to and settled), to inaugurate and nurture a strong and viable movement for freedom and elevation. Black abolitionists consequently adopted an integrationist platform, due largely to their faith in the universality of the American Dream. Blacks were convinced that, given certain conditions, they would become meaningfully free and elevated. They enthusiastically collaborated with white abolitionists, and invited some to the first National Negro Convention in Philadelphia in 1830. Notwithstanding this cooperation, black abolitionist philosophy reflected the peculiarity of the black situation. The convention movement epitomized a cardinal principle of nationalism—an affirmation of the uniqueness of the black experience. Between 1830 and 1835 free blacks organized five national conventions, dedicated solely to addressing issues pertinent to the black experience. This was followed in the 1840s by state conventions. The convention movement continued sporadically up to the Reconstruction period. Despite the involvement of whites in the early convention, and the cooperation between leading black abolitionists and William Lloyd Garrison, a leading white abolitionist, there was little doubt that the convention movement was essentially a black movement, and that blacks saw themselves as the prime movers.

Organizers of the conventions believed in the malleability of American society, and consequently pursued integrationist objectives. They were also legalistic and constitutional in their strategies, channelling their grievances and demands for political rights through state legislatures. This was particularly true of the state conventions of the 1840s. The integrationist orientation was due to the fact that blacks subscribed to the prevailing abolitionist ethics of moral suasion. Moral suasion, which dominated the abolitionist crusade for much of the 1830s and 1840s, was fundamentally a corrective and integrationist ideology that anchored the hopes of blacks for change on the cultivation of certain American middle class values—Thrift, Industry, Economy and Temperance. Blacks imbibed the notion that their problems stemmed from moral and material deficiencies, which could be alleviated through the cultivation of those middle class values. Moral suasion de-emphasized the racial factor, but moral persuasion failed.

By the early 1850s, Black Nationalism took on a militant and political character. As more and more blacks jettisoned moral suasion and the promise of the elusive American Dream, a new movement emerged which directed African American attention outward—Emigration. Emigration sentiments grew especially after the passage of the Fugitive Slave Law of 1850, which, among other provisions, pledged federal support for the apprehension and return of fugitives. This law underscored the depth of racism, and leading blacks interpreted it as an attempt to nationalize slavery. Many gave up on America. The state of despair and disappointment forced many to reassess their ideas and positions, especially with respect to colonization. One such was Henry Highland Garnet, who had delivered a speech at the Buffalo Convention in 1843 entitled, *Address to the Slaves of the United States,* in which he urged the slaves to revolt. He vehemently opposed colonization and unequivocally advanced the claims of blacks to American citizenship. Garnet's *Address* is popularly conceived as an expression of revolutionary nationalism. The motion to adopt the *Address* as an official declaration of the convention was, however, lost by just one vote. With increasing disillusionment and despair in the 1850s, Garnet reversed his earlier stance and began to advocate emigration, and identified Mexico, Central America and West Africa, as possible places of relocation for blacks. In 1858 he joined Whites in establishing the African Civilization Society, and was appointed its President. This society became one of the most active colonization/emigration forces of the 1860s. The main agenda of the society entailed the destruction of slavery through the promotion of commerce and industry in Africa. Like his black contemporaries, Garnet emphasized the economic potentiality of Africa, and advocated the emigration of a few, wealthy, enterprising and resourceful blacks who would plant civilization and Christianity in Africa.

However, the man who epitomized the culture of alienation, more than anyone else, and whose emigrationist ideas became dominant from the 1850s leading up to the Civil War was Martin R. Delany. Between 1852 and 1860, he led the emigrationist crusade, and provided both practical and ideological justification or rationalization for emigration. In two key publications; *The Condition, Elevation, Emigration and Destiny of the Colored People of the United States* (1852), and *Political Destiny of the Colored Race on the American Continent* (1854), Delany discussed the plights of blacks, and highlighted the difficulty associated with the quest for equality and freedom in the United States. Delany's nationalist philosophy began from a position of strength. In fact, like David Walker before him, Delany believed that blacks had even greater claim to America than whites. He debunked the myth of a liberal North, and strongly urged blacks to seek the realization of their destiny elsewhere. Blacks were, in his words, "a nation within a nation," an oppressed minority that perforce had to seek its own nation. He identified Latin America, the West Indies, Central America and Africa as alternatives.

Delany's writings and speeches galvanized the alienated. Those who believed in emigration responded to a call for a convention which assembled in August 1854 in Cleveland, Ohio. The convention set up a National Board of Commissioners with Delany as its first President. The emigrationists met in annual conventions for the next three years. In 1858, Delany was commissioned to undertake a scientific and investigatory trip to the Niger Valley of West Africa, specifically to gather information on the land, people and economic resources. He left for Africa in 1858 in company of the West Indian, Robert Campbell. They visited Liberia and Nigeria and travelled extensively in both countries. Delany returned to the United States in late 1860, his emigrationist convictions strengthened by his discoveries in Africa. He embarked on a series of public lectures designed to generate momentum for emigration. Delany also infused his emigrationism with a strong Pan-African or Pan-Negro nationalism. He advocated, as an effective counter to white hegemony, the solidarity of blacks across the Atlantic in a united front against a common enemy.

Emigration was, however, a minority movement. Most blacks refused to give up on America. To accept emigration was deemed tantamount to a voluntary surrendering of all claims to American citizenship. The majority of blacks remained optimistic and hopeful that positive change was possible within the country. Many likened emigration to the pro-slavery colonization scheme of the Colonization Society. From its inception in 1816–1817, blacks had condemned and rejected colonization as a sinister scheme designed to rid the nation of free blacks and thereby strengthen slavery. Delany's attempting to distinguish between emigration and colonization by describing the former as voluntary with a positive agenda and the latter as forced repatriation and proslavery failed. Led by Frederick Douglass, the integrationists favored instead the mobilization of racial and cultural identity, and the creation of racially based institutions and solutions that would further strengthen black racial and cultural distinctiveness, even while remaining in close proximity to mainstream white society. The Negro National Convention of 1853 in Rochester, New York, which Douglass spear-headed, advanced this cultural pluralistic strategy.

The outbreak of the Civil War temporarily halted the emigrationist drive, as even ardent emigrationist, like Delany welcomed the opportunities for integration created by the war. The war raised the hopes of blacks and there was almost a universal optimism for integration. Frederick Douglass, Martin Delany, Henry McNeal Turner, Henry Garnet, and other leading blacks, saw the Civil War as an opportunity to assist in dealing a crushing blow to slavery, defending the territorial integrity of the nation [as other blacks had done during the Revolution], and once again, demonstrating black fidelity, with the hope of ultimately realizing the elusive American Dream. Blacks rallied behind the Union, and selflessly volunteered their services. Unfortunately, their dream of integration remained unfulfilled. Blacks fought gallantly and helped to save the nation from disintegration, and proceeded during the brief period of "radical" Reconstruction to demonstrate capacity for political leadership and responsibility. The nation, however, appeared unprepared for the challenges of black freedom and elevation.

Disillusioned, Blacks once again turned outward. A renewed surge of Black nationalism developed into an exodus movement in South Carolina. The organizers turned to the newly established Black Republic of Liberia. Delany played a leading role in the rejuvenated exodus movement. He corresponded with the Colonization Society, and solicited aid for the repatriation of blacks to Liberia. Many, however, still averse to emigration, and confident that all avenues for redress within the nation had not been exhausted, sought the establishment of all-black communities [outside of the South]. Led by Benjamin "Pap" Singleton and Henry Adams [the Exodus Movement], thousands of blacks moved from Louisiana, Texas, Tennessee, Alabama and North Carolina to Kansas and Oklahoma in the 1890, where they set up several all-black communities.

The dominant nationalist strand among Blacks in post-Reconstruction era, however, remained external emigration. The most prominent leader of this movement was one who had staunchly defended integration during the Civil War—Henry McNeal Turner. The collapse of Reconstruction and the attempts by Southerners to revert to the **status**

quo antebellum raised further questions about the place of blacks in America. Many blacks came to the conclusion that they had no place in a nation that repeatedly trampled on them, and denied their basic human rights and privileges. The solution, once again, was the creation of an independent black state outside of the country. All attention focused on Liberia which had been settled by American freed blacks. A member of the all-black African Methodist Episcopal Church, Turner had been an ardent integrationist who very much believed in the American Dream. He served as a Union chaplain during the Civil War. After the war, he began a brief political career in Georgia. He was a delegate to the 1868 Constitutional Convention, and was later elected to the state legislature. Unfortunately, Georgia was one of the states where "radical" Reconstruction was never allowed to take root. No sooner had the black delegates taken their seats in the legislature than they were ousted by whites. Embittered, Turner gave up on the country and embraced emigration.

Turner was also determined to make whites contribute to the rehabilitation of blacks. He estimated that whites owed blacks the sum of $40 billion in reparations for centuries of enslavement and exploitation, and demanded this sum from the United States government to defray the cost of emigration. Needless to say, Turner got nothing. In desperation, Turner turned to the Colonization Society for assistance. In 1892 he started the Afro-American Steamship Company. Through sale of stocks to subscribers, the company hoped to finance trading expeditions to Africa, and also transport emigrants. He started a paper, the *Voice of Mission*, which became the organ of emigration and evangelicalism. In 1894, a group of white Alabama businessmen responded to his appeal by founding the International Migration Society to assist in financing emigration. Turner visited Africa three times between 1891 and 1895. According to one estimate, about a thousand blacks emigrated to Liberia under the auspices of the Migration Society.

Turner's nationalism has been described as the first case of mass emigration, which is different from the elitist emigration of earlier nationalists such as Delany. It is important to mention that Turner, as bitterly critical of America as he was, never meant to appeal to the masses. He, like Delany, appealed directly to the middle class whose resources and enterprises, he felt, were central to the success of emigration. While the middle class ignored him, the black masses, who felt more the pinch of deprivation and poverty, heard him and responded. By 1896, however, support for Turner had declined even among the poor masses. This downtrend, in part, was due to the negative reports associated with the poor handling of emigrants who went to Liberia and also with the emergence of a new leader—Booker T. Washington—whose ideas and values restored hope in the possibility of change within America. The age of Washington had dawned, and for the next two decades, optimism for meaningful changes through accommodation to American reality and subscription to its values would overshadow every other strategy.

The ideas of Alexander Crummell, a contemporary of both Turner and Delany, were also prominently featured in nineteenth century Black Nationalism. Crummell, born a free black in New York in 1819, developed a strong identity with Africa as a child. Reaching manhood, he witnessed and experienced the inhumanity and degradation that came with being black. And he too began to seek solutions in mobilizing racial consciousness and identity. He espoused a truly Pan-African Christian solution, grounded in the infusion of religion and western civilization, which was primarily undertaken by Africa's children in diaspora. He developed a strong sense of identity with Africa and felt that every black should do likewise. Crummell defined a genetic link between the plight of blacks and the condition of Africa, arguing that unless Africa was transformed, blacks elsewhere had little chance of meaningfully changing their own condition. Crummell's nationalism had a strong Christian character: It was not enough to simply develop the economic resources of Africa—Africa desperately needed religious salvation. Trade and religion only in combination would transform the continent.

Crummell moved to Liberia in 1853 and for about 20 years preoccupied himself with "saving the souls" of the natives. He established a mission in Liberia and converted many to Christianity. In speeches and writings, Crummell appealed to blacks, urging a quick response to the critical state of Africa. His commitment to the redemption of Africa was so strong and deep that not even the outbreak of the Civil War could induce him to return to the United States.

Like other Black nationalists of his time, Crummell had to deal with the dilemma created by his dual identity—African and American. Born and raised in America, Crummell had been socialized with American and European values, especially the notion of Anglo-Saxon superiority. Nineteenth century Black Nationalists developed similar condescending and paternalistic postures towards Africa.

The Pan-African orientation of Delany, Turner, Garnet, and Crummell, despite inherent contradictions, emanated from a strong awareness of historical and cultural affinity to Africa. The idea of Africa and African America linked by a common experience of slavery, racism, and colonization, and the idea of Africa as a foundation for the elevation and redemption of blacks worldwide, would be reactivated by twentieth century nationalists such as Garvey and Malcolm X.

SUGGESTED READINGS.

Howard Brotz ed., *African-American Social and Political Thought*, 1850–1920. NY: Transaction Publishers, 1972.

Bill McAdoo, *Pre-Civil War Black Nationalism.* NY: David Walker, 1983.

John T. McCartney, *Black Power Ideologies: An Essay in African-American Political Thought.* Philadelphia: Temple University Press, 1992.

Wilson J. Moses, *The Golden Age of Black Nationalism*, 1850–1925. NY: Archon Books, 1978.

Sterling Stuckey, *Ideological Origins of Black Nationalism.* Boston, 1972.

Slave Culture: Nationalist Theory and the Foundations of Black America. NY: Oxford University Press, 1987.

Okon Uya ed., *Black Brotherhood: Afro-Americans and Africa.* Lexington, MA: D.C. Heath, 1971.

Charles M. Wiltse ed., *David Walker's Appeal in four articles together with A Preamble To The Colored Citizens of the World, But In Particular, And Very Expressly, To Those of the United States of America.* New York: Hill & Wang, 1965.

STUDY GUIDE 13

1 In terms of location, what are the normal strategies of Black Nationalism?

2–4 Give the three most prominent slave revolts in the United States.

5 According to Wilson Moses, what was the cause of Black Nationalism?

6 In 1815, where in Africa did Paul Cuffe resettle some African Americans?

7 Name the capital of Liberia.

8 Name the father of Black Nationalist theory.

9 Name the first African American newspaper.

10 In 1829, who wrote the *Appeal*?

11 Were black abolitionists, for the most part, **emigrationists** or **integrationists**?

12 What late antebellum law pledged federal support for the apprehension and return of fugitive slaves?

13 In 1858, or so, who became the President of the African Civilization Society?

14 Was nineteenth century emigration a **majority** or **minority** advocated movement?

15–16 Give the most prominent leaders of the "Exodus Movement."

17 Henry McNeal Turner served in the State Legislature of what state?

18–19 According to Alexander Crummell, what two things were needed to transform Africa?

20 Name a twentieth century Black Nationalist mentioned in this chapter.

PART II

14

The Age Of Booker T. Washington

There are unique situations in history when the career of an individual aptly captures the essence of a much broader movement conceived in ideological terms. One such personality is Booker Taliaferro Washington (1856–1915), who is associated with Accommodationism—a historically deep-rooted ideological movement in the African American experience. The mention of his name today often reminds one of the ideological crisis of African American leadership from the 1890s up to the first two decades of the twentieth century—*i.e.*, the controversy over what strategy to adopt: accommodation or protest. Few men in the history of the African American experience dominated an epoch as completely as Washington. His personality and values so overwhelmed the decades from 1895 to 1915 that this period has gone down in history as the "Age of Booker T. Washington." The greatest accomplishment of this age, the one that seemed to reflect the mood of the epoch, was a "compromise" that resulted from a speech he delivered at the Atlanta Cotton Exposition in 1895. This "compromise," some suggest, set back the clock of black progress by at least half a century. The forces that nurtured Washington were precisely the ones prevailing in the South of the 1870s. Washington was indeed a child of his time. To probe deeper into the source and nature of the dominant forces and idiosyncrasies of his formative years is to glance into the inner dynamics of American society in the second half of the nineteenth century.

Born a slave in 1856 in Franklin county, Virginia, Booker T. Washington spent the first nine years of his life in slavery, becoming free after the Civil War. His parents then moved to Malden, West Virginia, where young Washington worked in the salt mines while also striving for knowledge. Driven by a thirst for learning, he moved to Hampton Institute [Virginia] in 1872. He arrived at the doorstep of Hampton hungry and without money. Washington worked as a janitor to pay for his room and board, and he relied on the contributions of philanthropists for his tuition.

Hampton was established in 1868 by Gen. Samuel Chapman Armstrong, veteran of the Civil War. It started as an institution designed specifically to train blacks in practical education. Armstrong thought education was the best means of smoothing the transition from slavery to freedom. In order for blacks to become useful to themselves and society, they had to develop an appreciation of the dignity and redeeming character of manual labor. Once properly sensitized to the utility of labor, blacks would expunge from their consciousness the dependency syndrome they had inherited from slavery. After this growth, they would have little difficulty acquiring the necessary vocational skills that would elevate them. Armstrong described the South as a land of opportunity and urged blacks to remain there, seeking the realization of their destinies.

The concept of utility is central to Armstrong's pedagogical philosophy. For him, the ideal black education would be infused with a utilitarian or functional consideration, which would create an education with a dual purpose: to improve the economic well-being of the individual and to harmonize discordant elements in society.

At Hampton, Washington was exposed to both liberal and industrial education. He graduated in 1876 as a firm believer in the potency of industrial education. After a brief period of teaching in Malden and at Wayland Baptist Seminary in Washington D.C., he returned to Hampton as an instructor in 1878. He taught at Hampton until 1881 when, on the recommendation of Armstrong, he was asked to assist in establishing a similar program in Tuskegee, Alabama [Tuskegee University].

Washington assumed his new responsibility with the passion, devotion, and determination of a fanatic. His immediate goal was to replicate his Hampton experience and training. From the start, Tuskegee emphasized practical education, the inculcation of Christian work ethics, and cleanliness. The students erected their living quarters and academic buildings; they cultivated the land, and produced their own foods. Spending more time on the farm and in practical workshops than in the classroom, they studied subjects such as brick-making, cabinet and mattress production, black-smiting, wagon-construction, modern agricultural methods, and housekeeping. As horrible as the experience of slavery was, Washington realized that it did confirm black expertise in agriculture and manual labor, and urged freedmen to build and develop upon this unique foundation.

The program Washington inaugurated at Tuskegee created no doubt in his faith and devotion to the Hampton model. However, his philosophy of education was also influenced by the prevailing ideological, cultural, and social currents of the world into which he was born and raised. Consequently, an examination of these currents and their contexts is central to understanding the ideological dynamics of his career.

The year he graduated from Hampton, 1876, was the very year of the crucial election that ended Reconstruction, ushering in a national compromise—the Compromise of 1877—that would significantly change the fortune of his race. The Compromise of 1877 was the culmination of developments that began at the onset of Reconstruction. Though blacks seemed integrated, their integration was into a very fragile and truncated relationship held together by the selfish political agenda of the Republican controlled federal government. Consequently, the commitment of the federal government to the elevation of blacks was at the very best questionable. This feeling towards blacks partly explains the ease at which conservative and reactionary forces regained political power and authority in Georgia, Tennessee, and Virginia. By the mid-1870s, it was becoming obvious that Republican support for blacks was on the wane.

The split in the rank of radical Republicanism also resulted from a changing political economy. The growing industrialization of the South and the potentiality for investment opportunities turned the North into a constituency, appreciative and sympathetic towards Southern aristocratic values. There were calls for a truce and **rapprochement** with the South in order to create and sustain a conducive atmosphere for investment and mutual economic growth. This was the beginning of the New South Movement. New South ideology combined propaganda and disinformation. The objective was to portray the South as a racially harmonious and politically stable environment in order to convince Northerners to cease further interference in the affairs of the region, especially on racial matters. New South ideologues such as Henry Grady described the South as a land of limitless opportunities and racial stability where blacks were supposedly satisfied and contented. There was, therefore, no need for any external interference in Southern race relations. This ideology won converts in the North, and the Compromise of 1877 was the result. Under the terms of this compromise, the federal government withdrew its forces from the South, giving Southerners absolute power and authority in shaping the destiny of the region. For Blacks, the compromise meant abandonment and betrayal, and it effectively marked the beginning of the end of political rights and participation. Put differently, the compromise inaugurated the restoration of ideals and values reminiscent of slavery days.

The second half of the nineteenth century was advanced by two philosophies: *laissez-faire* and Social Darwinism. Progress and elevation supposedly resulted, almost mechanically, from hard work, thrift, and Christian character. The main engine of social and individual progress was free competition, which allowed society to regulate itself without any intervention from the government or other external agency. This "free and fair" competition was supposed to advance the fortunes of those who faithfully upheld and lived by the precepts of Protestant ethics. *Laissez-faire* and Social Darwinism consequently tended to absolve the government of any responsibility or concern for social inequities and instead placed such responsibility squarely on the shoulders of individuals. Poverty, therefore, was not the consequence of social inequities or structural problems, but of the failure or inability of individuals *(i.e.* the poor) to uphold the canons of the Protestant work ethics. Those who reaped profits and amassed fortunes off the labor of the ordinary people felt relieved of any sense of guilt and responsibility.

This convergence, or "marriage of the minds," between the North and South, provided Southerners, or more appropriately "Redeemers," as they fondly called themselves, with an ideal climate to reshape Southern society in the old aristocratic image. Essentially, this reshaping entailed obliterating all the gains that blacks gained from the Civil War and Reconstruction such as: citizenship, the franchise, civil and political rights, and equal protection of the law. Between 1877 and 1889, Southerners, free of Northern interference, introduced lynching, criminal conviction, poll taxes, literacy tests, and the grandfather clause as legal and extra-legal means of circumscribing Black political rights. By 1890 and beginning with Mississippi, Southern states, one after the other, changed their constitutions to effectively eliminate Blacks as political participants. Stripped of political rights, Blacks were left to contend with marginal economic and social spaces—tenantry, peonage, and sharecropping. Essentially blacks confronted a vicious circle of poverty and misery.

For a brief period in the 1880s, the development of Populism seem to provide an avenue to political freedom for blacks, but due to mainstream political parties victories, this development was short circuited. The sudden revival of black political participation aroused fear of a possible resurgence of black political power, **a la** "radical" Reconstruction. Most Populists soon confirmed their racist consciousness by quickly abandoning Blacks. The solid South had emerged, and it became clear that blacks were identified only as marginal and subordinate members. All indications suggested a determination to keep blacks permanently subordinated and marginalized, peacefully if possible but with violence if necessary.

This was the world in which Washington attained maturity, and these were the social and cultural contexts that shaped his outlook. De-emphasized black political participation and power in consonance with the wish of the dominant culture, Washington offered blacks salvation through the economy. Tuskegee became his vehicle for demonstrating the potency and conservative nature of industrial education. The curriculum stressed economically practical disciplines, what he fondly called "the common occupations of life." These occupations did not threaten the political and economic hegemony of whites. He presented blacks as positive agents and factors whose services were central to the development of the South and the entire nation. He denied any intention on the part of blacks to oust whites or threaten their political dominance, and he stressed the need for economic cooperation between the two races. Southerners soon felt reassured and quickly overcame their initial skepticism. He, too, seized every available opportunity to underline the compatibility of the Tuskegee pedagogy with the prevailing normative values.

Washington became a national celebrity whose opinions were eagerly solicited by statesmen and philanthropists. He was frequently invited to deliver addresses, and he welcomed every opportunity to relieve whites of any apprehensions over the economic elevation of blacks. The zenith of Washington's popularity came in 1895 when he was accorded a rare opportunity to address the annual Atlanta Cotton Exposition. This speech became the defining moment of his career. Finally, here was the opportunity to sell his ideas to a wider audience. Washington's speech effectively marked the dawn of his age. Most critics agree that it also marked a turning point in his career, launching him into national fame and stardom. Washington became a black leader, many of his critics averred, not by the choice of blacks, but by the acclamation of whites.

Washington delivered a speech designed to harmonize the races and heal the existing racial antagonism. And he addressed both of his audiences—Southern whites and blacks. To blacks, he recommended agriculture as the key to economic elevation and ultimate freedom. He urged an appreciation of the importance and potency of manual labor. If blacks were to become elevated, respected members of the community, they had to acquire skills. Like Armstrong, his mentor, Washington loved the South and advised blacks to remain and attain economic elevation in the region. It is in the South, he said, that "the black man is given a man's chance." He encouraged blacks to cultivate habits of industry, thrift, self-help, and racial solidarity. He equally addressed the critical issue of education, underscoring the primacy of industrial over classical education. Industrial education would transform blacks into useful and functional members of society.

Washington depreciated and discouraged the pursuit of political rights and power; he stressed instead the primacy of economic power. He even favored suffrage restrictions based on property and education so long as they were equitably applied. He viewed this restriction as a viable solution to the problems of ignorance and poverty. Washington attached little significance to the political gains of Reconstruction; he described the time and efforts devoted to the acquisition of political rights and power during Reconstruction as a case of misplaced priority that was destructive in its consequence since it riveted the attention of blacks on duties and responsibilities for which they were not yet ready. He defined progress (*i.e.* Development) as a unilinear and cumulative struggle that begins at the bottom and progressively advances to the top. Washington identified industry as an elevating progression from bottom up that was the standard and most effective strategy of development. Consequently, he rejected calls for social equality. Equality **per se** was not a priority. The two races could remain socially separate, and still cooperate on issues pertaining to mutual progress. As he put it: "In all things that are purely social, we can be as separate as the five fingers yet one as the hand in all things essential to mutual progress." This statement became the centerpiece of the entire address, which most people remembered and considered as having aptly captured the mood of his age. In this single and often quoted sentence, Washington endorsed segregation. He left the impression that blacks equally and enthusiastically subscribed to the prevailing paternalistic and segregationist values and would willingly and faithfully accept and execute their assigned duties.

Washington assured Southern whites that their social and political dominance would not be challenged. Blacks were not interested in social and political equality and were not even ready for the exercise of such rights. He underlined the necessity and practicability of economic cooperation between the races. He appealed to the moral and economic sensibilities of whites and hinged all social development on the economic elevation of blacks.

Washington's speech reaffirmed themes blacks had espoused in the past. The debate on the efficacy of practical, industrial education is an old one, deeply rooted in the origin of organized black abolitionism. Leaders such as Frederick Douglas and Martin Delany advocated practical education on several occasions in the mid-nineteenth century. In the years immediately following the demise of Reconstruction, the subject was again prominently featured in debates and discourses among Black leaders. Even the issue of subordinating politics to economics was not unique to Washington. This idea was a central theme in debates among leading blacks during Reconstruction, and many strongly favored prioritizing economic elevation. Some, most notably Martin Delany, had also advocated compromise and accommodation to white paternalism. Though an unpopular minority view, acquiescence to white paternalism had been a component of black thought since the inception of Reconstruction, and some blacks stuck with the conviction to the end. This view partly accounts for the support, however minimal, that the Democrats were able to generate among blacks in the crucial election of 1876. This is also true of the concepts of self-help, racial solidarity, and the insistence that blacks should bear greater responsibility for their own advancement. Throughout the nineteenth century, leading blacks espoused and advanced strong faith in the gospel of wealth. There was, consequently, very little that was new or revolutionary in Washington's exposition address.

In Booker T. Washington, the big millionaires found a spokesman to induce blacks to seek the resolution of their problems in classic American middle class values, *i.e.*, to depend more on themselves and their own resources rather than on government or society. The national acclamation that followed his address distinguished Washington as a national black leader. He acquired the reputation of an apostle of peace and harmony. Gifts poured in from philanthropists. Andrew Carnegie donated the sum of six hundred thousand dollars to Tuskegee. As the "expert" on black affairs, Booker T. Washington became the avenue for dispensing government and philanthropic assistance to blacks, and he executed this function discriminatingly, making those resources available only to persons and institutions that toed the Tuskegee line, while starving all others of funds, especially institutions of liberal leaning such as Fisk and Atlanta University. In 1901, Washington received what amounted to a Presidential seal of honor when President Theodore Roosevelt invited him to dine in the White House. His fame also extended abroad, and he visited Britain, Germany, Italy, Austria and Denmark.

In 1896, the year after Washington's address, a mulatto, Homer Plessy of Louisiana, filed a suit before the Supreme Court challenging the state segregation law of 1890 on the grounds that it violated the equal rights protection guaranteed by the Fourteenth Amendment. In a landmark decision, the court upheld the legality of the Louisiana segregation law. It further held that the Fourteenth Amendment was never intended to eradicate racial segregation or to enforce social equality. Perhaps most significantly, the court reaffirmed the right of states to provide separate facilities, and that this right did not necessarily imply that one race was superior to the other. This case, popularly called *Plessy vs. Ferguson,* sanctioned the "separate but equal" doctrine, the leitmotiv of Jim Crow. It should be emphasized that this decision did not originate segregation. Segregation had always existed. What *Plessy* did was to encourage and embolden Southerners in their drive to subordinate blacks permanently. Lynching became a potent weapon of maintaining the color line, and impressing upon blacks an awareness of the racial boundaries, and of the importance of respecting those boundaries. Unfortunately, Washington himself was not immune from discrimination. He was forced to take back seats on Jim Crow sections of street cars and railroads. This compelled a reassessment of his philosophy, and he became critical of segregation and lynching, arguing, from a moral perspective, that both were destructive to the moral fibre of society. He secretly sponsored lawsuits against the exclusion of blacks from jury duty and the circumscription of franchise rights. Neither his moral pleas nor covert actions against segregation made any difference. The prevailing Social Darwinist culture discouraged any reliance on government. Blacks were, therefore, compelled to turn inward and exploit their own meager resources. Because *Plessy* followed on the heel of the exposition address, some have accused Booker T. Washington of complicity in the legalization of segregation. His ideas were seen as complementary to the normative values that denied blacks their rights and privileges.

To his critics and ideological opponents, Washington's leadership and policies felt oppressive, dictatorial, and vindictive. Nothing captured this feeling better than the concept they coined to describe his power, "Tuskegee Machine." Opposition to Washington and attempts to provide an alternative tradition of protest developed among a small group of northern black journalists, lawyers, and intellectuals, most notably Monroe Trotter, editor of *The Boston Guardian,* and W.E.B. Du Bois, a historian and sociologist trained at Fisk and Harvard. Trotter deplored Washington's tactics and ideas. He denounced accommodation as a very dangerous and harmful strategy and referred to Washington as the worst enemy of the Black race. It was Du Bois who first advanced a radical intellectual challenge to Washington. Du Bois had done research on the condition of blacks in some of the major cities, amassing a wealth of data on race relations. His findings provided a perspective on the black-white relationship that fundamentally differed from that of Washington. This notwithstanding, both men initially shared certain views. Du Bois also endorsed self-help and impartially administered discriminatory franchise based on education and property. Like Washington, he, too, stressed racial solidarity and cooperation, equally acknowledging the importance of industrial education, but he would not emphasize this importance.

By 1903, however, Du Bois's path began to diverge from that of Washington. He regarded Washington's pedagogical philosophy as anachronistic, since it taught fields that had become obsolete in the context of industrialization. He refused to surrender, or compromise on political rights and vehemently criticized Washington's advocacy of segregation. Du Bois traced the progress of segregation, disfranchisement, and the steady deterioration of black condition to Washington's policies. The policies indirectly helped shape the atmosphere that nurtured Jim Crow. Consequently, Du Bois deridingly tagged Washington's exposition address, "the Compromise of 1895," in obvious reference and juxtaposition with that of 1877. In an essay titled "Of Booker T. Washington and Others," Du Bois outlined his differences with Washington and identified what he called the major paradoxes or flaws in Washington's reasoning. First, Du Bois de-emphasized industrial education and opted instead for a pedagogy (classical or liberal education) that produced and nurtured exceptional men, bearers of culture and civilization, who he referred to as the Talented Tenth.

Neither the intellectual challenge of Du Bois nor the journalistic tirades of Trotter proved effective against the "Tuskegee Machine." It soon became obvious that some form of organization was desperately needed. In 1905, the first organizational attempt to combat Washington emerged—The Niagara Movement. Initiated by Du Bois and Trotter, the movement was formed to advance an alternative and counter **weltanschauung** to that of Washington. About twenty-nine men from fourteen states assembled on the Canadian side of the Fall in July of 1905 to launch a movement. The following year, with more in attendance, they met in Harper's Ferry, the scene of John Brown's bloody prelude to the Civil War. Here they dedicated themselves to an alternative tradition of black protest. The Niagara movement disclaimed the notion of Negro inferiority. The Negro, members maintained, would never bow to oppression, and they vowed to fight back, loudly protest, and assert their claims to every civil, political, and economics rights due to any free born American.

Washington marshalled every available influence and authority to stifle and undermine this new movement. His control of the Black press and rapport with White journalists gave him an inordinate power over his opponents who were intimidated and harassed. Monroe Trotter was arrested and jailed after a confrontation with Washington at the Boston Zion Church. It seemed as if the opposition was going to collapse. However in 1908, the faith of the Niagara Movement changed. Whites in Springfield, Illinois unleashed a reign of terror, beating and killing blacks. The atrocities provoked national indignation and touched the hearts of many white liberals. One of them, William English Walling, felt outraged enough to issue a call to white liberals for organized efforts on behalf of Negroes. Joining with a group of blacks in 1909, they formed a National Negro Committee, which changed its name in 1910 to the National Association For the Advancement of Colored People (NAACP). Its objective, inter alia, was to promote equality of rights and eradicate caste or race prejudice—an anti-Washington position. It had a much stronger organizational base for combating Jim Crow and the "Tuskegee Machine." Du Bois, who was then Professor at Atlanta University, left his job to join the new organization as Director of publicity and research and editor of its magazine, *the Crisis.* Several members of the Niagara Movement, including Trotter, refused to join because of its white leadership.

The NAACP immediately assumed a militant posture. Through publicity, protest, and litigation it advanced the case for equal rights and struggled to reverse the damages that Washington's ideas and values had done. It vigorously protested lynching and sponsored suits against segregation and discrimination. The first five years were difficult since Booker T. Washington remained very formidable. It was not until after Washington's death in 1915 that the NAACP was more effectively able to function. Washington, however, lived long enough to realize the failure of his accommodationist and paternalistic philosophy. Though in later life he revised his earlier views and became much more political and critical of segregation, the forces that he had inadvertently helped to strengthen had become formidable, and it would take almost four decades before any serious dent on Jim Crow would occur.

Disagreement persists over the place of Washington and his legacy to the African-American struggle. There are two contending schools of thought: The first avers that he sold out, betrayed his race, and undermined the efforts and accomplishments of earlier generations. According to this school, it was the 1954 *Brown vs. The Board of Education* decision that finally reversed Washington's negative legacy. The second school portrays Washington as a realist, one who knew that any strategy short of accommodation would have been counterproductive. Given the mood of the time, according to this school, blacks had no other viable alternative to accommodation.

Washington did not envision the total and perpetual subordination of blacks. This was not his goal. Very often, his means have been mistaken for his end. He applied a moderate, conciliatory approach to the pursuit of a radical end—the elevation of blacks. His determination to create a propertied class of Negro landowners and businessmen and encourage black entrepreneurship resulted in the founding of the National Negro Business League in 1900. He attached great importance to the attainment of racial harmony, even if it entailed concessions on terms temporarily disadvantageous to blacks. Consequently, Washington made short term concessions that he felt were necessary to ease racial tension and enhance the prospect of black elevation. It is important not only to distinguish between his immediate and long term goals but also to take due cognizance of the long term revolutionary implication of his short-term concessions. As he was quick to remark, "I plead for industrial education and development for the Negro not because I want to cramp him, but because I want to free him."

The age of Booker T. Washington witnessed significant and far-reaching developments in the African American experience. It should be remembered that there was virtually nothing that he did or advocated that had not been said or tried by earlier black leaders. He borrowed from his predecessors, often verbatim, without acknowledgment. Had Washington acknowledged his ideological mentors, perhaps posterity would have been a little gentler on him.

SUGGESTED READINGS

John B. Child. *Leadership, Conflict and Cooperation in Afro-American Social Thoughts.*

William E. B. Du Bois. *Soul of Black Folk: Essays and Sketches.*

Louis R. Harlan. *Booker T.* Washington: *The Making of a Black Leader,* 1856–1911. *Booker T Washington: The Wizard of Tuskegee,* 1901–1915.

John T. McCartney. *Black Power Ideologies: An Essay in African-American Political Thought.*

August Meier. *Negro Thought in America, 1880–1915: Racial Ideologies in the Age of Booker T. Washington.*

Booker T. Washington. *Up From Slavery: An Autobiography,* "The Virtue of Industrial Education."

Leslie H. Fishel and Benjamin Quarles, eds. *The Negro in America: A documentary History.*

John White. *Black Leadership in America: From Booker T. Washington to Jesse Jackson.*

STUDY GUIDE 14

1 Expand the "T" in the name of Booker T. Washington [hereafter printed as BTW].

2 "Accommodationism" became the ideology for what black leader during the 1890s and the turn of the century?

3 At what 1895 event in Atlanta did BTW make his historical address?

4 In what state was BTW born?

5 At what school did BTW matriculate as an undergraduate?

6 Name the mastermind behind Hampton Institute [University].

7 Give the location of Tuskegee University.

8–9 What two Compromises are discussed in this chapter?

10–11 What two philosophies dominated American life in the second half of the nineteenth century?

12 Name the group of southerners who reshaped the south after the "fall" of Reconstruction?

13–17 Give at least five of the legal and extra-legal means adopted in the post Reconstruction years to curtail the political gains of African Americans in the post Civil War years.

18–19 Give two antebellum black leaders who showed similar views as BTW on practical education.

20 What American President invited BTW to the White House to dine?

21 Name the 1896 case that ushered into law the "separate but equal doctrine."

22 Name the policy of race separation that developed in the south after the "fall" of Reconstruction.

23–24 Name two of the race leaders who attacked BTW's leadership.

25 The "talented tenth" was a part of whose philosophy?

26 Expand the abbreviation NAACP.

27 Name the 1905 organization founded by Du Bois and Trotter that became a central part of the NAACP, an organization which Trotter refused to join?

28 Name of the official magazine of the NAACP.

29 In what year did BTW die?

30 What 1954 law case reverse the *Plessy* Case?

15

Black America's Response To World War I

As early as 1911, observers of international politics and European developments could see Europe heading for war. They saw an inevitable clash between Germany and her satellite nations and western Europe. Germany and its allies were determined to control Africa and Asia while extending their influence on the European continent. The western European nations, led by England and France with the support of Russia, were just as determined to curb Germany's expansionist designs. The vast majority of the people of the United States and their political leaders seemed oblivious to the growing tension and when it exploded into all-out warfare in the summer of 1914 they were caught by surprise.

Black Americans as a community were less aware of European developments than their white counterparts. Blacks were deeply involved in their own struggle for freedom and equality at home. The twentieth century in America had opened on a sour note for blacks. They had been the victims of four brutal race riots in the first decade of the century: Statesboro, GA, 1904; Atlanta, GA, 1906; Brownsville, TX, 1906; and Springfield, IL, 1908. In each case the black community had been invaded by angry white mobs. Blacks suffered immensely from the unwarranted attacks and their pleas to the federal government for help fell on deaf ears.

The spirits of black America were lifted somewhat in 1912 by the campaign promises of Democratic presidential candidate, Woodrow Wilson. "Should I become president of the United States," Wilson told blacks, "I will administer justice to the colored people in every matter; and not mere grudging justice, but justice executed with liberality and cordial good feelings." Although skeptical of the Democratic party which they identified with slavery and the oppression which followed in its aftermath, they were encouraged by Wilson's promises. Disappointed by President Theodore Roosevelt's [Republican] reaction to the race riots during the first decade of the century and angered by Republican presidential candidate, William Howard Taft, who told black graduates of Biddle University in 1906, during his commencement address, that blacks and whites could not live together in harmony and that "your race is adopted to be a race of farmers, first, last, and for all times," blacks saw Wilson as their only choice.

Blacks who supported Wilson's successful bid for the presidency were quickly disappointed by his actions in the area of race relations. The President, by Executive Order, segregated all federal jobs and facilities in the nation's capitol and began phasing blacks out of the civil service. Nor did he actively oppose the flood of bills introduced into Congress during his first year in office which called for the removal of all blacks from the armed forces and the barring of all people of African descent from immigrating to the United States. They were further disheartened by the President in 1915 when he violated the sovereignty of Haiti and sent marines into the country to keep order which resulted in the deaths of hundreds of Haitians. In the same year he screened the motion picture *Birth of A Nation* [based upon Thomas Dixon's novel, *The Clansman*] in the White House and praised the violently anti-black, pro-Ku Klux Klan film, describing it as "history written with lighting." The film ignited a wave of violence against blacks throughout the South, including the 1916 live burning of Jessie Washington by a cheering white mob of men, women, and children in Waco, Texas. Rocked by Wilsonian racism at home and abroad, blacks paid little attention to the outbreak of war in Europe in 1914 and Wilson's proclamation of neutrality. Their first concern was their fight against lynching and other injustices at home.

By late 1916, Wilson's proclamation of neutrality had passed into armed neutrality due to German submarine attacks on unarmed American and Allied passenger and merchant ships. In early 1917 Congress and the nation's political leaders knew that it would be only a matter of time before the United States entered the European war on the side of England, France, and the other Allied nations. In November of 1915 during his campaign for reelection, Wilson asked Congress to enact legislation to expand the nation's ground and naval forces, not for war, but so that America would be prepared to defend itself if the European war spilled across the Atlantic. Some observers believed that Wilson's preparedness campaign was the first step toward entering the European war.

Following his reelection in 1916, Wilson moved closer and closer toward war. By the spring of 1917 Washington, D. C. was immersed in war talk. The talk of war naturally raised the question of how to raise, train, and equip an army and who would serve. Some members of Congress favored a system of compulsory Universal Military Training which would require all young men to serve in the armed forces. Even progressive reformers, who generally opposed the United States going to war, supported the concept. "Compulsory military training," said one, "is a melting pot which will break down distinctions of race and class and mold us into a new nation and bring forth . . . New Americans." Southern Congressmen, even those who supported American entry into the European war, were opposed to Universal Military Training. These legislators had sponsored bills in 1912 to remove all blacks from the armed forces and believed that Universal Military Training would lead to the enlistment of large numbers of blacks. Perhaps they believed that blacks who had benefited from military training would use that training to aid the black community in its struggle against southern injustice.

On April 6, 1917, the United States joined the Allied Nations of Europe (England, France, Russia, and Italy) in war against the continent's Central Powers (Germany, Austria, and Turkey), thereby transforming the European war into World War I. The United states went to war, according to President Wilson, not to conquer but to "make the world safe for democracy." The United States' entry into WWI provoked a spirited debate in the black community over whether it should support the war effort. But, anti-war sentiment, however, was not representative of the thinking in the black community as a whole.

The vast majority of blacks supported the nation's entry into WWI. They believed, as one black newspaper editor wrote, that the war was "a God-sent blessing" and an excellent opportunity for blacks to earn the respect of whites and to advance the cause of the race by heroic wartime service. Even W.E.B. Du Bois, editor of the national voice of the National Association for the Advancement of Colored People (NAACP), *The Crisis,* who had initially opposed the nation's entry into the war and was one of Wilson's bitterest critics, believed by 1918 that it was important for the future of blacks to demonstrate their support for the war effort. In July, 1918, he published in the Crisis an editorial entitled "Close Ranks." He believed, as did many others, that black support for the war effort would result in grater freedom and democracy in the post war era.

Even before Du Bois's "Close Ranks" editorial, the vast majority of blacks were doing what he suggested. They were especially active in the five loan campaigns to raise funds to pay the cost of the war and the campaign to increase food production. Mary B. Talbert, president of the National Association of Colored Women, reported that black women alone purchased more than $5 million worth of bonds in the Third Liberty Loan drive. Black businesses also purchased large amounts of bonds. The vast majority of blacks still resided in the South at the outbreak of the war and most of them were farmers. Consequently, they played a major role in the drive to conserve and increase food production. Herbert Hoover, the director of the Food Administration, appealed to black farmers directly for help and in 1918 he appointed Ernest Atwell as director of black food raising and conservation projects. Blacks also generously supported the fund raising campaigns of the Red Cross and other wartime support agencies.

The war also opened up tremendous economic opportunities for blacks in urban, areas which led to a mass exodus from the South. High wage industrial jobs in the North had been traditionally filled by native white workers and European immigrants, but the outbreak of war in 1914 slowed immigration to a trickle and the war's demand for manpower used up much of the available white labor thereby creating a severe labor shortage while the demand for industrial production increased dramatically. To fill the labor vacuum, northern industries sent agents South to entice blacks as well as whites to move North to work in their factories. The majority of blacks in the South were dependent upon cotton for their existence and times were hard. In 1914 and 1915 economic depression in the South sent wages in the cotton fields down to seventy-five cents per day, hardly enough to support a family. Although economic opportunity was the major reason blacks left the South in huge numbers, there were other factors: lynching, the injustice of southern courts, and the denial of voting rights and civil rights in general. Even before the war southern blacks viewed the North as the "promised land," and with the encouragement of industrial agents and the black press, they left the South by the thousands.

White northern factory workers and southern employers were alarmed by the massive black migration. Many of the industrial jobs in urban America were controlled by labor unions which denied blacks membership and they were opposed to the employment of non unionized black labor. Since many of the black workers worked for wages below the union scale, unionized labor viewed them as scabs.

By 1918 many southern homes were without cooks and maids, houses and churches formerly occupied by blacks were empty, and plantation owners faced financial ruin because there was not enough labor to harvest crops. "We must have the Negro in the South," declared the Macon, Georgia Telegraph. "It is the only labor we have, it is the best we could have and if we lose it, we go bankrupt." Several white southern newspapers urged blacks to stay in the South and many communities resorted to police harassment of northern industrial recruiters and potential black migrants in an effort to keep the region's cheap labor force.

Just as blacks flooded Northern cities to take advantage of the economic opportunity offered by industrial employment, they also flocked to Army recruiting station, the only branch of the armed forces that blacks could join, and volunteered their services after war was declared on April 6. There were only four units of black troops when war was declared (Ninth and Tenth Calvaries and the Twenty-Fourth and Twenty-Fifth Infantries), and once they were brought up to full strength with selections from the volunteers, the remaining volunteers were rejected due to a quota which restricted black enlistment. Some of the existing black National Guard units, however, were utilized. As early as March 1917, two weeks before the official declaration of war, the all black National Guard in the District of Columbia was called to active duty to protect the capitol. But the majority of blacks who served in the Army were not inducted until after President Wilson signed the Selective Services Act (the draft) into law on May 18, 1917.

Registration for the draft began on July 5, and more than 700,000 blacks registered. Before the end of the draft, two million blacks registered and 367,710 were inducted into the various branches of the Army. Although blacks only made up about ten percent of the nation's population in 1917, they were drafted at a rate of thirteen percent. Thirty-six percent of all black registrants were declared fit for military duty compared to twenty-five percent of white registrants. The discrepancy was caused by several factors. Among these was the racism of southern draft boards. A few southern draft boards used the draft to rid their communities of as many black males as possible.

Blacks also suffered discrimination in the army at the hands of the all-white officer corps and the War Department. Officials in the War Department made it clear in May of 1917 that all blacks in the Army would be subordinate to white officers. Under pressure from Southern congressmen, led by Senator John Sharp Williams of Mississippi who wanted to make sure no black officers in the Regular Army were placed in command of white troops, the War Department removed Lieutenant Charles Young, a West Point graduate and the senior black officer in the Regular Army, from his command. Young was sixth in line for promotion to the rank of Brigadier General, a rank he would have easily made due to the speed of wartime promotions. But the War Department abruptly ordered Colonel Young to report to Letterman Hospital in San Francisco, California, for examination to determine his fitness for active duty. Army doctors said he was suffering from Bright's disease and (high blood pressure) and ordered his retirement. Young vehemently protested and rode on horseback from his home in Ohio to Washington, D. C. in an unsuccessful attempt to prove his fitness. In 1918, five days before the armistice ending the war was signed, Colonel Young was called back to active duty and sent on a mission to Liberia where he contracted fever and died in 1922.

War had been declared in April, 1917, the Army's high handed dismissal of Colonel Young took place in June and July, and by the summer the War Department was being flooded with complaints from black troops and leaders in the black community charging discrimination by white civilians, law enforcement officials, and white officers. The complaints came from throughout the nation, but the most serious ones came from the South. Tension between black troops and white civilians in the South often led to violent physical confrontations. The most violent clash between white civilians, local white police officials, and black troops occurred in Houston, Texas in August of 1917. In July the all-black 3rd Battalion, 24th Infantry was sent to Houston to guard the construction of Camp Logan. The men of the 24th Infantry were not welcomed and they were expected, by local authorities and civilians, to behave in the same fashion as local blacks, accepting brutality, harassment, and insulting racial epithets without retaliation or comment. According to the battalion's white commander, the general attitude among local police and white civilians was that the soldiers' was negated by their race. He reported that white construction workers at Camp Logan "lost no opportunity to refer to the 24th Infantry as 'niggers'; the city police and people generally did the same. . . and no efforts were made in any respect to discourage the use of this appellation." Tension between the troops and the local community led to open violence when some local whites fired into the soldiers camp under the cover of darkness. Some of the soldiers armed themselves and left the camp in pursuit of their assailants. The resulting confrontation left sixteen whites and four black soldiers dead on the streets of the city.

For defending themselves the soldiers of the 24th Infantry were forced to pay a heavy price including court martials and trials. The trials resulted in twenty-eight death sentences, thirteen of which were carried out on December 11, 1917, before the cases could be reviewed and before the respective families were notified. President Wilson reluctantly commuted ten of the remaining death sentences to life imprisonment after his office was flooded with letters protesting the earlier executions and requesting leniency for those remaining on death row. As a result of the Houston incident and growing racial friction in the Army, Secretary of War, Newton D. Baker, appointed Emmett J. Scott, a Houston native who had served as Booker T. Washington's secretary for eighteen years, as his special assistant for black affairs. Scott, however, was able to do little to improve Army race relations.

Although deeply troubled by the reports of racism in the Army, black leaders still felt that it was in the best interest of the race to support the war effort. Black men wanted to fight for democracy abroad with the hope that it would mean greater democracy at home, but they wanted to be more than just foot soldiers, they also wanted to serve as officers. Fourteen officer-training camps were opened after war was declared but none of them accepted blacks. General Leonard Wood was adamantly opposed to blacks attending white officer-training schools. In July, 1917, one month before the explosion at Houston, a black officer-training camp was established at Fort Des Moines, Iowa. On October 15, it graduated 639 officers, all below field rank. The graduates were assigned to the 92nd Division where they served under white officers of higher rank.

The vast majority of blacks drafted into the Army worked as laborers and stevedores and were assigned to the 92nd and 93rd Divisions, the principal combat units. Only one of every five black draftees sent to France saw combat duty, but those performed heroically. The combat records of the 92nd and 93rd Divisions were quite different. The 92nd was under the command of General Charles C. Ballou and other white officers that he described as being of the "lower grades." Ballou's characterization of his officers was apparently accurate because the division performed poorly when forced into battle. The white officers charged that the poor performance record of the division was due to the cowardice of black troops under their command. But according to French accounts, the poor performance of the 92nd was due to a lack of competent leadership. Black troops under French command "have done splendidly," said a French military report in October, 1918, "but owing to inexperience, particularly in the higher ranks, American divisions employed in large blocks under their own command, suffer wastage out of all proportion to result achieved, and generally do not pull more than a small fraction of their weight."

The record of black regiments fighting under French officers was far superior to those which fought under the command of white American officers. This was especially true of the 369th Infantry of the 93rd Division. Several members of the 369th won individual recognition for their heroism under fire and the entire regiment earned the French Croix de Guerr (Cross of War) for bravery and gallantry in the face of the enemy. The Germans nicknamed them the "Hell Fighters." Testimonials to the efficiency and good conduct of the 369th and other black soldiers came from all sectors of French society. General John J. (Black Jack) Pershing, the commander of the American Expeditionary Forces who had served extensively with black troops before the war in Mexico in pursuit of Pancho Villa and in other areas, was one of the few white Americans officers who favorably commented upon the performance of black troops in battle.

One of the many reasons for the excellent record of the 369th Infantry, 93rd Division, was their reception and treatment by the French. While not on duty, the men moved about freely in French society and associated socially with French men and women. The experience was exactly opposite from what they were accustomed to in training camps in the states. Some white Army officers were so alarmed by the fraternization between black troops and the French people until they took it upon themselves to warn the French about the "dangerous" position in which they were putting themselves. American officials privately warned French officers not to treat black troops as equals because they were rapist and could not be treated with civility, and that they had to be lynched and burned in the states in order to control their behavior. The warning was followed in August of 1918 by the publication and circulation of an official army pamphlet entitled *"Secret Information Concerning Black Troops"* which urged the French to completely segregate themselves from black troops least their women be assaulted and raped.

When demobilization began after the war one of the goals of Army officials was the removal of all black troops from service. It was relatively easy to discharge black soldiers who had been inducted into the service as national Guard units from the states, but it was much more difficult to dismiss the black regiments that made up the Ninth and Tenth Calvaries and the 24th and 25th Infantries. These units had been created by Congressional legislation in 1866 and 1869 and could not be disbanded without congressional approval. The continuation of these units disturbed many of the white soldiers being discharged.

Although some black soldiers remained in France after the war, the majority of them were eager to return home where they were quickly demobilized. The rapid discharge of thousands of black soldiers drew storms of protest from the leadership of the black community. Not only were black leaders upset by the rapid dismissal of WWI veterans, the soldiers were upset by the reception they received. In the North there was a short lived period of jubilation as black veterans were greeted with ticker tape parades in New York City and in Buffalo. There were also warm greetings in St. Louis and Chicago, but there was little recognition of black veterans in the South. The Ku Klux Klan had been revived in the South in 1915 at Stone Mountain, Georgia, and by the end of the war it had launched a program for the preservation of white supremacy. Throughout the South, black soldiers, some still in uniform, were attacked by white civilians and Klansman. More than twenty blacks, ten of them soldiers, were lynched in the South in the first year after the war.

For those blacks who expected greater freedom in the United States after the war, the post war era greeted them with a return to prewar normalcy. The editor of the Crisis understood their disappointment and tried to spur them into action for greater home front democracy in May 1919 when he wrote: "We return. We return from fighting. We return fighting. Make way for Democracy! We saved it in France, and by the Great Jehovah, we will save it in the USA, or know the reason why." Despite the Crisis rallying cry, the war had little impact on the status of blacks. "I confess personally," wrote Emmett Scott in 1933, "a deep sense of disappointment, of poignant pain that a great country in time of need should promise so much and afterward perform so little."

SUGGESTED READINGS:

Bennett, Lerone. *Before the Mayflower: A History of Black America.*

Franklin, John Hope. *From Slavery to Freedom.*

Haynes, Robert, *A Night of Violence: The Houston Race Riot of 1917.*

Myrdal, Gunnar, *An American Dilemma.*

Study Guide 15

1–3	Name the leading three (3) European nations that vied to stop Germany's pre-WWI attempts for supremacy.
4–7	Give four (4) sites of major race riots in America during 1900–1910.
8	Who was elected President of the United States in 1912?
9–11	Give the political party affiliation of each person below:
9	Theodore Roosevelt
10	William Howard Taft
11	Woodrow Wilson
12	What black led Caribbean nation did the United States invade in 1915?
13–14	Name the title (**13**) and the author (**14**) of the novel upon which the motion picture *Birth Of A Nation* was based?
15	Name the U. S. President voted to office in the Election of 1916.
16	In what year did the United States enter WWI.
17–20	Name the leading Allied Nations of WWI.
21–23	Name the leading Central Power nations of WWI.
24	According to President Woodrow Wilson, why did America enter WWI?
25	Expand the abbreviation NAACP.
26	Name the editor of *The Crisis* during the WWI era.
27	With what organization was *The Crisis* affiliated?
28	"Close Ranks" was a pro-WWI article written by whom?
29	Where did blacks generally migrate during the WWI era?
30	What year was the Draft Bill signed into law?
31	Who was the highest ranking black military officer in 1917?
32	In 1917, where was the Camp Logan race riot?
33–34	During WWI, what two Divisions of the U. S. Army were mainly composed of black troops?
35	Give John J. Pershing's nickname.

16

Harlem Renaissance
A Historical Perspective

> "Why is it important for us to know Paul Roberson and Dr. DuBois and the men and women of the Harlem Renaissance? Because they are a vital and heroic part of our history. Because a people who are ignorant of their history are condemned to repeat their history. Because so many young people believe that the Black Liberation Movement began two or three hours after they joined the issues and they themselves invented militancy . . . We need desperately to know that this generation is not the first to produce artists and writers and historians who identified with Africa and proclaimed that Black was beautiful."
>
> John O. Killens

This chapter is an introduction to an unusually productive period in American History that saw a flourishing in literary and artistic talent among African Americans. As well, there was a flourishing of productivity in other areas of life, particularly in politics, business, and entertainment. All of these activities were in response to the economic and social conditions of the times and the confluence of African Americans striving for social equality.

The Harlem Renaissance was an extension of the on going struggle of African Americans to equally share the benefits and opportunities of American life with other Americans. This time can best be defined as an African American protest movement of the 1920s characterized by racial assertiveness and an outburst of literary and artistic expression. The protest was subtle and artistic. A number of political and social organizations were formed during this period in an effort to improve the plight of African Americans. The movement had Harlem as its "capital," but it spread throughout urban areas of the nation. Through poetry, novels, essays, paintings, short stories, histories, plays and music these voices spoke out against social and economic injustices in America, segregation, lynching, poor working conditions, and they promoted increased racial consciousness and revitalization of their African heritage. Their work went beyond mere protest and portrayed African American culture as inherently rich and vital. Literary circles, salons, poetry clubs, new magazines, and newspapers emerged in New York and other urban areas.

While the Harlem of today is painfully ugly, the glory of its past is hauntingly beautiful. The mid-nineteenth century Harlem, located in upper New York's Manhattan, was an isolated and poor rural area, inhabited by squatters living in shanty shacks. By the 1920s it had been transformed from a community of poor squatters to a white middle class community of mixed ethnic groups and then transformed again into one of the nation's largest and most densely populated African American communities. Harlem was the cultural capital of "Black America" and the center of the Harlem Renaissance or the "New Negro." The soul of Harlem at this time is best captured in a poem by Langston Hughes: "Strange/ That in this Nigger place I should meet life face to face;/ When, for years, I had been seeking/ Life in places gentler-speaking,/ Until I came to this vile street/ And I found Life stepping at my feet!"

The rapid growth of Harlem was a product of the urbanization and population growth of New York. As the city expanded, so did its population. By 1881, Manhattan's elevated railroad lines had been extended to Harlem. And as Harlem's transportation facilities improved, so did its residential potential. Land speculators moved in hoping to make a quick fortune. Houses, townhouses and expensive apartments went up in anticipation of an influx of white residents, which did not materialize. A deflated real estate market, the result of overbuilding by white speculators in Harlem, created an oversupply of well built houses. Astute aggressive African American businessmen such as realtor Philip A. Payton, Jr. snatched Harlem's newly developed real estate from middle class white hands and converted it into the most elegant African American community in the world. It was linked to downtown Manhattan by major avenues and the public transportation system. For the first time in New York's history, decent living accommodations were available to African Americans, and they flocked to Harlem to fill houses as fast as they became available. Wartime prosperity enabled large numbers of African Americans from all classes to save and invest in Harlem property. Perhaps the best known African American to achieve the American dream was Mrs. Mary Dean, known as "pig foot Mary," for the southern style pigfeet she sold from a pushcart in the streets of Harlem. She invested in real estate and made a fortune.

By 1920, Harlem, geographically defined by the Harlem River on the East, Eighth Avenue on the West, 125th street on the south and 145th street on the north, had become the home of every major African American business in downtown New York. Churches, insurance companies, small businesses, real estate firms, fraternal orders, settlement houses, the YMCA and YWCA, the Urban League and the NAACP all moved to Harlem. Harlem Hospital hired its first black nurses and doctors in 1919. The first group of African Americans to move into Harlem were members of the middle class with money. They formed social clubs, held cocktail parties and dances which supported the rapidly growing cultural life. Later the working class along with those of talent and creativity were drawn into this prosperous black community where they could live in comfort, and reach the widest African American audience in the world.

As more intellectuals came to Harlem, the more attractive it became for others. One newspaper editorialized Harlem as "a community in which Negroes as a whole are better housed than in any part of the country." Rev. Adam Clayton Powell, Sr., Pastor of the Abyssinia Baptist Church, called Harlem "the symbol of liberty and the Promised Land for Negroes everywhere." Langston Hughes, a noted African American poet referred to it as a "magnet" for African American intellectuals, and a magnet it was. Allain Locke, sometimes referred to as the "Father of the Harlem Renaissance, wrote of Harlem, "Negro life is seizing upon its first chance for group expression and self-determination." It was perhaps this sense of possibility that served as the magnet to bring together African Americans from diverse backgrounds and interests, creating the largest concentration of African Americans in the world.

Attracted by stories that work and money were abundant in New York, a host of writers, thinkers, artists, entrepreneurs, actors and musicians came to seek their fortune, to seek each other, and to organize and inspire their race to seek better economic and social opportunities. Musicians came in large numbers, especially the blues and jazz players. It was this coming together of people that gave birth to the Harlem Renaissance where African Americans from across the nation met and shared their experiences, dreams and ideas. They talked in crowded apartments, in social centers, read their latest works to fellow writers, helped each other to find housing, food, jobs, publishing outlets and in general encouraged each other. From this networking came a new writing style and new ways of looking at the world in which they lived. Harlem seemed to have taken on magical connotations, and African Americans thought their community was special. Harlem became the center from which the voice of intellectual African Americans would be heard around the world.

Most historians place the beginning date for the Harlem Renaissance around 1920, but its roots extend back to earlier years. The artists and thinkers of the 1920s owe much to their predecessors, earlier movements, and organizations. A variety of social and historical forces contributed to the rise of Harlem as a cultural and intellectual center for African Americans. The migration of African Americans from the rural South to urban centers in the North, early civil rights leaders and organizations, World War I, the Red Summer of 1919, and an increase in educational opportunities for African Americans were among the contributing factors.

The Harlem Renaissance of the 1920s and 1930s represent a high point in the creation of a rich and varied body of literature, the mastery of literary craftsmanship and the definition of specific cultural problems by African Americans. As stated by Allain Locke, "the Negro was shaking off the psychology of imitation and implied inferiority and creating a literature concerned with the human behavior of individuals and their lives." Many African American writers examined the mores of African American life in an honest and forthright manner. They portrayed the plight and promise of African Americans and protested segregation, discrimination and oppression. They revitalized African pride and became the moral spokesmen for the African American community.

During this period, many powerful figures emerged, and their many expressions have become great models of arts and letters. A cursory look at some of these artists follows: Claude McKay, considered as the first significant writer of the Harlem Renaissance, wrote both prose and poetry. *Harlem Shadow,* a volume of poetry published in 1922, was widely received, and, combined with his other works, stimulated action. "If We Must Die," one of his noted poems, was his angry response to the Red Summer of 1919. In 1923, Jean Toomer, made a significant contribution to the movement with only one work—a series of stories and lyrics about African American life in the rural South, entitled *Cane.* This work is characterized by objectivity, strong feelings and racial pride. Countee Cullen was recognized as a poet while still in high school and published his first book of poems, *Color,* in 1925. *Color* contained verses delicately dealing with the race problem. During this same year, some of his works began to appear in *Vanity Fair,* a popular white magazine. His "Ballad of the Brown Girl" and "Copper" were published in 1927. Today he is considered one of the major poets of the twentieth century. *Opportunity, Crisis, The Messenger, Challenge, The Voice, The Crusader, The Emancipator* and the *Negro World* provided an unprecedented forum for the works of numerous African American poets and writers of this period.

As for African American Literature, Jessie Redmond Fauset's 1924 novel *There is Confusion,* presents both the pride and the attitudes of middle class African Americans confronted with racial problems. Fauset wrote three other books, all of which are considered innovative contributions to African American literature. As literary editor she had a significant influence on other writers. Walter White, in addition to being a noted civil rights leader, was a prolific writer and a supporter of the arts during the Harlem Renaissance. He spent much of his life denouncing racism and rallying African Americans against racial intolerance through his books, syndicated columns, magazine articles and speeches. He worked to promote black artists and performers, often hosting social affairs whose guest list included members of the white literary establishment, black literary figures, etc. He wrote six books, three of which appeared during the Renaissance era, and numerous articles including a chapter in Allain Locke's *The New Negro.* His *Fire in the Flint,* published in 1924, is about the tragic treatment of black life in the South. *Flight* is a story of a young woman's search for identity. His third work, *Rope and Faggot* is a biographical treatment of Judge Lynch and an incisive analysis of lynching. Nella Larson dealt with pertinent social problems of black women in America and Europe in her works which include *Quicksand* (1928) and *Passing* (1929).

The names of Langston Hughes and Zora Neale Hurston have become apt synonyms for the Harlem (or Negro) Renaissance. These two prolific writers are examples of black rebellion as they sought both to gain acceptance and end oppression by proving their competency through written expression. Combined with the other writers of this period, Hughes and Hurston looked to their roots, and the subsequent mythology surrounding it, for subjects on which to write. They saw literary expression as a natural forum for protest against slavery. Interestingly enough, they garnered first applause from white audiences. It is of interest to note that these two, Hughes the poet, novelist, translator, and journalist; and Hurston, female novelist, anthropologist and playwright, have survived via the literary and social efforts to attain popularity to this day. Indeed, their works are now essential to the American literary canon.

Langston Hughes (1902–1967), a native of Joplin, Missouri, sought success by experimenting in several genres. He subsequently became the most prolific writer of the period, and, perhaps, the most prolific writer in American history. Through poetry, drama, fiction, and newspaper contributions, he portrayed the urban experience of working class blacks in America. Love of life and heritage permeates all of his works. *Weary Blues* (1926) is a collection of verse that reflects his love of music and his belief that music is pertinent to the black experience. The poems are mostly simple lyrics, reflecting a gentle protest consistent throughout his works. As well, there are experimental poems with sea as the subject. "Mother to Son," appearing in this volume is perhaps the most poignant expression of gentle, sad protest. Here, the author presents encouraging words from a mother to her son, explaining "life for me ain't been no crystal stair." Further, she make an apt comparison of life to climbing a rough stair. This poem continues to be especially popular in the black community. *Weary Blues* is often referred to as the signal of the advent of the Negro Renaissance. Other anthologies published by Hughes include *Fine Clothes to the Jew,* 1927, and *Montage of a Dream Deferred,* 1951. *Not Without Laughter,* a novel published in 1930, is heralded as a fine example of an American boy's rite of passage into manhood. This author is also well known for his post-Renaissance offerings, as well as the Jesse B. Simple legends.

This period was one of racial assertion and poetic freedom. It is interesting to note that males dominated the printed pages. But even so, Zora Neale Hurston left an indelible mark on the African American and African tradition of literary genres. She became one of the foremost collectors of African American folklore. A novelist and dramatist, she struggled for exposure both during and after the Harlem Renaissance. Regarded as forward and ahead of her times, her talents were not given full range, yet they were characterized by a boldness that affirmed blackness in a time when it was not the accepted thing to do. Hurston had the courage to produce an honest rendering of life, time, and place. Her works include a short story collection, *Mules; Man of the Mountain; Their Eyes Were Watching God,* and *Seraph on the Suwannee,* her last novel. Other works include *Dust Tracks on A Road, Color Struck,* a drama; *The Great Day,* a musical revue; *Tell My Horse,* non fiction; *Polk County,* a drama; *Mule Bone,* a comedy about black life, co-authored with Langston Hughes.

Hughes and Hurston joined with other African American writers in founding *Fire,* a literary journal devoted to black culture in America. Unfortunately, a fire in the editorial office killed this effort early on. When Hurston died in 1960, the event received scant notice. However, revived interest in her work has occurred, largely impart to the efforts of Robert Hemenway and novelist Alice Walker, who reclaimed and edited some of Hurston's works that are finally receiving their appropriate acclaim.

The African Americans of this period used varied mediums of expressions: Music, dance and drama were witnessed as great works of art. Theater personalities and organizations, singers and musicians fed the period. The 1921 musical "Shuffle Along" with Eubie Blake and Noble Sissle has been given credit as the single impetus for the period. In addition to marking the beginning of the commercialization of the Harlem Renaissance, "Shuffle Alonge" is credited with legitimizing ragtime music and jazz dancing. Many of its tunes became world famous such as "I'm Just Wild About Harry." It became a veritable theater model. As the twenties began, songs of true African American origin, spirituals and blues, were virtually unknown, being sung mostly in African American homes and churches. W.E.B. DuBois called these sorrow songs. Similarly, blues were songs in African American businesses. Popular figures of this era included Bessie Smith, Alberta Hunter, Ethel Waters (first to sing W. C. Handy's "St. Louis Blues"). Jazz came to New York from out of town musicians such as trombonist Charles Irvis and trumpeters June Clark and Bubber Miller. And the streets of Harlem were ready for it. After "Shuffle Along" premiered, jazz became popular in uptown New York. This led to the opening of African American dance studios to teach the new dances. Harlem saw the proliferation of night clubs, many of which catered to whites only. The Cotton Club, known as "The Aristocrat of Harlem," Connie's Inn, and Ed's Paradise were the three most popular spots in Harlem. Among the African American actors of note were Charles Gilpin, who starred in Eugene O'Neill's *Emperor Jones* in 1920 and Paul Roberson in *All God's Children Got Wings* in 1924. DuBose Hayward's dramatization of his novel *Porgy* and Marc Connelly's *Green Pastures,*1930 were plays which offered significant exposure of African Americans actors though the playwrights were white. Most plays by African Americans were performed in little theater groups, although writers like Willis Richardson and Frank Wilson contributed several plays to be aired in the African American community. It may be added here that musical revues that were mostly imitative of the white culture and sometimes blackfaced, received favorable hearing on Broadway. Such titles include "Strut Your Stuff," "Struttin' Hannah from Savannah," "Town Topics," and "Watermellon."

In summary the Harlem Renaissance is a term used to designate a period in American History, during the 1920s and 1930s when there was a rich surge of African American art and letters, not only in Harlem, New York where there was a large concentration of artists, but in many other areas of the nation. As African Americans became increasingly aware of the discrepancies between the promise of freedom and the realities of their experiences, they seized the opportunity to:

1 Write about their culture and tradition
2 Confront racism via artistic expression
3 Write about the economics and social problems in the United States
4 Protest injustices
5 Improve the culture and civilization by their art
6 Create art for arts sake
7 Create art for escape
8 Transform feelings of hate and hurt into accepted forms of expressions

Due to the climate of neglect, indifference and rejection much of the literature created during this period never reached the reading public and even today much of this literature is inaccessible to the general public. Langston Hughes' poem, "Ballad of the Landlord" was banned from the Boston school system for a long period of time. The Great Depression of the 1930s led to a wane in artistic creativity by African Americans however the artistic output among African Americans saw a rebirth in the 1960s as increased awareness and opportunities formed the setting for new self-expression and revelation of the African American artist in American life.

Suggested Readings:

Thadious Davis, *Nella Larsen: Novelist of the Harlem Renaissance.*

Hugh Gloster, *Negro Voices In American Fiction.*

Alain Locke, ed., *The New Negro: An Interpretation.*

Study Guide 16

1 Mainly, in what decade did the Harlem Renaissance occur?

2–3 Give two alternate names for the "Harlem Renaissance."

4–5 What two things mainly characterize the Harlem Renaissance?

6 Name the "father" of the Harlem Renaissance.

7 In what year did the "Red Summer" occur?

8–13 Name six of the magazines or journals available to artists of the Harlem Renaissance for publication of or about their works.

14–25 Give the artists that created or are identified with each work below:

14 *Cane*

15 *Color*

16 *Harlem Shadow*

17 "If We Must Die"

18 "Jesse B. Simple"

19 *The New Negro*

20 *Not Without Laughter*

21 *Passing* (1929)

22 "Shuffle Along"

23 *Rope and Faggot*

24 *Their Eyes Were Watching God*

25 *There Is Confusion*

17

Between the Wars and World War II

When Woodrow Wilson became President of the United States in 1913, his administration became known as "New Freedom." Apparently, however, this Freedom applied to all Americans except African Americans. For during his administration, black people were faced with many setbacks.

Before the WWI, the Ku Klux Klan had been resurrected to continue its war on African Americans with a new aggressiveness. In November, 1915, William J. Simmons became the Imperial Wizard of the Klan resurrected at Stone Mountain in Georgia. This new Klan aimed its agression at blacks, Jews, immigrants and Catholics. Although the new Klan was stronger outside the south, it eventually came to dominate the governments in Texas and Oklahoma.

During Wilson's administration, America's foreign policy also began to affect the black world. In 1915, for example, the United States intervened in Haiti after her European creditors complained of the country's inability to pay off its debts. Through force, Hati turned over its customs department, public works and constabulary forces to America. This resignation lasted until 1934. Then, in 1916 until 1924, American troops entered the Dominican Republic in order to prop up the government and bring stability to the country. In 1917, the United States acquired the Danish Virgin Islands for a reported $25 million. The islands were used to provide more naval defense for the Panama Canal. In 1927, citizens of the Virgin Islands became American citizens.

During these events on January 18, 1919, the Treaty of Versailles was signed, ending WWI. Discussions formulating this treaty had taken place in Europe between January and June, 1919. Back "in the States," the year 1919 started off with the ratification of the Eighteenth Amendment, otherwise known as the Prohibition Amendment. Then the Red Scare Movement broke out in America, led by Attorney General A. Mitchell Palmer. This movement, whose objective was to purge America of "all the 'commies' (Communists) hiding under every rock in America," featured the infamous Sacco-Vanzetti Case of 1921 where the two defendants were accused of a robbery in Braintree, Massachusetts and executed in 1927. And in the midst of all this activity, there was the chilling "red summer of 1919," during which over two dozen race riots ocurred. Longview, Texas; Washington, D. C.; Tulsa, Oklahoma; Elaine, Arkansas; Chicago, Illinois and Knoxville, Tennessee all simmered. In the nation's capital, a riot lasted from July 19 to July 23; and, in Chicago, a riot continued from July 27 until August 6, 1919.

During this destruction, W. E. B. DuBois was in the "construction business." He helped organize the Pan African movement, in which Congress put forth a black agenda for the peace discussions at Versailles talks that met in Paris between February 19–21, 1919.

The decade after the peace of WWI was known in America as "the Jazz Age." This period was characterized by assembly line production; motion pictures (which became talking pictures in 1927); cars; and the air age with advanced air planes. The Jazz Age was an age of speed. KDKA became the first commercial American radio station, broadcasting out of Pittsburgh, Pennsylvania. But for African Americans, these years were, in many regards, still the bleak years. Fear of violence and lynching during this time was a continuation of the fear experienced in the years of southern migration between October, 1922 and October, 1923 during which over one-half million blacks migrated from the south. But, World War I had aroused new hope in the African American. And for some who had become disillusioned with "America's democracy," there was the infiltration of the communism philosophy. But not all was bleak, because in these same years, civil rights groups like the NAACP and the Urban League began to exert influence and power. Not all was gloom for black folks. For example, this was the era of Jack Johnson—the World's first black heavyweight boxing champion, who hailed from Galveston, Texas.

In politics, the Republicans won the 1920 presidential election with the "dark horse" candidate, Warren G. Harding, a U. S. Senator from Ohio. He wanted a "return to normalcy." Unfortunately, he died on August 2, 1923, and his vice-president, former governor of Massachusetts, Calvin Coolidge, became president. During the 1924 presidential campaign, the Democrats denounced the Ku Klux Klan at their national convention. Much of the conservatism of this period came to a head in the so-called Scopes-Monkey Trial of 1925. John T. Scopes was put on trial in Tennessee for violating the states laws by teaching scientific evolution. Clarence Darrow, Scope's lawyer defended the "Modernist" interpretation of evolution, and William Jennings Bryan, the fundamentalist, presented the opposite view point. Although Scopes was convicted, this case helped to open up America to the teaching of modern science.

In the black world, on August 25, 1925, A. Phillip Randolph led the emerging organization of the Brotherhood of Sleeping Car Porters. This group became the first successful labor union with a black origin. As a result of its success, blacks became a part of other labor unions. In February 1926, Carter G. Woodson began the celebration of "Negro History Week." This event took place during the second week of the month; later, it would be expanded into "Black History Month." Carter G. Woodson also founded The Association for the Study of Negro Life and History, which publishes *The Journal of Negro History*. This publication is intended for professionals, but, for the laymen, he began publication of the *Negro History Bulletin*. Reflecting the trend of the day, the name of the Association was changed in the 1970s to The Association for the Study of Afro-American Life and History.

In 1920, Marcus Garvey began the U.N.I.A. (Universal Negro Improvement Association) in Harlem. This association became the first mass movement organization among black Americans. This type of organizing paved the way for organizations to come and also helped in creating the movement discussed in the last chapter titled "The Harlem Renaissance." For the black world, the Harlem Renaissance brought forth a rebirth of learning and creativity, but for the white world, it brought more white admirers to advocate the cause of blacks.

In the south, the white groups that helped to bring about change were (1) the Commission on Interracial Co-operation that had been founded in 1919. (2) the Southern Conference for Human Welfare founded in 1938; and (3) the Southern Regional Council founded in 1944. White groups desiring racial change tended to be urban liberals or people motivated by religion.

In 1927, Dr. Lawrence A. Nixon, a black El Paso dentist, began a series of court challenges to regain the franchise for blacks fighting the Texas "white primary" laws. These cases included (1927) *Nixon v. Herndon*, and (1932) *Nixon v. Condon* that invalidated the white primary. Unfortunately, this activity gave the white community new energy and a new desire to keep black folks away from the ballot.

The Courts became the scene of action for a number of cases affecting the black community. In the decision of *Powell v. Alabama* in 1932, the courts, acting under the 14th Amendment, decided to make the appointment of a trial lawyer for the defendant mandatory . In 1935, the Courts gave a setback to the 1932 *Nixon* case. In *Grovey v. Townsend*, the courts approved the Texas white primary. Also in 1932 in *Norris v. Alabama,* the Courts stated that deliberate exclusion of blacks from juries was *prima facie* evidence of racial discrimination. Three years later, in *Missouri ex rel Gaines v. Canada,* the Courts required states to provide equal educational facilities for African Americans. Finally, in 1941, the Courts decided in *Mitchell v. U. S.* to strike down segregation in interstate commerce.

But, for most Americans, the years between WWI and WWII were characterized not by the action of the Courts, but by the action of the Executive. In late June, 1928, the Democratic National Convention was held in Houston, Texas. Perhaps as a symbol of the times, this Convention was preceeded by a lynching. Robert Powell, a colored man, was lynched on June 19. This became the last lynching of a black man in Houston, and, as is typical with lynchings, no one was ever convicted with Powell's murder.

On October 21, 1929, the Stock Market crashed, causing the depression to take shape. By the end of 1931, ten million Americans were unemployed. In 1932, appromimately four and a half million more Americans were added to the unemployment rolls. Between 1929 and 1932, over eighty-five thousand businesses failed. Income declined from $81 billion in 1929 to $53 billion in 1932 and $41 billion in 1932. Soup kitchens, bread lines, and apple-sellers became the orders of the day. Herbert Hoover, the Republican U. S. president, supported reliance on individual initiative and limited governmental assistance as a solution to America's problems with the depression.

In 1932, Franklin D. Roosevelt won the executive race by a landslide victory. In his presidential inaugural address, Roosevelt said, "The only thing we have to fear is fear itself." FDR, to alleviate effects of the depression, began the "New Deal,"a campaign aimed at helping the "forgotten man."

In the black community, most people were used to the inadequate feeling of not having enough of anything. Things simply got harder during the depression. For example, during the 1930s, the south spent seven dollars to educate a white child, but only two dollars on an African American child. On April 6, 1931, this decade also witnessed the "Scottsboro Boys" trial in Alabama where several young black men were accused of raping a white woman. This trial became an ugly affair mixed up with communism. By 1932, blacks began switching from the Republican Party to the Democratic Party. A factor in this switch was not only the "crumbs" of the "New Deal" coming to the black community, but Mrs. Eleanor Roosevelt's close work with the black community. On a whole, the "New Deal" operated with mixed rules based on color. For example, in Houston, Texas, an average black person on relief received only $12.67, whereas an average white recipient received $16.86. The New Deal measures receiving the most headlines for discrimination in the black community were the PWA, the CCC of 1933, the NYA of 1935 and the Social Security Act. By 1933, FDR was operating with a "Black Cabinet" whose cabinet members included Mary McLeod Bethune, William H. Hastie, Eugene Kinckle Jones, L. A. Oxley, Robert L. Vann, and Robert C. Weaver. Unfortunately, these years also witnessed a population migration. Between 1935 and 1940, 8.15 percent of America's black population migrated to a different part of the countryin order to improve their economic conditions, increase their educational opportunities, and improve their social conditions. Prior to the war years, the NAACP in 1933 began a concentrated attack on segregation. During July 1940, what would eventually become a major case began in Houston, Texas: Dr. Lonnie Smith was refused a ballot in a "white primary." On May 26th, 1941 in *United States v. Classic,* the Supreme Court held that the government could regulate elections in which federal officials were elected.

The rumblings of war could be heard in the distance. On a simple basis, one might say that due to Japanese aggression and German Nazism, World War II resulted. For instance, it had been thought that in the August, 1936 Olympic Games in Berlin, Adolf Hitler had seen some of the fallacies in his superman Aryan theories with the heroism of Jesse Owens and Ralph Metcalfe. But in the United States, this military conflict was opening on a sour note. A. Phillip Randolph was threatening a "March on Washington" set for July 1, 1941. This march was serious business, and President Roosevelt responded. On June 25, 1941, Roosevelt signed into law Executive Order 8802—the Fair Employment Practice Act—to eliminate racial discrimination in wartime industries and various government apprenticeship programs. The march was then called off. On December 7, 1941, the Japanese attacked Pearl Harbor. Accoring to FDR, this "day would live in infamy."

On this day Dorie Miller became a hero. The "system" made no provisions for black men to fight in combat. In the Navy, black men, such as Dorie Miller, could only serve as stewards, messmen and other menial positions. In the heat of battle, however, Miller became a gunner. In WWI, black men had fought to "make the world safe for democracy." And the world was safer for all people, except for the Negro in America. Now, because of racism, WWII was beginning with the black man fighting the war as half-of-a-man. Regardless, black men and black women became an essential and necessary part of World War II.

On February 19, 1942, the Japanese Americans got a chance to feel what blacks in America had been feeling for over three hundred years. The Executive Relocation Order forced Japanese Americans to evacuate from the West coast. 1942 also saw the beginning of a wartime employment pickup for blacks. In the Spring of 1945, on April 12th, at Warm Springs, Georgia, FDR died. Harry Truman, from Missouri, became the new President. On August 6, 1945 the United States dropped an atomic bomb on Hiroshima, Japan. Then on August 9th, an atomic bomb was dropped on Nagasaki. At Potsdam, Germany a conference was held to finalize the meaning of WWII. Truman, Joseph Stalin of the Soviet Union, and Clement Atlee (replacement for Winston Churchill) of Great Britain drew up Japanese surrender terms.

A few days later (October, 1945), a Pan African Convention was held at Manchester, England to push "black demands" for the end of the War. After all, the Potsdam conference just concentrated on the world as seen by the eyes of whites.

In America, there had been another type of war going on alongside WWII. In June, 1943, CORE (the Congress of Racial Equality) had been founded. On April 3, 1944, another atomic bomb-like explosion had rocked America: This was the earlier mentioned case of Dr. Lonnie Smith, originating in Houston, Texas. In this case of *Smith v. Allwright.*, the U. S. Supreme Court reversed the Townsend decision and granted blacks the right to vote in Democratic (white only) primaries.

The next year, on October 23, 1945, the Brooklyn Dodgers signed Jackie Robinson to a baseball contract: He broke the baseball color barrier. On February 26, 1946, Heman M. Sweatt filed an application to enter the University of Texas. And in June 1946, the U. S. Supreme Court, in the case of *Irene Morgan v. Commonwealth of Virginia*, banned interstate bus segregation. In the same month, boxer Jack Johnson died.

The Nuremberg (Germany) trials also started in 1946; these were the World War II war criminal trials. Twelve of the defendants from these trials were sentenced to death. Still, from a panoramic perspective, a German in America would have probably received better treatment than a black man.

After 1948, Truman's administration became known as "the Fair Deal." In 1948, there was the restrictive racial covenant case of *Shelley v. Kraemer.* At this same time, America became deeply involved in a "cold war." This turn of affairs brought forth the trial of *Paul Robeson v. Jackie Robinson* in 1949 explaining black folk's loyalty to the United States and their "dislike" of communism.

On June 5, 1950, the U. S. Supreme Court decided the *Sweatt* case, ordering the University of Texas to desegregate. This verdict was similar to that in the *McLaurin* case in Oklahoma. The Courts seem to have been looking favorably at blacks as a people. Adding more positiveness to this black trend was the Pulitzer Prize Committee which presented Gwendolyn Brooks its prize for her book of verse entitled *Annie Allen.* Ralph Bunche also added to this list by claiming the Nobel Peace Prize for 1950 for his mediation in the Arab-Israeli Conflict. Finally, there seemed to be a light at the end of the tunnel. Or, was this the calm before the storm?

Suggested Readings

Howard Jones, *The Red Diary*.

STUDY GUIDE 17A

1	Whose Presidential administration became known by the cliche "The New Freedom?"
2	Where in 1915, was the KKK resurrected?
3–6	What groups became the obects of hate for the new KKK?
7	What new territory did the United States acquire in 1917?
8	What treaty ended World War I?
9	U.S. Constitution.
10	Who "led" the "Red Scare Movement?"
11	What was the infamous 1921 "witch-hunt" case that centered on two immigrants accused of robbery in Massachusetts?
12–17	Name six of the major race riots of the Summer of 1919?
18	Name an African American leader of the 1919 Pan African Movement.
19–22	What four facets of life helped to characterize "the Jazz Age?"
23	What became America's first commercial broadcasting station?
24	Name the world's first heavyweight boxing champion that was black.
25	In 1920, who was elected President of the United States?
26	Who succeeded the above (**#25**) person in 1923 as President of the United States?
27	Give an alternate name for the John T. Scopes trial of 1925.
28–29	Give the names of two interpretations of the evolution of man.
30	Who founded the Brotherhood of Sleeping Car Porters and Maids?
31	Who began the celebration of "Negro History Week?"
32	Name the organization the above person (**#32**) founded.
33	Expand the abbreviation U.N.I.A.
34	Who founded the U.N.I.A.?
35	When did the Stock Market crash?
36	In 1932, who won the American presidency?
37	In what state were the "Scottsboro Boys" placed on trial?
38	What white female stoodout in helping the black community during the New Deal?
39–44	Name the members of FDR's "Black Cabinet."
45	Under what philosophy did pre-World War II Germany operate?
46–47	Name two black heroes of the 1936 Berlin Olympics.
48	Name the mastermind behind the 1941 March on Washington.
49	Give an alternate name for the 1941 Executive Order 8802.
50	When did the Japanese attack on Pearl Harbor occur?

Study Guide 17B

1	Name the black hero from the Japanese attack on Pearl Harbor.
2	In 1942, what group of people were negatively affected by the Executive Relocation Order?
3–4	On what two Japanese cities did the U. S. Drop A-bombs in 1945?
5	Expand the abbreviation C.O.R.E.
6	What constitutional case eliminated the all-white primary?
7	Who broke the color line in professional baseball?
8	What was the restrictive covenant case?
9	Who won the 1950 Pulitzer Prize for poetry?
10	Who won the 1950 Nobel Peace Prize?

18

The Immediate Years of the Brown Case

[White] school boards relied on the "separate but equal" doctrine announced by the Supreme Court in Plessy v. Ferguson. Plaintiffs argued that segregated public schools were not "equal," could not be made "equal," and thus denied equal protection of the laws.

Derrick Bell.

The Supreme Court in the 1954 *Brown v. Board of Education* decision concluded that in the field of public education the doctrine of "separate but equal" has no place. It is significant to note that in subsequent years the High Court had little difficulty in terminating state-imposed racial segregation in a variety of public facilities. However, the High Court contradicted its mandate relative to public education. The contrariety emanated from the fact that the High Court actually delayed implementation of its mandate to desegregate public schools. In *Brown v. Board of Education II*, one year subsequent to the original decision in *Brown*, the High Court, having established that segregated public education was illegal and "inherently unequal" it addressed the issue of remediation. The High Court concluded that defendants (southern school systems ordered to desegregate) should consummate movement toward full compliance with *Brown* and that plaintiffs (African American students) should be admitted to public schools on a racially nondiscriminatory basis "with all deliberate speed."

Significant movement did not occur "with all deliberate speed." A number of years were to pass before the High Court would reach a point where it would no longer tolerate the delays and obstructions posed by recalcitrant southern school systems. However, it was not until 1968 that the Supreme Court finally determined that the time for all deliberate speed had been exhausted.

The struggle of blacks in America is well documented, both in this book and elsewhere. They have endured over two hundred years of the denial of basic human rights, followed by over a hundred years of the denial of full civil rights guaranteed by one of the most celebrated documents in Western civilization—the Constitution of the United States. The Plessy decision of 1896, followed by the institutionalization of Jim Crow [code phrase for segregation] were, seemingly, all part and parcel of a society intent upon maintaining separate and unequal status for blacks and whites. The status of African Americans changed very little up through the early part of the twentieth century. However, the intensification of racial prejudice and discrimination following the end of Reconstruction persuaded many former slaves to seek refuge in the north.

Much of the migration was a consequence of the blatant prejudice and discrimination practiced in the south under Jim Crow.

World War II, the war to end racism in Europe, saw African Americans play a prominent role in that war. African Americans gave their lives in the cause for liberty abroad, yet were lynched at home because of racial hatred. The impetus behind the U.S. involvement in the war (to end racial genocide and repression in Europe) brought new vigor and a greater commitment to the push for civil rights at home. The conclusion of the war was reminiscent of the circumstances that existed at the end of the Civil War and World War I. Just as black soldiers who fought in the Civil War and World War I had high expectations of a society that they fought to preserve, so did the blacks that fought and sacrificed in World War II. This did not occur. Even during the war African American soldiers were subjected to discrimination and mistreatment by white American soldiers.

In 1947 Harry S. Truman created the President's Committee on Civil Rights. The Committee recommended that new legislation be enacted to protect the voting rights of African Americans. However, Congress failed to act on the Committee's recommendation. Congress was remiss in enacting even an anti-lynching law. President Dwight D. Eisenhower took up the initiative of Truman by attempting to pass civil rights legislation. Despite Eisenhower's initial efforts, and the efforts of President Truman, it was not until 1957 that the first Civil Rights Act was passed in the twentieth century.

Legislation enacted in the twentieth century prior to the *Brown* case was only minimally successful in terms of combating discriminatory practices. Even the decree handed down in the *Brown* decision was not effectively administered until the 1960s. It is curious to note, that as significant as the *Brown* decision was, in terms of setting a legal precedent to dismantle a dual society, it carried little weight of enforcement. The enforcement component was not put into place until ten years later, with the enactment of the 1964 Civil Rights Act.

There were a number of court cases litigated by the NAACP prior to *Brown*—each chipping away at racial segregation and racial discrimination. In 1935 Donald G. Murray, was a twenty year old African American and a resident of Baltimore, Maryland. He had recently graduated from Amherst College and was seeking to enter the University of Maryland's law school. The Maryland Court of Appeals ruled in 1936 that Murray must be admitted to the law school without delay. Herman M. Sweatt, was an African American mailman, who applied for admission to the University of Texas law school in 1946. To circumvent Sweatt's admission to the all white law school, the state of Texas hastily constructed a separate law school for African Americans at the all black Prairie View College. In 1950 Sweatt was ordered to be admitted to the University of Texas law school. George W. McLaurin, was a sixty-eight year old African American who applied to the University of Oklahoma's doctoral program in education in 1948. He was admitted to the University of Oklahoma, but was made to sit alone in an anteroom outside the regular classrooms. In 1950, on appeal, the Supreme Court granted McLaurin the right to attend classes with his white classmates. Ada L. Sipuel, a twenty one year old African American female who applied to the University of Oklahoma all white law school in 1946, was denied admission. The state of Oklahoma argued that a law school for Negroes would soon be constructed and that Sipuel could wait until the facility was opened. The Supreme Court in deciding the case, concluded that Sipuel had a right to attend the University of Oklahoma law school, but the fact that she would be isolated and roped-off from the rest of her white classmates did not violate her constitutional rights. While these cases were not a frontal assault on *Plessy*, they did establish that equal educational opportunity was an issue the High Court was willing to address, in spite of the immutability of Plessy.

Brown v. Board of Education turned out to be the case that would provide the opportunity for a frontal attack on Plessy. There were actually five school desegregation cases scheduled by the Supreme Court during the time of *Brown*. *Brown* was actually four cases consolidated into one—all dealing with the issue of school segregation. The four suits all challenged the constitutionality of state imposed school segregation. The common denominator in the five school desegregation cases to reach the Supreme Court was the NAACP.

Despite the outward cohesiveness of the legal cadre of the *Brown* team, there were struggles within the ranks about the most judicious strategy to pursue. There was disagreement over whether to seek equalization of resources and facilities (which would have kept them within the confines of Plessy) or to seek a bolder strategy by trying to overturn Plessy (*i.e.*, the separate but equal doctrine). Plessy was the target that all the segregation litigation had been pointing to over the years. It was the foundation upon which segregated schooling rested. Overturning Plessy would open the gate to the elusive ideology of equal educational opportunity. The NAACP had heretofore chosen its cases carefully. It had been critical to select cases with wider implications than just the mitigation of individual suffering by African Americans. It sought cases that would tear at the heart of Jim Crow; causes that would have a transforming impact on race relations in the U.S. Consequently, the NAACP sought cases that were amenable to class action suits. Class action suits would bring relief, not only to the individual, but to all members of a class similarly situated.

The early years of preparing for the assault on the separate but equal doctrine were characterized by a series of legal trial and error, attempting to make the best decision about which cases to litigate, deciding what regions to choose, and deciding what corrective measures to pursue. Throughout the late 1940s, cognizant that the NAACP had little, if any, hope of winning an all out war on *Plessy,* Thurgood Marshall had favored arguing within *Plessy* in the struggle against segregation in graduate and professional school cases.

Despite the overwhelming evidence presented by the NAACP legal staff, the long list of expert witnesses, the precedent of earlier litigation, and the weight of an overpowering oral argument in 1953, the High Court, nonetheless, insisted upon *Brown* being reargued in 1954. Furthermore, no directives were established for the implementation of *Brown.* In 1955, when this oversight was finally addressed it did so without establishing time lines or uniform conditions. It simply argued for desegregation "with all deliberate speed." This lack of assertion and direction would prove to be the basis on which the south would forestall any meaningful desegregation for over a decade.

The *Brown* decision represented nearly twenty-five years of litigation and struggle by the NAACP, documenting claims and supporting allegations of constitutional infractions. The impact of the *Brown* decision was to reverse the "separate but equal" philosophy established fifty-eight years earlier in the *Plessy* decision.

The Court ruled that separate facilities were "inherently unequal" and that it needlessly stamped a badge of inferiority on colored children that carried over into other areas of life. *Brown* set the stage for the dismantling of a dual society—one black and one white.

It should be noted that *Brown* did not expressly overturn the decision in *Plessy.* The Court simply concluded that in the field of public education the doctrine of separate but equal has no place. It is interesting also to note, that public education was explicitly referred to by Chief Justice Warren in communicating the position of the Court. However, the Court chose to delay desegregation efforts in public education while vigorously pursuing it in other areas.

Jim Crow policies were voided by the Supreme Court in auditoriums, bathhouses, beaches, courtroom seating, municipal golf courses, streetcars, buses and swimming pools. Lower courts usually did the same. Nevertheless, as significant as the *Brown* decision was, it still did not address the issue of how to remedy nearly fifty-eight years of state sanctioned segregation. Having concluded that segregated educational facilities denied constitutional guarantees under the equal protection clause, the next step for the High Court was to seek remedial strategies.

Brown II (1955) undertook the task of mandating the implementation of desegregating state imposed dual school systems outlawed in the 1954 *Brown* decision. Since most of the state-sanctioned *(i.e., de jure* [of law]) segregation occurred in the South, the High Court focused its early efforts below the Mason-Dixon line. Initially, the High Court invited all states requiring (or permitting) segregated public school facilities to present their rationale before the Court. Instead of the High Court rejecting the pleas of state officials guilty of operating dual school systems, the High Court reasoned that because of the complexity of full implementation of the constitutional principles involved, it would be necessary to remand the cases to the district courts. The district courts, in turn, admonished that orders and decrees should be carried out so as to admit plaintiffs to public schools "with all deliberate speed" on a nondiscriminatory basis.

The effect of this policy by the Supreme Court was to allow the defendants to delay, for a considerable period of time, the implementation of the desegregation mandate. However, the expectation of the High Court was that a "prompt and reasonable start toward full compliance," would be made with "defendants carrying the burden of showing that requests for additional time [were] necessary in the public interest and consistent with good faith compliance at the earliest practicable date."

It is interesting to note, however, that the first school desegregation case to reach the High Court—the review of a petition by the Little Rock, Arkansas School Board requesting a stay of its 1958 school desegregation plan—was denied. Aside from this case, the High Court could be considered woefully remiss in its effort to carry out the mandate in *Brown* for the next ten years.

Minimal desegregation occurred within the first decade subsequent to *Brown*. The decree in *Brown II* was responsible for the elimination of Jim Crow conditions in a wide range of civil areas. However, as late as the 1963–64 school year only 1.17 percent of the African American students in the eleven states that comprised the Confederacy, attended school with white students. By the 1964–65 school year the percentage rose to only 2.25. But, by the 1965–66 school year, the percentage had grown to 6.01 with the enforcement guidelines of the 1964 Civil Rights Act. It was also in 1964, that the High Court finally exhausted its patience with the procrastination of recalcitrant school boards. "All deliberate speed" had expired, the patience of the High Court had run out.

Perhaps no other area of the civil rights struggle more accurately reflects the pulse of the struggle than events surrounding the public school desegregation effort. From 1954 to the present, very little has been established relative to a definitive position by the federal courts in desegregation litigation outside of establishing that dejure segregation is prohibited under the equal protection clause. *Defacto*, segregation, which has been just as pernicious, has been nearly impossible to effectively root out. Since it is essentially an artifact of segregated housing patterns—where students are obligated to attend their neighborhood school—attempts to end it resulted in massive busing of students within school districts. The High Court began to finally move on the lack of compliance, by southern school districts, in 1964. This initiative was prompted by the defiance of the Prince Edward County Board of Education. Rather than comply with a desegregation decree, the school board closed all its schools.

Prince Edward was not the first southern school system to use school closings as a strategy for combating desegregation decrees by the federal courts. In 1957 the governor of Arkansas closed the public schools to circumvent a federal mandate to integrate Little Rock's schools. "Massive resistance" emboldened Governor Orval Faubus to resist the attempts of the federal government to integrate Central High School in Little Rock, Arkansas in 1957. His attempt to halt integration of Central High by nine African American students, led by Daisy Bates, eventuated in the closing of all the schools in the state. This scene was repeated in Virginia in the struggle over desegregating the public schools the following year.

Within a year of *Brown II* (1956) the White Citizens Council of America was established. Its expressed purpose was to create a ground swell of white resistance ("massive resistance") to desegregation (especially school desegregation) throughout the South. This movement was successful in coercing local school boards, state and local politicians, business leaders, and ordinary citizens throughout the "Old Confederacy" to maintain a hard line against desegregation" stance. Notwithstanding, the relatively late affirmative position assumed by the High Court, it did appear to support its earlier decisions in both *Brown I* and *Brown II*. But that support was not evidenced until 1968. In 1968, *Green v. County School Board of New Kent County*, the High Court essentially rejected the "freedom-of-choice" plan as an effective desegregation strategy. The disposition of the Court was considered significant by those who believed that the *Brown* mandate could not be effectively implemented while public schools remained identifiable by race.

It is important to note, that in rejecting the freedom-of-choice plan by the New Kent County School Board, the High Court did not preclude freedom-of-choice plans as a workable strategy. However, in a footnote to its opinion the High Court echoed the sentiment of the Civil Rights Commission that said in effect, freedom-of-choice plans tend to perpetuate segregation unless both African American and white parents are committed to the spirit of disestablishment of dual education systems. Nevertheless, when African Americans did opt to attend all-white schools, under the freedom-of-choice plans they typically encountered numerous acts of violence and threats directed at them, especially those that requested transfers. Often, the entire African American community suffered as a result of some Black families attempting to exercise their free choice. Local newspapers often contributed to the turmoil by publishing the names of African American applicants for transfer.

Mainstream opposition to school desegregation was clearly evident in 1968. It played a key role in politics, not only at the local and state levels, but also at the national level. A case in point was the presidential administration of Richard Nixon. It should be pointed out, that the disposition by the Nixon administration was significant to the point, that the Supreme Court felt it necessary to enter the controversy over the administration's retreat.

With the retreat from the enforcement of school desegregation by the Nixon Administration and the indecision on the part of the judiciary, regarding its policy on desegregation litigation, the direction in which school desegregation was moving was uncertain. In an attempt to resolve the burgeoning controversy over school desegregation, the Supreme Court defined the limits of judicial authority to enforce compliance with reasonable and workable desegregation plans in *Swann v. Charlotte-Mecklenberg Board of Education*. The High Court emphasized that elimination of illegally segregated school systems through the use of neighborhood schools or student assignment is not acceptable because it presently appears to be neutral. Prior segregation policies may require a more drastic approach in remedying the present segregated status of dual school systems. *Swann* has also been credited with establishing the limited use of black/white student ratios as a basis for remedial assignment and for establishing that the transportation of students is a legitimate strategy for inclusion, in an effective desegregation plan.

The immediate years, following the *Brown* decisions, were a time of tremendous activity and struggle for civil rights by the African American community. Yet, it is doubtful that the attitude and determination displayed by the African American community—to engage in a social revolution, that would forever change the state of race relations in this country—would have occurred when it did, without the 1954 *Brown* decision. The magnitude of *Brown* will probably not be fully realized until well into the twenty-first century. How numerous have been subsequent legal decisions premised on *Brown*? A host of minority (ethnic and cultural) groups, along with women, have all benefitted from *Brown*. *Brown* may well be the most important decision ever rendered by the United States Supreme Court.

Brown arguably can be considered the catalyst for much of the civil rights activities of the mid-twentieth century. But it was not the only struggle for humanity by the African American community. As Constance Baker Motley argued, those were historical times and not subject to control by any group or organization. Concomitant with the struggle to desegregate the public schools were struggles to desegregate other areas of American society. *Brown* appeared to touch off a new defiance in the African American community.

SUGGESTED READINGS:

Derrick A. Bell, *Race, Racism And American Law.*

Brown v. Board of Education II, 349 U. S. (1955).

Robert H. Brisbane, *The Black Vanguard, Origins of The Negro Social Revolution, 1900–1960.*

W. Haywood Burns, *Voices of Negro Protest in America.*

Carter v. West Feliciana Parish School Board, 396 U. S. 290 (1970).

Cooper v. Aaron 358 U.S. 1 (1958).

Coppedge v. Franklin County Board of Education, 394 F. 2d 410 (4th Circuit 1968).

Charles V. Dale, Legal Analysis of H. J. Resolution 56.

Griffin v. Prince Edward County Board of Education, 377 U. S. (1967).

"The Road to Brown," California Newsreel, San Francisco, CA, 1990.

Richard B. Wilson, *It is So Ordered: The Supreme Court Rules On School Segregation.*

STUDY GUIDE 18

1 Give the case that stated in the field of public education, separate but equal has no place.

2 In what 1896 case was the "separate but equal" doctrine first announced?

3 Jim Crow was a code name for what?

4 Name the first 20th century black person admitted to the University of Maryland.

5 Name the first 20th century black person admitted to the University of Texas.

6 Name the first black person admitted to the University of Oklahoma.

7 In its simplest, *de jure* means what?

8–14 As a result of desegregation cases like *Brown*, whom actually was desegregated?

15 In what city did Daisy Bates help to desegregate the schools?

19

The King Era and Turmoil

In 1955, African Americans in Montgomery, Alabama embarked on a year-long boycott of the city busses to protest the city's segregation law that required them to surrender their seats when the section reserved for white passengers filled up. Mrs. Rosa Parks, a seamstress and a member of the Montgomery chapter of the National Association for the Advancement of Colored People (NAACP), sparked this boycott when she refused to surrender her seat to a white man on December 1, 1955. She was arrested for violating the city's segregation statute and jailed. Local NAACP leader, E. D. Nixon bailed Mrs. Parks out of jail and called a rally to organize the community to boycott the city busses. Reverend Martin Luther King, Jr. was chosen to lead the year-long boycott, and his inspired leadership of the boycott not only helped African Americans in Montgomery to win the boycott, it also won him national recognition as the leader of the nonviolent, civil rights movement.

It was somewhat ironic that King's leadership of the Montgomery bus boycott would make him one of the greatest African American leaders of the twentieth century. Unlike most African Americans, in 1929 he was born into a relatively comfortable life in Atlanta, Georgia. After a sheltered childhood, he attended Morehouse College, Boston University, and Crozier Theological Seminary. None of his familial and educational background seemed to destine him for the leadership of the nation's greatest social movement. Nevertheless, after he became pastor of Montgomery's Dexter Avenue Baptist Church in 1954, events soon thrust the mantle of leadership upon him. Despite a background that did not include the hardship that most African Americans of his era encountered, he met the challenge of leadership and took the African American freedom struggle to a new level.

In fairness, although King emerged to lead the nonviolent, civil rights movement and the Montgomery bus boycott seemed to be the catalyst for over a decade of struggle by African Americans for civil rights, the African American freedom movement preceded King and Montgomery. Indeed, as historians Lerone Bennett and Vincent Harding have shown, the African American freedom movement had been ongoing. For example, in 1941 Reverend Adam Clayton Powell Jr. led a boycott of the New York City busses and won jobs for blacks as bus drivers and mechanics in that city. Eight years after the New York City bus boycott, African Americans in Baton Rouge, Louisiana under the leadership of Reverend T. J. Jemison boycotted that city's busses and forced the city officials to agree to fairer seating arrangements for African American passengers. These precedents in New York City and Baton Rouge made Montgomery possible.

But without a doubt the victory in Montgomery helped to increase the pace of the African-American freedom movement. The victory in Montgomery combined with several other factors in the 1950s to aid the civil rights movement's development. From 1935 to 1954, the NAACP won a series of cases in the courts challenging the legal basis of racial segregation—most notably the *Brown v. Board of Education*, Topeka, Kansas case of 1954 which outlawed segregated schools. After World War II, many African Americans grew impatient with the slow pace of gaining their full citizenship rights as Americans. In the war they had fought and died to defend the rights of others abroad; now they were ready to take action for themselves. The democratic posturing of the United States in its "cold war" with the Soviet Union also helped to quicken the pace of the movement. Many African Americans questioned how the United States could represent itself abroad as the land of freedom and democracy and still deny its black citizens their basic citizenship rights. All of these factors came together in the 1950s to encourage African Americans to use direct action tactics in the quest for their own freedom. Following King's leadership and that of other civil rights leaders, they began to use nonviolent, civil disobedience tactics such as sit-ins, pray-ins, wade-ins, marches, and demonstrations to win their rights as American citizens.

To take advantage of the spark lit by the Montgomery bus boycott among African Americans as well as to organize the civil rights effort more effectively, in 1957 King and other ministers formed the Southern Christian Leadership Conference (SCLC). As King later wrote, SCLC was organized to use nonviolent, direct action against segregation and unjust laws. SCLC's strategy was to use public opinion against southern racism and racist oppression. Through demonstrations, sit-ins, wade-ins, pray-ins, marches, and civil disobedience, SCLC was going to expose and challenge segregation on all fronts nonviolently. They also hoped to redeem white southerners through love (agape); they were going to use moral persuasion to convince white southerners that segregation and race hatred were wrong and unchristian.

In theory, the nonviolent methods and civil disobedience advocated by King, SCLC, and others in the movement seemed practical and workable. In practice, turmoil resulted. King, SCLC, and others who walked in the marches and participated in the demonstrations found that they met resistance at every point. Even before the organization of SCLC, southern white politicians such as Strom Thurmond of South Carolina and James O. Eastland of Mississippi had urged their constituents to resist the Brown decision. In fact, they urged their constituents to use what was called at that time, "massive resistance." As it was carried out by white southerners opposing the civil rights movement, "massive resistance" took the form of beatings for civil rights workers, the use of cattle prods and police dogs on demonstrators, and the more subtle forms of intimidation such as economic pressure and social ostracism for whites who refused to follow the segregationist line. It also meant the bombing of black churches and a resort to violence by whites in the Ku Klux Klan, the White Citizens Councils, and other whites who opposed desegregation.

By 1957, "massive resistance" had already had a disruptive influence on the civil rights movement. Several southern states had outlawed the NAACP, subpoenaed its membership rosters, and forced the organization to spend money and needless time in the courts defending its right to exist. At least five race-related murders had been committed against participants in the civil rights movement. Moreover, not one southern school district had desegregated.

In this atmosphere of "massive resistance," King participated in a Prayer Pilgrimage to Washington, DC, the first "March on Washington." On May 17, 1957, exactly three years after the United States Supreme Court's Brown decision, King addressed 35,000 people at the Lincoln Memorial. In the speech he called for an end to segregation and violence in the South. He called for black pride and dignity. He also called for the passage of a civil rights bill to guarantee and protect the right to vote of African Americans in the South.

The 1957 "March on Washington" coincided with Congress's deliberations over a new civil rights bill. In August, 1957, Congress passed the bill over the filibuster and protest of southern congressmen. The Civil Rights Act of 1957, as the new civil rights bill was called, was the first civil rights measure passed since 1875. Although a fairly weak measure, the act established the Civil Rights section of the Justice Department and created the Civil Rights Commission. It also empowered federal prosecutors to investigate the exclusion of blacks from voting in the South. The act was the first indication in some time that the United States government intended to enforce its laws in the South.

While the march and the civil rights bill were positive achievements for the movement in 1957, they were overshadowed by the violence and racial hatred that occurred in Little Rock, Arkansas when nine black students attempted to desegregate Central High School. When Arkansas state NAACP president Daisy Bates gathered the student volunteers who would become the "Little Rock Nine" to desegregate Central High School, she did not know that she was provoking an incident that would result in a conflict between state and federal authority. Arkansas's governor, Orval Faubus, decided to use the Arkansas National Guard to prevent the nine students from attending Central High School. But President Dwight Eisenhower decided to act and force Faubus and the whites in Little Rock to observe the law of the land. He ordered Faubus to protect the entry of the nine black students into Central High School. When Faubus withdrew the Arkansas National Guard in protest, Eisenhower sent the 101st Airborne Division of the United States Army to protect the nine black students attending the school. Eisenhower's action to demonstrate the power of the federal government over the states provoked angry reaction throughout the South. Southerners claimed that Eisenhower's action violated the authority of the Arkansas governor and made a mockery of home rule in the South. Faubus and his supporters invoked the outdated concept of "states' rights" to protest forced desegregation.

The Turmoil in Little Rock proved to be symbolic of the continued violence and resistance that blacks and whites met in their efforts to desegregate the South. Faubus, and later, governors Ross Barnett of Mississippi and George Wallace of Alabama became southern heroes as they encouraged resistance to desegregation. They invoked "states' rights" and other outdated constitutional theories such as "nullification" and "interposition"—to justify their resistance to desegregation and to enflame the passions of their white constituents to resist integration at all costs. The rhetoric used by Wallace, Faubus, Barnett and other segregationists encouraged violence and turmoil, and it made the civil rights movement one of the most violent movements in American history. Their rhetoric also made the blacks and whites in the movement victims of organized violence against which they had no protection. Moreover, the rhetoric and the accompanying violence that it sparked showed Americans how deep racial hatred was in America. Americans saw the violence and disorder that accompanied the attempts to desegregate schools in Little Rock, New Orleans, and Mansfield, Texas on the evening news and many were shocked that an allegedly peaceful, nonviolent movement could expose the nation's shortcomings to the world and belie the nation's claim that it was a democracy and a land of opportunity. This was one of the most significant achievements of the civil rights movement—exposing American racism to the world.

In a direct action tactic, students from North Carolina A&T State University began a sit-in at the Woolworth lunch counter in Greensboro, North Carolina on February 1, 1960. This sort of became a movement to be matched by students elsewhere. It resulted, after beatings, etc., in the desegregation of lunch counters, etc. Southern University in Baton Rouge, Louisiana got in on this action. Texas Southern University in Houston began a similar movement!

Nowhere was the violence and racial hatred that the movement engendered more obvious than in Birmingham, Alabama. In the Spring of 1963, King, SCLC and other civil rights organizations began a desegregation campaign in Birmingham called "Project C." Birmingham was symbolic of segregation in American society. It was considered to be the most segregated city in the South. Birmingham's public safety commissioner, Alonzo "Bull" Connor, enforced the city's racial segregation laws with a vengeance and a zeal unmatched by any law enforcement officer in the South. The campaign in Birmingham became a testing ground as well as turning point for the movement. Connor had his police force arrest and jail 100s of men, women, and children. The Birmingham police used police dogs, cattle prods, and fire hoses on marchers and demonstrators. Connor's men whipped heads and arrested so many people that the jails overflowed. After the jails were full, Connor had demonstrators placed in pens that were usually used to hold livestock. This appalling spectacle of violence and brutality in Birmingham was also beamed to the nation daily on the evening news. Due to the excessive force used by Connor's law enforcement officers, some demonstrators began to retaliate and a full scale war erupted in Birmingham. President John F. Kennedy was forced to send in troops in order to restore order in Birmingham.

King was arrested in Birmingham. From his jail cell he wrote the now famous "Letter from A Birmingham Jail." The letter has become an important historical document in the civil rights movement because in it King explained the reasons for the African American freedom movement and justified what his critics called his "untimely" actions in Birmingham. He described three indignities, slights, and humiliations that African American citizens experienced on a daily basis in American society. He castigated his critics—especially the white church—for failing to address the issue of full citizenship for African Americans. He also stated that a movement for freedom would never be "timely" for those who wanted to deny freedom to those seeking it. In short, in his "Letter from A Birmingham Jail," King was able to put forward the need for, the objectives, and principles of the civil rights movement.

After the intervention by the Kennedy administration, Birmingham's city officials agreed to end the city's racist practices against African Americans. City officials agreed to open public facilities to black citizens and to end such practices as forcing blacks to buy clothing and shoes without trying them on. But the appalling spectacle of an American City using brutal force to enforce second class citizenship on some of its citizens because of their skin color had a dramatic impact on all Americans as well as people around the world. For African Americans Birmingham became the catalyst for a massive march on Washington to demonstrate for a new civil rights bill and to dramatize their plight in American society.

The second march on Washington was planned by A. Philip Randolph who had planned a similar march in 1941 to protest the exclusion of African Americans from the defense industries and the continuation of segregation in the American armed forces. After President Franklin D. Roosevelt issued Executive Order 8802 creating the Fair Employment Practices Commission to investigate discrimination in the defense industries, Randolph called off his march in 1941. In 1963, however, the "March on Washington" plans had national support at the grassroots level and coincided with congressional debate and consideration of a civil rights bill that outlawed three discriminatory practices dramatized by the Birmingham campaign. Planned primarily by Randolph's associate Bayard Rustin, the second "March on Washington" took place on August 28, 1963. All of the major civil rights organization—the NAACP, SCLC, Congress of Racial Equality (CORE), Student Nonviolent Coordinating Committee (SNCC), and the National Urban League (NUL)—participated in the second march and it attracted over 200,000 people. King made his famous "I Have A Dream" speech, offering a vision of America's future based on racial harmony rather than racism and segregation.

By this time, however, there was some dissent in the movement. The deterioration of the Birmingham campaign into retaliatory violence by African Americans demonstrated that many of them had had enough of nonviolence. Some African Americans in and outside of the movement criticized the strategy of nonviolent, civil disobedience as foolhardy and as one that only subjected movement participants to beatings and being killed. The most important critic of this strategy was Malcolm X. Born Malcolm Little in Omaha, Nebraska in 1925, Malcolm X was the national spokesman of the Nation of Islam, a black nationalist organization founded by Elijah Muhammad in 1934. Malcolm X was a former pimp, hustler, thief, dope pusher, and con man, who, as he claimed, was "saved" by Mr. Muhammad to preach the gospel of Black Nationalism and the separation of black people from the devil white man in America. Malcolm X emerged as the voice for a new generation of young blacks who were fed up with nonviolence, the slow pace of civil rights, and who wanted to take action to win their freedom "by any means necessary." Malcolm X disagreed with King and other civil rights leaders over the strategy of nonviolence and considered a movement based on moral persuasion in the face of white violence suicide.

Malcolm X was especially critical of the "March on Washington," which in 1963 was seen as one of the movement's most successful achievements. Malcolm X called the march the "farce on Washington" because as he charged, it accomplished little. He said that the march had begun as a grassroots "revolutionary" movement to use civil disobedience and other revolutionary tactics to disrupt "business as usual" in the seat of the government. But the "Big Six" civil rights leaders—King of SCLC, Whitney Young of the Urban League, James Farmer of CORE, Roy Wilkins of the NAACP, John Lewis of SNCC, and A. Philip Randolph—had taken over the march and turn it into a peaceful circus where people gathered together, sung "We Shall Overcome," heard some speeches, and then went home without accomplishing anything. He further accused the "Big Six" of selling out to the Kennedy administration to take over the march and circumvent those African Americans who intended to use more violent and revolutionary means of winning their rights as American citizens.

Malcolm X's charges had some merit. The "Big Six" did control dissent at the march. John L. Lewis, the newly-elected chairman of SNCC, had prepared a speech which stated the following:

> This nation is still a place of cheap political leaders who build their careers on immoral compromises and ally themselves with open forms of political, economic and social exploitation. . . . The party of Kennedy is also the party of Eastland. The party of Javits is also the party of Goldwater. Where is our party?

Lewis had also planned to state that: "We cannot depend on any political party, for the Democrats and the Republicans have betrayed the basic principles of the Declaration of Independence." He called the civil rights bill introduced by the Kennedy administration "too little and too late." Lewis never delivered these words because King, for whom all the members of SNCC had tremendous respect, and Rustin convinced him to delete those words from his speech.

Both Malcolm X and Lewis were right: the "March on Washington" failed to achieve anything. Southern congressmen held up the civil rights bill introduced by Kennedy for months. Less than a month after the march, members of the Ku Klux Klan in Alabama responded to the march by bombing a church in Birmingham and killing four young black girls. The bombing seemed to symbolize one of the most violent years in the civil rights movement: in June, Mississippi state NAACP secretary Medgar Evers was murdered in front of his home in Jackson; two other participants in the movement were also murdered in race-related killings in Alabama.

The killings, beatings, and the continued resistance to black citizenship rights in the South had a negative impact on some of the participants in the civil rights movement. It disillusioned some; but it radicalized others to forego nonviolence and take a more militant stand for their rights as American citizens. This was especially the case for the young men and women who became members of SNCC (pronounced "Snick"). Black and white students organized SNCC in the Spring of 1960 to use the methods advocated by King—nonviolent civil disobedience and passive resistance—to end segregation and racial oppression in the South. Many of these students had participated in the sit-in movement which occurred in February of 1960 in cities such as Greensboro, North Carolina and Nashville, Tennessee, and had learned how direct action tactics could bring about social change. They had first sought to ally with King and SCLC, but Ella Baker, a former NAACP organizer and executive director of SCLC, had urged them to form their own organization. They organized SNCC on the campus of Shaw College in Raleigh, North Carolina in order to coordinate their own efforts against segregation and to assist King who had inspired them to join the movement.

The members of SNCC attempted to raise the direct action movement to its highest level. They took the freedom rides to challenge segregation in interstate transportation. They became the foot soldiers of the movement in demonstrations, sit-ins, pray-ins, and voter registration drives led by King as well as those led by their own organization. They went to the rural areas of Alabama, Georgia and Mississippi—places where even King and other movement participants would not venture—to organize voter registration drives and to convince blacks to participate in the democratic process. They also became the chief casualties of the movement. Many were beaten, jailed, and even killed in their visionary efforts to bring racial justice to the South. This caused their eventual disillusionment as well as their radicalization.

While SNCC members were being beaten and arrested for trying to register African Americans in rural Mississippi, Alabama, and Georgia to vote, they soon learned that their efforts meant nothing unless King was present. For example, in the Albany, Georgia voter registration and direct action campaign of 1961 and 1962, SNCC organizers and field workers worked in the city for months in the face of threats, beatings, and going to jail to mobilize blacks to challenge segregation and to register to vote. But King came to town, got arrested, and diverted the attention of the media and the people in the city away from SNCC's overall campaign in Albany. Due to the national and international attention that King's presence brought to Albany, city officials decided to negotiate with SCLC leaders, but not with SNCC organizers. Immediately upon King's departure from Albany, however, city officials reneged on some of their agreements. SNCC organizers almost had to start from scratch again with demonstrations and a voter registration drive to renew their efforts against segregation in the city. To members of SNCC, the dependence of the movement on King's charisma was hurting the movement. It also appeared that the movement to end segregation would only go as far as King allowed it to go because the media tended to focus national attention only on King.

SNCC members began to break away from King's influence. First they questioned his use of a large share of the money donated to civil rights organizations to maintain a large SCLC staff in Atlanta. They also charged that King never accounted for the funds that he collected. Secondly, there were dissenting attitudes among SNCC members about nonviolence, and what many of them considered to be the ridiculous attempt to love white racists who were beating and harassing them at every point in the movement. Finally, SNCC members lost their faith in the federal government; they believed that King placed too much faith in the federal government to protect civil rights workers from violence. SNCC had found that the FBI, federal marshals and other federal government officials often did nothing but stand by as southern whites—police and civilians—beat and injured them. In fact, instead of protecting civil rights workers, the federal government seemed anxious to prosecute them—the federal government had literally jumped at the opportunity to indict and prosecute several SNCC members for obstruction of justice after a court case during the Albany campaign.

The key turning point in the radicalization of SNCC came in the "Freedom Summer" project of 1964. Using the voting rights provision of the Civil Rights Act of 1964 (which was finally passed in February of 1964) and with the encouragement of Attorney General Robert Kennedy, SNCC planned a project to go into Mississippi and register African-American voters. Less than ten percent of the state's black population was registered to vote. SNCC planned to register African Americans, organize the black electorate, and make democracy work in Mississippi. Some 700 black and white students descended on Mississippi to register blacks to vote and to organize a political party. Most of the whites in the "Freedom Summer" project were from northern colleges and universities and had not been involved in previous SNCC activities. This fact, along with the growing resentment among some SNCC members about the role of whites in the movement, led them to question the sincerity of the new recruits. SNCC members knew that the whites participating in the summer project would leave at the end of the summer and return to their safe and secure, middle class homes. Thus, there was even a proposal to exclude whites from participating in the summer project, but it was voted down. SNCC members decided to use these northern white students as hostages: they thought that the racist whites in Mississippi would be less likely to harass and intimidate these northern whites as they had done black SNCC workers who had been in the state since 1961. They also believed that the nation would have more concern for the lives of white students than for those of African Americans. SNCC members were both right and wrong. The federal government did intervene eventually to investigate the harassment of workers in the summer project. But racist whites in Mississippi beat, harassed, jailed, and even murdered the white students just as they had done the black SNCC workers for years.

The "Freedom Summer" project started badly. First, while SNCC was still conducting orientation sessions for the summer project at Miami University in Ohio, three civil rights workers (James Chaney, Michael Schwerner, and Andrew Goodman) disappeared near Philadelphia, Mississippi, in Neshoba county. Their bodies were found six weeks later buried under a dam near Philadelphia and they had been beaten and murdered by members of the Ku Klux Klan, including the sheriff of Neshoba County. Secondly, before the project began, there were racial confrontations between black and white members of SNCC. Veterans of the organization who had been in rural Alabama, Georgia, and Mississippi thought that the newer members did not take the project and the work seriously enough. SNCC veterans lashed out at the recruits and invited them to leave Oxford, Ohio.

Despite these difficulties, the project began and SNCC succeeded in organizing a multi-racial party called the Mississippi Freedom Democratic Party (MFDP). The new party had 60,000 members. It held elections and sent delegates to the 1964 Democratic National convention in Atlantic City, New Jersey. The intent of the MFDP was to challenge and unseat the Mississippi "regulars," the state's Democratic party which was all-white and which had practiced racial discrimination in its selection of delegates.

At the convention, the National Democratic party refused to unseat the Mississippi "regulars" and replace them with the MFDP delegates. Vice President-to-be Hubert Humphrey attempted to compromise with the MFDP by giving the MFDP two nonvoting, at-large seats on the convention floor. But under SNCC's influence the MFDP refused the compromise. They refused to compromise with racism. They considered the MFDP more legitimately-constituted than the regular Democratic party of the state because it was multi-racial; the Mississippi "regulars" excluded sixty percent of the state population from participation because it excluded African Americans from membership. King and Roy Wilkins tried to convince the members of the MFDP to accept the compromise, but they voted to reject it. After a valiant attempt to take the seats of the Mississippi regulars who walked out of the convention, the MFDP left the convention without accomplishing their objective of empowering African Americans in Mississippi.

The failure of the MFDP challenge in Atlantic City only increased the disillusionment of SNCC members with the American democratic process. The SNCC-led MFDP left the convention feeling betrayed by the Democratic party and convinced that the American political system was corrupt and irredeemable because it was willing to compromise with racism. SNCC members began to feel that the white power structure of the United States could not be changed by anything short of a real revolution. They also felt that white liberals in the Democratic party such as Humphrey had betrayed them. The "Freedom Summer" project was a failure and it disillusioned members of SNCC about the ability of the democratic process to meet the needs of the poor and the specific needs of the African Americans. This setback also began the end of SNCC's commitment to integration.

The limited success of SNCC's "Freedom Summer" project was not obtained without some suffering. Three more people were killed, eighty others were beaten, thirty-five churches were burned, and thirty other buildings were bombed. To SNCC members, after the summer of 1964, all of the suffering and sacrifice seemed to have gone for nothing. It also hurt the credibility of African Americans in the MFDP who had sacrificed their livelihoods to join the party and had nothing to show for it. Fannie Lou Hamer of Ruleville, Mississippi, for example, had joined SNCC in 1962. For registering to vote, she was forced to leave a plantation where her family had sharecropped for eighteen years. She was later jailed and beaten for attending a voter registration school. She had served as an example for Mississippi blacks as a home-grown activist who had stood up for her rights as an American citizen in spite of the threats on her life. After the MFDP's rejection in Atlantic City, she had difficulty convincing other Mississippi blacks to risk everything just to vote.

In the summer of 1965, SNCC held another voter registration drive, but the drive had little success. The organization divided along racial lines. Black members wanted whites to have a lesser role in the organization. While whites argued that their skin color should not determine their ability to serve the movement. The key issue in the organization became who would control the civil rights movement and what tactics should the movement use. Blacks felt that whites were holding them back because whites always urged moderation and nonviolence, even on the issue of self defense. Many African American members of SNCC were adopting the stance of Malcolm X that they had to defend themselves against the terrorist attacks of white racists and the Ku Klux Klan. Other conflicts also emerged in SNCC. Chief among them was the conflict over the role of women in SNCC—women were often relegated to typing and secretarial duties. Another conflict emerged over the interracial, romantic relationships that had formed in the organization. All of these conflicts emerged in the organization and led to its eventual downfall.

Before SNCC actually ceased to function as a civil rights organization, two more events occurred in the movement which dramatized the conflicts in the civil rights movement and the emerging rift between King's tactic of nonviolence, civil disobedience and the self determination and self defense that many SNCC leaders were advocating. The two events that set the stage for SNCC's demise as well as the eventual split in the civil rights movement were the Selma campaign of 1965 and the Meredith "march against fear" of 1966.

SNCC's Selma, Alabama campaign mirrored that of the organization's earlier one in Albany, Georgia. Once again, SNCC came into conflict with King's SCLC. For three years SNCC organizers worked valiantly in the city of 29,000 people to convince the city's African American population to register to vote. Just as valiantly, the city's white power structure, led by Sheriff Jim Clark, fought SNCC; voter registration activities by preventing blacks from registering to vote and by intimidating those blacks encouraged by SNCC to register to vote. By January, 1965, SNCC's voter registration project had virtually failed. Several residents invited King and SCLC to Selma to revive the voter registration campaign. In March, 1965, SCLC organizers began demonstrations to support the voter registration campaign. As SCLC increased its demonstrations in Selma, Selma's white authorities increased their resistance to the voter registration campaign. In February, 1965, an Alabama state trooper killed Jimmy Lee Jackson, age 26, during a demonstration. Jackson's death prompted a call for a march on the state capital of Montgomery to protest it. As the planning for the march proceeded, the members of SNCC voted against participating in the march because it was led by SCLC and because many of them were moving away from "symbolic" demonstrations that they felt only depleted the energy and funds of the movement. Some also felt that SCLC leaders would once again hold a big march and leave town.

Several members of SNCC dissented about the organization's decision not to support or participate in the Selma to Montgomery march. Among them was John Lewis, SNCC's chairman. He decided to participate in the march anyway, but he did so as an individual and not as a representative of SNCC. On March 7, 1965, as the marchers approached the Edmund Pettus bridge at the edge of Selma, they were attacked, gassed, and beaten by the Alabama state police. Lewis had his skull fractured by a trooper's billy club.

Following this violent confrontation, a second, and then a third march was organized to protest the violence meted out to the marchers by the Alabama state police. (Right after the second unsuccessful march on March 9, Reverend James Reeb was murdered by local whites.) On March 21, King and over 8,000 people left Selma for the third march to Montgomery. Arriving in Montgomery on March 25, King gave another one of his famous speeches at the Alabama state capitol. SNCC voted to participate in this third march. Members such as Stokely Carmichael saw it as an opportunity to do more organizing of African Americans in Alabama's rural counties.

By the end of the Selma campaign, the members of SNCC had moved away from nonviolent, civil disobedience as a tactic capable of providing African Americans full equality in the United States. They were also in disagreement with King over the viability of such tactics. In addition, their experience in the South had shown them that the equal participation of African Americans in the Democratic party was also an impossibility. Right after the Selma to Montgomery march, SNCC organizer Stokely Carmichael moved to Lowndes County, Alabama to organize an independent, black political party to challenge the exclusion of African Americans from the political process in that county. Prior to Carmichael's arrival less than 100 blacks were registered to vote in Lowndes County out of population of over 12,000. Carmichael organized the Lowndes County Freedom Organization (LCFO), an independent black political party, and over 900 African Americans voted in the county's next election.

Following his success in Lowndes County, in 1966 Carmichael became the new chairman of SNCC, succeeding John Lewis. His election as chairman symbolized SNCC's new direction. Independent black political action and the self defense advocated by Malcolm X emerged as SNCC' new approaches to empowering disfranchised African Americans in the South. Shortly after his election, another one of the major events in the civil rights movement provided Carmichael the opportunity to announce SNCC's new approaches to a national audience.

In June, 1966, James Meredith began a "march against fear" to prove that an American citizen could walk across the South without being harmed. Four years earlier, Meredith had faced hate-filled, white mobs to become the first African American to attend the University of Mississippi. He planned to march from Memphis, Tennessee to Jackson, Mississippi to defy white racists. One day after his march began, Meredith was shot by a sniper. Several civil rights leaders and organizations, including King, Carmichael, and Floyd McKissick of CORE rallied to continue Meredith's march. From the start, however, Carmichael and members of SNCC made demands that demonstrated their new approach to the movement. First, they wanted to ban all whites from the march. With the urging of King, they moderated their position to allow white participation. Then, Carmichael insulted Roy Wilkins of the NAACP and Whitney Young of the Urban League and caused both men to withdraw their organizations from the march. King, Carmichael, McKissick were able to resolve their disagreements over the handling of the march and proceeded with the march from Memphis to Jackson. Due to King's presence the march attracted considerable media attention.

Carmichael and members of SNCC decided to use the march as a vehicle to demonstrate their new approaches of self defense and black self determination. When the marchers reached Greenville, Mississippi, Stokely Carmichael mounted the platform at a rally and called for "Black Power." To King's embarrassment and chagrin, "Black Power" became the rallying cry of the march and it soon emerged as the rallying cry for many of the younger generation in the movement.

The cry of "Black power" scared white Americans. The media interpreted "Black Power" as a call for African Americans to use retaliatory violence against whites indiscriminately. Although Carmichael later described "Black Power" as a call for black pride, black self determination, and black political empowerment, the media and the critics of "Black Power" continued to distort it as black violence against whites. The critics of "Black Power," of course, had two reasons for distorting the meaning of the concept. First, several American cities, including New York City in 1964 and Los Angeles in 1965, had already experienced urban civil disorders where African Americans had engaged in random violence against law enforcement officers and other symbols of white power. Secondly, white racism was so entrenched in the American psyche that just the idea of African Americans rejecting white power and acting independently was automatically equated with black racism and black violence against whites. Moreover, it was clear to many whites, even white liberals, if "Black Power" began to compete against white power, then it would be as violent and relentless in its oppression of whites as white power had been of blacks. Empirically, it was very easy to equate white power with violence. That was why the critics equated "Black Power" with violence.

Despite King's efforts, by 1966 the civil rights movement had departed from the tactic of nonviolent, civil disobedience. The generation influenced by Malcolm X was no longer willing to accept beatings, going to jail, and being killed just to integrate into American society. Through his charisma and personal dynamism King had held the movement together for ten years. But 1966 was the turning point for the movement and for America. During the last two years of his life, King would witness some of the bloodiest and most violent civil disorders ever to occur in the nation. Ultimately, he would become a victim of the violence and bloodlust that he had preached against and deplored for one-third of his life.

Although in 1964, Martin Luther King had received the Nobel Peace Prize, he later played that down when he declared he just wanted to be remembered as a drum major for peace. That "peace" came on April 4, 1968 when he was slain in Memphis, Tennessee where he had gone to help sanitation workers "combat" the city government.

Suggested Readings:

Louis E. Lomax, *The Negro Revolt.*

STUDY GUIDE 19

1 What lady began the Montgomery, Alabama bus boycott?

2 What church in Montgomery, Alabama did Martin Luther King, Jr. [hereafter MLK] pastor?

3 What 1954 case outlawed segregated schools?

4 In 1957, who ordered federal troops to Little Rock, Arkansas?

5–6 In what state was each person blow a leader?

5 Daisy Bates

6 Fannie Lou Hamer

7 What Executive Order outlawed discrimination in the defense industry?

8 Who made the "I Have A Dream" speech?

9 Where/what event was the "I Have A Dream" speech made?

10 Malcolm Little was better known by what name?

11 The Edmund Pettus Bridge leads to what city?

12 Who coined the phrase "Black Power?"

13–19 Expand each abbreviation below—

13 CORE

14 LCFO

15 MFDP

16 NAACP

17 NUL

18 SCLC

19 SNCC

20–22 Name the three Civil Rights workers killed near Philadelphia, Mississippi during the "Freedom Summer."

23–30 Give the organizational affiliation of the following persons—

23 Stokeley Carmichael

24 James Farmer

25 MLK

26 John Lewis

27 Malcolm X

28 Floyd McKissick

29 Roy Wilkins

30 Whitney Young

20

Twentieth Century Black Nationalism

Black nationalism, no less than American nationalism, not only led to the break from English colonial domination, but is also the outgrowth of the realization that, for no fault of their own: 1) African Americans were systematically excluded from the full benefits of American citizenship; 2) this exclusion was more by design than mere coincidence; and, 3) only through a coordinated racially united effort, can the problem be resolved.

Black nationalism is not, never was and probably never will be monolithic. Instead, the black nationalist quest has taken on the varied characteristics of its many and different practitioners. Essentially, however, there are three variations of black nationalism. These are radical or revolutionary, reactionary and moderate.

Radical nationalists are leftists. That is to say that these individuals seek to infuse socialist or Marxist dogma into a revolutionary strategy and profess a willingness to use armed resistance, if necessary, to bring about change. Such change, usually entails not only severance of the relationship with the oppressive majority, but an overthrow of the entire social, economic and political order. Radical nationalists are just as concerned about the political regime that governs as they are about the race or ethnicity of the governing group(s).

Reactionary forces of nationalism, on the surface, may appear similar to the radicals or revolutionaries. Like their left wing brothers, these right wing proponents, espouse a militant rhetoric; seek to establish a separate identity on land or a portion of land away from whites, and seek to break from the white domination and control. Both may view the existing government as a colonial force, the oppressed black citizenry as victims of colonialism, and may seek to get rid of the dominating colonial force (in this instance, the United States government). However, reactionary nationalists usually seek to replace the system in question with one not tremendously different. In short, faces may change, but the system of government and socio-economic and politic principles of the colonial power are, for the most part, retained. A reactionary regime, however, may give legitimacy to itself through strict adherence to a religious or mythical ideology.

The moderate nationalists borrow from both the revolutionary and reactionary elements. Rhetorically speaking, the moderate nationalists criticize the establishment. For example, moderates blame government action or inaction for the lack of improvement in the black standard of living, high crime rates, unfair distribution of wealth, economic chances, and so on. Moderates emphasize that the depraved individual (or status of those in perpetual poverty) is a product of governments failure to look out for the welfare of all its citizens. On the surface, these moderates blast government shortcomings and name-call (that is blames whites specifically for the problems encountered—often times using statistics to back up such claims). But unlike revolutionaries, and for that matter reactionaries, moderate nationalists have no intention of creating a separate country. Instead, moderate nationalists seek to use education and the first amendment rights of freedom of expression to carry their message throughout the country. Moderates, in a true sense, structure, and have no designs on changing the system (though such individuals may have problems with specific individuals of elites administering these institutions).

While political scientists and sociologists may question the specific distinctions made above, there is certainly agreement that nationalist individuals and organizations may vary in their functions approaches, and these can be categorized. Nationalist individuals and organizations may also vary in their emphasis. Some may concentrate on political issues and take specific pro-African American positions. Others may focus upon art, artistic expression, and ideas with more emphasis upon preserving vestiges of the African past and exposing Americans to black culture and its influence upon other world cultures. Still other nationalists may emphasize economic freedom. In short, it is appropriate to speak of political nationalism, cultural nationalism and economic nationalism, and such a distinction is neither confined to nor excluded from radical, reactionary or moderate nationalists.

The roots of twentieth century black nationalism go back to the nineteenth century when brave black men, collectively and individually, critically analyzed the African presence in the United States, and sought both immediate and long range solutions to the problems of race in the United States. The Black Conventions movement is an example of a collective effort. The movement began in the 1830s and continued into the 1890s. It not only opposed the institution of slavery, but promoted the ideals of black economic development nationalism. After the end of slavery, the movement's thrust was for the procurement of black political rights, educational opportunities and legal rights. Brave individuals, such as Martin R. Delaney, Edward W. Blyden, Alexander Crummell, and Timothy Thomas Fortune addressed socio-cultural and economic aspects of nationalism. In addition, W. E. B. Du Bois and Booker T. Washington, though not in agreement on the best manner in which the racial problem should be addressed, each made a significant contribution to the development of twentieth century black nationalism in the United States.

In 1852, Delaney (1812–1885) wrote, *The Condition, Elevation, Emigration,* and *Destiny of the Colored People of the United States,* in which he advocated the mass emigration of blacks to Latin America or some part of East Africa. Only through emigration, he suggested, could African Americans develop to their full potential and enjoy rich lives. Edward W. Blyden, in the post-bellum period, continued the emphasis on black emigration as a solution to the United States' race problem. In addition, Blyden encouraged that blacks shed themselves of Western values and standards, and consider non-Western ones instead. Specifically, Blyden suggested that Islam offered blacks a world view which could assist blacks in their quest to eliminate oppression. Alexander Crummell (1819–1898), while embracing a strong commitment to Christian values and a belief that Christianity could pave the way to black liberation, strongly insisted that blacks control their own social, political and economic institutions. Fortune (1856–1928), organized the Afro-American League in 1890. The League advocated black solidarity and encouraged economic and social nationalism. Specifically, the League created an Afro-American bank, endorsed industrial education, job training, and promoted cooperative economics. However, the league succumbed to the pressures of an internal black power struggle of the late nineteenth century and faded out in 1893. It resurfaced as the Afro-American Council, in 1898, and thrived until 1908.

Booker T. Washington and W. E. B. Du Bois, men at odds regarding the best approach to combating America's race problem, each contributed something positive to black nationalism. Washington (1856–1915), certainly endorsed accomodationism in social and political matters. In fairness to Washington, however, these represented areas where white Southerners were in fact using legal and extra-legal means to reduce black participation. Had Washington taken any other position it would not have improved the situation, but most probably would have cost him the support of white benefactors. However, Washington whole-heartedly advocated black economics. Among the goals of the

National Negro Business League, which Washington founded in 1900, was to achieve racial economic independence, promote self-help, and race loyalty. This theme, economic independence, would become an important component of each twentieth century black nationalist organization or movement. Du Bois (1868–1964), agreed with Washington's view of black economics, some even argue that the idea may have originated with Du Bois. Du Bois promoted racial unity, advocated racial leadership by the "Talented Tenth" (a well trained and educated black elite), and insisted upon full participation of African Americans in American life. If Washington gave black nationalism concrete fiscal and monetary strategy, then Du Bois provided a philosophy or strategy for combating racial oppression.

Certainly, in the twentieth century, numerous black nationalist organizations surfaced in the United States. Most were short-lived. In 1917, Cyril Briggs established the African Blood Brotherhood for African Liberation and Redemption (ABB), a revolutionary and Pan-Africanist organization. Its primary focus, according to Aingred G. Dunston, was "to ally racial consciousness to the goals of class consciousness." In 1933, Frank Thorn, William Henry Hastie, and Bedford Lawson, formed the New Negro Alliance (NNA), one of several groups involved in the Jobs for the Negro Movement. Founded in Washington, D. C., the organization advocated black economic nationalism. Specifically, the NNA encouraged picketing and boycotting businesses and chain stores operating in African American communities without black workers. The organization was effective in the quest of Washington, D. C. blacks to attain some control of the local economic institutions until its dissolution in the 1950s. From 1968 to 1971, the Republic of New Africa (RNA) promoted black separatism and establishment of an independent country in several lower South states with large African American populations. The founders, Robert F. Williams, and brothers Milton and Richard Henry, advocated mass emigration of blacks into the designated lower South states in an effort to establish electoral majorities, thus securing control using constitutional means. The organization also advocated the use of violence, and its demise followed an August 1971 shoot-out between New Republic members and Jackson, Mississippi police. The Revolutionary Action Movement (RAM), organized in 1963, was a classic example of a revolutionary nationalist organization. This short-lived organization, which collapsed in 1968, sought waging urban guerrilla warfare in the quest for African-American nationalism. RAM did not limit its targets to whites. The group planned unsuccessful assassination attempts of Roy Wilkins of the NAACP and Whitney Young of the Nation Urban league. RAM considered that both black men were aligned too much with the establishment.

Some organizations, however, have endured or have had a lasting impact on the country, either directly or indirectly through their influence upon some other organization(s). These would include the Moorish Science Temple Movement, Universal Negro Improvement Association, Nation of Islam, Student Non-Violent Coordinating Committee, and the Black Panther Party for Self-Defense.

One of the earliest attempts to combine black nationalist theory with a new non-Western life-style was Noble Drew Ali's Moorish Science Temple Movement, which originated at Newark, New Jersey, in 1913. According to John White in *Black Leadership in America*, Ali, as would Elijah Muhammad of the Nation of Islam several years later, insisted that African Americans "would find salvation only when they realized that they were Moorish Americans of Asiatics, whose true African homeland was Morocco." Ali emphasized black economics and strong dedication to religious principles. Like Booker T. Washington, he believed that blacks had to believe in themselves as a people and work for the survival of the race. The movement gained strength in the late 1920s with the influx of large numbers of former Universal Negro Improvement Association members (also called Garveyites).

Scholars debate whether the Garvey Movement stimulated the cultural renaissance or vice versa. To be sure, in the early twentieth century, black Americans experienced a cultural and literary awakening that has forever changed the black perception of race and the black race's contribution to America, and indeed the world. The advent of the "New Negro", more aptly called the Harlem Renaissance, covered the period 1920 throughout the early 1940s. it was a period when black artistic or expression,—whether literary, sculptural, pictorial, or performing—became acceptable. Black themes and examination of life from black perspectives were welcomed also. This open environment encouraged the growth of cultural nationalism. Black art and artists exhibited racial pride, and went a long way in creating an atmosphere conducive to the establishment of black nationalist organizations and movements.

The Universal Negro Improvement Association (UNIA) was established in Jamaica by Marcus Garvey in 1914. It appears that the organization both gained and contributed to the spirit of the Harlem Renaissance. Garvey observed that throughout the Americas, race had become a precondition for opportunities. He, therefore, envisioned a world organization to procure justice for people of African ancestry wherever they may be; improve their lives; serve as an advocate of and provide economic, social and political guidance to an enslaved people. Garvey established a branch office of the UNIA in New York City in 1916. Within months more than a thousand members had been enrolled in Harlem. Growth in Harlem was so rapid that the branch office there became international headquarters. By 1919, the UNIA had thirty branch offices throughout the United States and claimed two million members.

The UNIA was organized as a government in exile, with a Declaration of Rights of the Negro Peoples of the World, and Garvey serving as the Provisional President of Africa and President General and Administrator. In addition, the UNIA created titles and distinctions, such as Knight of the Nile, Earl of the Congo, Viscount of the Niger and Baron Zambesi. The organization adopted a flag with the colors red, black and green, and embraced the motto: "One God! One Aim! One destiny!" The UNIA published a weekly newspaper, *The Negro World*, which was called one of the best newspapers in America. Other UNIA economic ventures included purchasing or renting auditoriums for meeting places throughout the country (called "Liberty Halls"); operating the Black Star Line, and steamship company; and incorporating a Negro Factories Corporation. In addition, the UNIA was involved in social-political and cultural pursuits. The Black Cross Nurses was organized to aid blacks who were routinely discriminated against by the Red Cross. The movement had its own church, the African Orthodox Church, which developed a black oriented theology. Also, there were para-military units such as the African Legion, the Universal Africa Motor Corps, and the Black Eagle Flying Corps.

In an era when black organizations and a cultural renaissance were in full swing, the UNIA was targeted by unsympathetic groups and individuals. The Garveyites focus on separation from white society was attacked by integrationist including William Monroe Trotter and W. E. B. Du Bois. The Association's down-fall, however, was Garvey's 1923 Federal Court conviction for selling Black Star Line stock when the company was insolvent. He was fined $1000 and sentenced to five years imprisonment. In spite of comebacks attempt the UNIA never was the same. By 1930 the organization was defunct. Nevertheless, the UNIA became the proto-type for future black nationalist organizations in the United States.

The nation of Islam (NOI), is a black nationalist and religious organization founded in Detroit around 1930 by W. D. Fard (Members of the NOI are commonly referred to as Black Muslims.) Fard taught that blacks could obtain success through discipline, racial pride, knowledge of God, and physical separation from white society. In June 1934, Fard mysteriously disappeared and was succeeded by Elijah Muhammad (born Elijah Poole). Muhammad proclaimed that Fard was Allah (God) and had selected him as his messenger. Muhammad also moved the organization's headquarters to Chicago. The Nation of Islam promotes integrity, honor and cleanliness; practices abstinence from intoxicants and control substances; and, publishes its own newspaper, "Muhammad Speaks." In many ways the NOI, though basically reactionary, was the most ambitious black nationalist organization of the twentieth century. Placing emphasis on economic nationalism and self-help, the NOI purchased and farmed thousands of acres of southern farmland; invested in business dealings; and negotiated independently with foreign governments. The Nation of Islam also has its own educational system, a para-military force comprised of men—Fruit of Islam (FOI), and a female counterpart—Muslim Girl Training (MGT).

One of the most effective spokesmen for the NOI was Malcolm X (born Malcolm Little, also known as Malcolm Shabazz and, after his pilgrimage to Mecca, Saudi Arabia, as El Hajj Malik al-Shabazz). During the late fifties to 1963 he served as Muhammad's national representative and the Nation of Islam gained national attention and a strong following. In 1963, Malcolm X lost favor with Elijah Muhammad, and in 1964 he resigned from the NOI to form the Muslim Mosques, Inc., and the Organization of Afro-American Unity. Outside of the NOI, Malcolm X worked more closely with civil rights and human rights groups and organizations. It was outside of the NOI that he developed his black nationalist philosophy. In a 1963 speech titled "Ballots or the Bullet," Malcolm X specifically defined economic and political nationalism as follows:

> The political philosophy of black nationalism only means that the black man should control the politics and the politicians in his community. . . .
>
> The economic philosophy of black nationalism only means that we [blacks] should own, operate and control the economy of our community.

Malcolm X's definitions of black political and economic nationalism are significant because later organizations, including the Student Non-Violent Coordinating Committee [SNCC] and the Black Panther Party would borrow heavily from them. Ironically, Malcolm X, who was assassinated in February 1965, allegedly by members of the NOI, became more popular following his death.

When Elijah Muhammad died in 1975, the Nation of Islam split into two distinctively different and competing factions. Muhammad's son Imam (Reverend) Warith Deen Muhammad took control of the larger faction which was renamed the American Muslim Mission, and later the Muslim American Community. Warith introduced his followers to internationally accepted practices of the Islamic religion. The smaller, more reactionary faction refused to deviate from Elijah Muhammad's teachings, retained the name Nation of Islam, and follow Louis Farrakhan (born Louis Eugene Walcott). Farrakhan became prominent when he replaced Malcolm X as Muhammad's national representative.

The Student Non-violent Coordinating Committee (SNCC), was established in 1960 as the student wing of the civil rights movement. Initially, SNCC accepted the non-violent approach of the Rev. Dr. Martin Luther King and the Southern Christian Leadership Conference (SCLC). The organization, however, began to move towards the left, and by the time of James Meridith's 1966 March Against Fear, SNCC was advocating the selective use of violence and a black nationalist program. As SNCC openly advocated the use of violence, law enforcement surveillance increased and the organization began a steady decline.

The Black Panther Party for Self Defense was organized in Oakland, California, in 1966. The founders were Huey Newton, Bobby Seale, and Eldridge Cleaver. Stokely Carmichael, a former chairman of SNCC, was among the more vocal of the party's early membership. The organization was formed for the purpose of monitoring police activities against blacks in Oakland where there were numerous abuses of power. The program expanded to include a political agenda and self-help programs. Politically, in the words of Marshall Hyatt, the Panthers subscribed "to the belief that African Americans constituted an oppressed black colony within a white mother country." To liberate blacks from American oppression, the Panther Party platform borrowed from Malcolm X's concepts of black political and economic nationalism. The Panthers advocated that blacks should control the economics and politics of their own communities, secure decent housing, educational opportunities, legal justice, and, be exempted from military service. In the area of self-help, the Panther Party organized community-based programs such as the free breakfast program for school children.

The Panthers confronted police hostility wherever it surfaced, and refused to retreat from its confrontational demeanor. Standing up against the white oppressor improved the organization's status among the young and urban blacks, and resulted in increased membership in the period 1969–72. Cells of the organization began cropping up even in the South. This led to heightened law enforcement activity against the Panthers. Shootouts between Panthers and law enforcement officials occurred on the East Coast, West Coast, and in the Midwest. The most prominent alleged shoot-out involved a joint FBI-Chicago Police Department early morning raid of the Panther organization in Chicago, which resulted in the death of Fred Hampton. By the mid-1970s, panther membership had declined immeasurably, and the organization was defunct by 1980.

The Black Panther Party presents a puzzle to the student of black politics in the United States. The organization was revolutionary in that it called for a new American order and self-determinism for African Americans. Blandishing firearms, the Black Panthers were militant and stood firm to its principles even when faced with an insurmountable foe, the Federal Bureau of Investigation and local law enforcement cooperation. Yet, the organization worked within the constraints of the American judicial system, evidenced by successful court actions freeing members from prosecution—most notably, Huey Newton's acquittal of murder charges. Nevertheless, the Panthers revolutionary philosophy and discipline influenced future generations of black nationalists.

SUGGESTED READINGS

Martin Delaney, *The Condition, Elevation, Emigration and Destiny of the Colored People of the United States.*

C. Eric Lincoln, *The Black Muslims in America.*

Malcolm X with Alex Haley, *The Autobiography of Malcolm X.*

Elijah Muhammad, *Message To The Black Man In America.*

John White, *Black Leadership In America.*

STUDY GUIDE 20

1–3 Give the three (3) variations of *Black Nationalism.*

4–7 Name four (4) of the leading nineteenth century black nationalists.

8 Give the author of *The Condition, Elevation, Emigration, and Destiny of the Colored People of the United States* (1852).

9 In 1900, who founded the National Negro Business League?

10 The "Talented Tenth" was whose idea?

11–12 What black men were the leading targets for assassination by RAM in the 1960s?

13 Who founded the Moorish Science Temple Movement?

14 Expand the abbreviation UNIA.

15 Who established the UNIA?

16 What were the colors in the UNIA flag?

17 The Black Star Line was affiliated with what group?

18 Give the non-physical person that founded the NOI.

19 Elijah Muhammad came to lead what group?

20 Give Elijah Muhammad's birth name.

21 Give the synonym for Allah.

22 Who was El Hajj Malik Shabazz?

23 Expand the abbreviation SNCC.

24 Give the common name of Louis Eugene Walcott.

25 Expand the abbreviation SCLC.

26 Where was the Black Panther Party founded?

27–29 Give three prominent founders of the Black Panther Party.

30 Fred Hampton was a member of what group?

31–35 Give the group affiliation for each item below:

31 Earls of the Congo

32 FOI

33 "Liberty Halls"

34 *Muhammad Speaks*

35 *The Negro World*

21

A Survey of African-American Literature from the Past to the Present

African American literature takes its roots in Africa and merges them with that which has been taught by the Europeans. The literature is the written words that have been preserved through their oral tradition. One may conclude that the early writers were griots who remembered the stories, myths, and traditions, and finally these African Americans decided to transfer their oral form of communication into written expressions. From the earlier literature to the more contemporary writings, one can trace the various themes, forms and styles. Much of the literature is a reflection of the specific time periods and the talk of the day. A vast change in African American literature can be seen through five stages: **Literature before the Emancipation Proclamation, Literature after the Emancipation Proclamation, Literature of the Harlem Renaissance, Literature after the Harlem Renaissance,** and **Literature of the Contemporary Era**. Since this survey is limited to one chapter, only those noted writers who best exemplify the framework for each period are highlighted.

Literature Before the Emancipation Proclamation

African American writers before the Emancipation Proclamation stood alone and were not recognized for their contribution; in fact, their work was said to be of "poor quality." Phillis Wheatley, noted for her poetry, was one of the earlier writers during this period. Her book, *Poems on Various Subjects, Religious and Moral* was published in 1773 in London. Some of her noted works appear in anthologies such as "Anthology Virtue," "On Being Brought From Africa to America," "An Hymn to The Morning," "On Imagination," and "An Hymn to The Evening." Note the biblical reference and the use of rhythm in "On Being Brought From Africa to America":

> 'Twas mercy brought me from my Pagan land,
> Taught my benighted soul to understand
> That there's a God, that there's a Saviour too:
> Once I redemption neither sought nor knew.

> Some view our sable race with scornful eye,
> "There colour is a diabolic dye."
> Remember, Christians, Negroes, black as Cain,
> May be refined, and join the angelic train.

Wheatley's poems indicate that she has a broad knowledge of Christianity and a deep religious commitment. As presented in the preceding poem, Phillis Wheatley has a great concern for all people. Her style of writing as well as her poetic diction can be found even in some of the contemporary works. Further readings about Wheatley and her works can be found in *The Poems of Phillis Wheatley*, edited by J. Mason, 1966, and *Critical Essays on Phillis Wheatley*, edited by W. Robinson 1982. Although Phillis Wheatley has become known for her earlier writings, Jerome Klinkowitz in "Early Writers: Jupiter Hammon, Phillis Wheatley, and Benjamin Banneker" states that [Jupiter Hammon] is generally regarded as America's first black poet, though this rank is determined by formal publications within the structures of "genteel white society" (1) Nevertheless, other writers noted for their contributions are James Madison Bell, and George Marion McClellan. These writers were not given the necessary recognition because works by African-Americans were not viewed as valuable.

Like Phillis Wheatley, Harriet Wilson's novel, *Our Nig*, has also been unrecognized for its merit. *Our Nig* is the first novel written by a Black woman in this country. The novel highlights a young girl's life as a servant, and how she deals with education and religion. Wilson sheds light on the depth of the harsh treatment of the little servant-girl. Like the classic slave narratives, Wilson's novel is a statement of equality.

Another group of writers that emerged was known for their contribution to the "Abolitionist Movement" including Frederick Douglass in The Narrative of the Life of Frederick, Olaudah Equiano in *Equiano's Travels*, and Harriet A. Jacobs in Incidents in the Life of a Slave Girl. These writers wrote their personal autobiographies in the form of slave narratives addressing various issues and themes from religion and education to the unfair treatment of blacks. Each piece of literature illustrates how religion and education enhanced the author's chance at freedom. Frederick Douglass was probably the most vocal and the most radical of the three writers. Since *Equiano's Travels* is the earliest work of the three, one can conclude that it is a trope for the slave narratives that were written later. For example, like Equiano, Douglass' and Jacob's narratives indicate ownership by including the phrase "written by himself." Equally important, the narratives all start at a particular point in the character's life and ends with freedom and working in the "Abolitionist Movement" for the freedom and equality of all Blacks.

Douglass, Equiano, and Jacob's works are known as classical slave narratives. These works fall into the same category as *Our Nig* by Harriet Wilson although *Our Nig* is not considered a slave narrative because the young servant is not called a slave; however, after considering the extent to which she is brutalized, she is no more than a slave. Therefore, all four works are constructed in the same style. Other writers who wrote for the cause of the abolitionist movement are Frances Harper, Charlotte Forten, William Wells Brown, and Jupiter Hammon. Blyden Jackson's *A History of Afro-American Literature vol. I* serves as an excellent conclusion for the writers who produced literature during the abolitionists movement. Jackson says that:

> [The] black abolitionists did not all (or, as a matter of fact, any) die when slavery was ended at the end of the Civil War, although they tended, by that time, all to be quite mature and beyond a second birth in their interpretations of the world and their reactions as writers to their own such interpretations. The generalization can be applied to them that they did not cease to be abolitionists in their creative urges even as they grew old. From about 1830 to about 1895 they were the prevailing force in Afro-American literature, the Age of the Abolitionists.

From Jackson's account of the abolitionists writers, they continued to write for a common cause even after the great "Emancipation Proclamation." However, much of the abolitionists' concerns spilled over into African American literature that appeared later.

Literature After the Emancipation Proclamation

After the Emancipation Proclamation in 1863, another kind of literature surfaced known as "protest literature." Because of the many Jim Crow laws, "protest literature" was written as a plea against racism, hatred and discrimination. The Emancipation Proclamation freed the slaves; however, blacks were still controlled and mistreated by whites who previously owned them. As a result, the African Americans began to address the various issues of the day in their literature. Among the protest writers were W.E.B. DuBois, Booker T. Washington, Charles W. Chesnut, *et al*. DuBois is noted for his many works including his most noted piece *The Souls of Black Folk*, a collection of essays discussing the problems of African Americans. Like many of his predecessor, he was very outspoken and was labeled a radical for his powerful diction. His literature is unique and straight forward, and his works are often quoted even in contemporary literature.

Although Booker T. Washington in his work *Up From Slavery* appears in the same category as W. E. B. DuBois, his ideas were quite different. Blyden Jackson refers to Washington as the "greatest of black accommodationists and also a black writer, [who] delivered the address which so completely confirmed him in the favor of white America, especially among its high and mighty. . ." DuBois viewed Washington as an educated black man who tried to satisfy the white men in society. In modern day terms, Booker T. Washington may be called a "sell-out." DuBois' works are written more in the folk tradition and make use of the dialect while Washington's works appear to the more educated man. Paul Laurence Dunbar and other writers also make use of the folk tradition which may be found in *Folks From Dixie*, and *The Hear of Happy Hollow*. Like many early writers, James Weldon Johnson took his stories and poems from the Bible and elevated them. Some of the biblical stories include "Go Down Moses," The Prodigal Son," "Let My People Go," and "The Crucifixion." His most noted novel is *The Autobiography of an Ex-Coloured Man*. However, Johnson is most known for writing the Negro National Anthem, "Lift Every Voice."

LITERATURE OF THE HARLEM RENAISSANCE

Soon after the protest literature, another kind of literature emerged known as the literature of the Harlem Renaissance which surfaced during the 1920's. The Harlem Renaissance writers consisted of writers such as Claude McKay, Langston Hughes, Zora Neale Hurston, Countee Cullen, Nella L. Karsen, Arna Bontempts and others. Unlike the early writers, the Harlem Renaissance writers were very popular and have always been remembered for their contribution and the barriers that they had to break through. The Harlem Renaissance was a period when Black writers came together to share their literature, their ideas, and their experiences. The sharing of thoughts gave the writers insight on how to best present themselves in written form and how to best appeal to their readers. There was no single issue that caused the Harlem Renaissance. Trudier Harris in *Afro-American Writers From the Harlem Renaissance to 1940* says that

The Harlem Renaissance was spurred by a variety of factors. The depletion of southern soil and the industrial opportunities afforded by World War I encouraged more black Americans than ever to leave the country for the city. Visible black communities were therefore emerging in a number of urban areas, including Chicago, Detroit, and Philadelphia. Returning black veterans had also made it clear that, after fighting for democracy on foreign soil, they were no longer content to accept second-class citizenship in their own country. Consequently, there was a renewed spirit of racial mobility in the country, as well as a series of riots that indicated the extent to which blacks were willing to go to bring about change.

All of these factors contributed to the making of the Harlem Renaissance, and these are all reasons why the Black writers of this period began to speak out and to come together for a common cause. Many of the same issues can be found in the literature written by the Harlem Renaissance writers. These writers came to Harlem from diverse places. Perhaps Harlem at that time should have been referred to as the "Black creative writer's world." Many of the writers together established a journal called *Fire* and produced their own works because like modern day black writers, it is sometimes difficult to get work published, especially if it is not satisfying to the "powers that be." The literature of this period does not follow the conventions established by the Europeans, although there are some of the same characteristics, the writers have their own styles, their own forms, and their own themes that are much different from any other. For example, Langston Hughes in his works appealed to the "Black Masses" by using humor in his works.

Hughes simply mixed the serious with the comical, and therefore, one can enjoy reading a piece of literature that may normally be sad, harsh or unappealing. Among his works are his first novel *Not Without Laughter* (1930), a collection of short stories *Laughing to Keep From Crying* (1952), *The Ways of White Folks* (1934), *Simple Speaks His Mind* (1950) and many others. Langston Hughes is also noted for his poem "Mother to Son" which is often quoted during various occasions. The first seven lines of "Mother to Son" reads as follows:

> Well, son I'll tell you:
> Life for me ain't been no crystal stair.
> It's had tacks in it,
> And splinters,
> And boards torn up,
> And places with not carpet on the floor-
> Bare.

As indicated, the poem discusses the trials of a mother's life and she explains these trials to her son. "Mother to Son" is perhaps one of Hughes more serious poems.

One of the best women writers during the Harlem Renaissance was Zora Neale Hurston who is most noted for her novel *Their Eyes Were Watching God* (1937). Like many writers who broke barriers, Hurston steps out of the ordinary and creates a powerful black woman character that is unlike any other piece of African American literature during that period. Similar to other writers during this period and even to those writers before and after the Harlem Renaissance, Hurston's works also are written in folk tradition using the dialect of the people. Through the use of language, Hurston allows her readers to examine the gender differences by way of her characters Janie, Joe Starks, and Teacake. Some of the same trends may be found in Hurston's other works such as *Of Mules and Men* (19), *Seraph on the Suwanee* (1948), and *Jonah's Gourd Vine* (1948).

Yet another writer during the Harlem Renaissance, Countee Cullen, was similar to James Weldon Johnson, being that he centered many of his works around religion. Among Cullen's works are *On These I Stand* (1947) a collection of his poems, "Yet Do I Marvel" one of his best known poems, "The Black Christ", and *Color* (1925). *Color* was one of Cullen's most noted works, for during the Harlem Renaissance many African-Americans were concerned about the color "Black" and being proud of the fact that they were black. For example Trudier Harris says that the 1920s were an age of focus on color, and the volumes published during that period attest to that fact. [Claude] McKay's *Harlem Shadows* (1922) led their way, followed by Cullen's *Color* (1925) and *Copper Sun* (1927), Bennett's *Bronze* (1922), Thurman's *The Blacker the Berry* (1929), and George Schuyler's *Black No More* (1931). There were "dark towers," "ebony flutes," "weary blues," and many other indications that the writers were captivated with a sense of their own people.

The preceding pieces of literature shed light on the fact that the Harlem Renaissance writers were proud people, and they were people who sat out to publicize that black people had something to offer. They had to be heard. Perhaps it is during this period that James Brown developed his theme "Say it Loud, I'm Black and proud." nevertheless, the Harlem Renaissance writers made a mark that will never be forgotten.

LITERATURE AFTER THE HARLEM RENAISSANCE

Writers who came immediately after the Harlem Renaissance appeared during a time called the Depression Age. The literature of this period dealt with many issues including the unfair treatment of blacks as a race. Some of the noted writers are/were Richard Wright, James Baldwin, Ralph Ellison, Ann Petry and LeRoi Jones. This period of depression is reflected in the literature where authors were concerned with themselves and their identity as African American people. For example, this theme of unfair treatment can be found in Wright's *Native Son* (1940) and *Black Boy* (1937). The two novels speak of black men in a "Jim Crow" society. John M. Reilly in his chapter titled "Richard Wright" says that

> It was characteristic of Wright to stress such objective facts, for his early encounter with Jim Crow society, his poverty and limited opportunity for education or employment, and his migration in 1927 to the South Side of Chicago made him a representative participant in black social history and gave him his inevitable literary topic.

In *Native Son,* Wright's character Bigger Thomas is a reflection of the society in which he lives, identical to Wrights very own life in South Side Chicago. The novel reflects the unfair chance that blacks are given, the poor education and the poor living conditions. The same kind of treatment and literary themes appear in *Black Boy.* Wright's treatment of the black male and his oppression is further illustrated in his extraordinary collection of short stories titled *Eight Men* (1961)published only a year after Wright's death in 1960. His other noted works are *Uncle Tom's Children* (1938), The Outsider(1953) and *Savage Holiday* (1954).

The use of imagery is very much alive in the literature. John M. Reilly points out that there is a lack of understanding which is embedded as a metaphor in *Native Son.* Certainly imagery is presented in Ralph Ellison's *Invisible Man,* for the unnamed character is invisible because society fails to recognize him as a black man. Similar to the unnamed character, Bigger Thomas is frustrated because he does not have the same wealth, statues and knowledge as the white man. Both blacks and whites are blind, for they fail to converse and to understand each other.

Ralph Ellison's works are similar to Richard Wright when approached from a thematic point of view. As mentioned earlier, *Invisible Man* also addresses the struggles of a black man and his quest for his own identity. The unnamed character goes unnoticed and eventually lives underground which serves as a metaphor for the novel. Ellison's novel is much like Wright's short story "The Man Who Lived Underground" found in Eight Men. Joanne Giza in "Ralph Ellison" says that

> Several excellent articles have been written using folkloric elements as a basis for discussing Invisible Man. Praising Ellison for defining the ideological and technical possibilities of American Negro materials more accurately and effectively than any work in our literary history, 'Gene Bluestein, "The Blues as a Literary Theme" (MR, Autumn 1967), explores in great detail Ellison's use of folklore 'to create a distinctly national expression which yet speaks in broadly human rather than racial or regional terms'—in short, to provide a portrait of the American.

In examining the novel in terms of its use of folklore, one can clearly see a pattern of how Ellison's novel fits in the context of earlier works such as *Br'er Rabbit* and more contemporary works such as Toni Morrison's *Tar Baby.* Certainly the works changed from period to period; however, the literature continues to have some of the same characteristics.

Another noted writer whose works stand out is James Baldwin. Among his works are *Another Country* (1963), *Go Tell It on the Mountain* (1953), *Nothing Personal* (1964), a collection of short stories *Going to Meet the Man* (1965) and *The Amen Corner* (1968). Finally, LeRoi Jones, who changed his name to Amiri Baraka, is also a well known writer of this period. Jones is said to be one of the most prolific writers of his time. Because he is so outspoken, one may classify him as a radical and place him in the category with writers such as W. E. B. DuBois. Some of his works are *Home, The Dead Lecturer* and *The Autobiography of LeRoi Jones.*

Literature of the Contemporary Era

During the 1950s and 1960s, African American writers struggled together for equal rights and the black women basically supported the black males. However, after that period the women began to realize that they needed to make a contribution concerning their role in society. Although black women writers have been writing for some time, it is only around the early 1970s that a vast number of black women writers began to create their own world through the use of the pen. In fact, they also began to deal with their oppression by the black man. Women writers who emerged during this period were Alice Walker, Toni Morrison, Maya Angelou, Bell Hooks, and Terry McMillian. Alice Walker presents her "womanist" theory to identify the black woman within the feminist movement. Walker also presents a most graphic picture of male/female relationships in her literature. Examples can be found in *The Third Life of Grange Copeland* (Walker's first novel), and *The Color Purple.* Various relationships occur within the two works. In The Color Purple men often mistreat women. Mr__. ill-treats his wife Celie, and Harpo mistreats his wife Sophia. In addition, Celie is also abused sexually, mentally, and physically by her stepfather. However, the female characters eventually conquer the male characters and create their own identity. The same issues are presented in *The Third Life of Grange Copeland.* The two Black male characters, Grange Copeland and his son Brownfield are depicted as negative characters. However, Walker takes her character Grange through a change and not only does she present him as a negative character, but she also depicts him as a positive character. This is just one example of how the women writers indicate the various kinds of black males.

Walker's depictions of the black male is similar to that found in Toni Morrison's works. Morrison also deals with the Black male character; however, she also focuses on a lot of other aspects. In fact, she does a lot of exploring and creating in her works. Like Walker, Morrison allows her characters to go through various experiences and changes. For example, Milkman, in *Song of Solomon*, goes through a lot of experiences on his journey in search of his identity. He is depicted as a negative black male character in the beginning of the book. However, the more he learns about his heritage, the more he moves toward becoming a positive black male character. Morrison also presents mythical characters such as Solomon in *Song of Solomon* and the ghost like character, Beloved, in *Beloved*. Morrison's mixture of the real with the surreal is what makes her works most complex. The treatment of black male characters can also be found in other works such as *Tar Baby* and *The Bluest Eye* by Toni Morrison, *Waiting to Exhale* by Terry McMillian, and *I Know Why the Caged Bird Sings* by Maya Angelou.

African-American literature in all of its stages illustrates the various changes that have taken place from the beginning to the present day. The literature before the Emancipation Proclamation chronicled the life of the African slave in America, and it preached against the evils of the institution of slavery. After the Emancipation Proclamation, the literature was used as a form of protest against the results of enslavement of a people. However, the Harlem Renaissance ushered in a new attitude among writers. The emphasis was on expression of creativity rather than writing to please one particular group. Literature after the Harlem Renaissance concentrated on writers who dealt with the plight of the race. Finally, the Contemporary Era ushered in the black female fiction writers who attempted to depict the African American community from a feminist or womanist point of view. The various themes, trends, forms and styles have all made African American literature rich in heritage and have promoted the preservation of the oral tradition of the African culture.

Suggested Readings

Charles L. Blockson, *The Underground Railroad.*

Joanne Giza, "Ralph Ellison." *Black American Writers Bibliographical Essays,* vol. 2. ed. M. Thomas Inage.

Trudier Harris, *Afro-American Writers Before the Harlem Renaissance.* DLB vol. 50.

—*Afro-American Writers From the Harlem Renaissance to 1940.* DLB vol. 51.

Blyden Jackson, *A History of Afro-American Literature,* vol. 1.

Jerome Klinkowitz, "Early Writers: Jupiter Hammon, Phillis Wheatley, and Benjamin Banneker." *Black American Writers Bibliographical Essays,* vol. 1. ed. M. Thomas Inage, *et al.*

George McMichael, *Anthology of American Literature.*

William Still, *The American Negro His History and Literature: The Underground Railroad.*

STUDY GUIDE 21

1–5 Give the five (5) stages of African American Literature.

6–7 By what names did the immediate post 1863 African American Literature become known?

8–12 Give five (5) writers of the Harlem Renaissance.

13 Who created the character "Bigger Thomas?"

14 Give Leroi Jones's new name.

Give the author for each work below:

15 *The Amen Corner*

16 *Another Country*

17 *The Autobiography of an Ex-Coloured Man*

18 *Beloved*

19 *Black Boy*

20 *The Bluest Eye*

21 *The Color Purple*

22 *Go Tell It On The Mountain*

23 *Harlem Shadows*

24 *I Know Why The Caged Bird Sings*

25 *Invisible Man*

26 "Mother to Son"

27 *The Narrative of the Life of Frederick*

28 *Native Son*

29 *Not Without Laughter*

30 *Of Mules and Men*

31 *Our Nig*

32 *Poems on Various Subjects, Religious and Moral*

33 *Simple Speaks His Mind*

34 *Song of Solomon*

35 *The Souls of Black Folk*

36 *Tar Baby*

37 *Their Eyes Were Watching God*

38 *Up From Slavery*

39 *Waiting to Exhale*

40 "Yet Do I Marvel"

22

African Americans in the Military

The military is a part of our heritage, and the African American soldier has served in the military throughout history. Only in the past ten years has there been a consistent effort to recognize the African American military members.

To look at the true contributions of the African American in the military, one has to travel back in time. The African American's contribution to the military success of this country can be traced back to a pre-Revolutionary era. Although very limited records are available, it is known that African American slaves were inducted into the military district's militia by the Control Officer in charge of each district prior to 1700. These individuals served diligently, and many died in defense of their districts throughout the South and as far North as far as what is now called the New England States.

The African American military member has always been a symbol of valor and pride. He served in the Queen Anne War, the Tuscarora War, early Indian Uprisings in the territories, and fought gallantly during the fortification of St. Augustine. These individuals were fighting for freedom while still in servitude. All have heard of Crispus Attucks, Salem Poor, Peter Salem in the American Revolutionary War, and possibly Seymour Bull, but those names are just the tip of the iceberg. Crispus Attuck's death was a continuation of the bravery that has always been exhibited by the African American. Although killed by a British military member, Crispus Attucks was not a uniformed member of local militia. Others like him fought in and out of the militia beside their masters during the War of 1812, the Mexican War, and other skirmishes on land and sea.

The Civil War

The African American became a controversial member of the United States in the early 1800s. This controversy became so intense that a civil war resulted. At the center of this controversy was the issue of slavery or servitude. While still in servitude, the African American military men were a major factor in the armies of the Union and the Confederate forces. African American Union Soldiers were present at all major battles and distinguished themselves in a heroic fashion throughout the Civil War. Their dedication and loyalty, frequently to their owners, was recognized by all who served with them. In some states these troops were rewarded by being given what was considered challenging responsibilities.

African Americans have always been a large contingent of the volunteer forces. They worked as laborers, body servants, and cooks to supposedly release other more capable individuals to fight or defend the territory. It also must be remembered that the service of the African American at the beginning of the Civil War was refused by both the Union and Confederate armies. Their acceptance into the military was predicated on the availability of outstanding Caucasian military leaders who could train and indoctrinate them in the ways of the military. The Union Army trained and developed what is now considered to be the first recognized Colored Troops in the United States. Not only were African American military men heroes during this period, they were awarded the highest honor in the military.

After the Civil War, some African Americans continued in the military, while others left the military upon completion of their commitment. They became rather disenchanted with the lack of recognition and promotions. Few attained the rank of Captain during the war, and even fewer were given the opportunity to develop leadership qualities.

The Indian Skirmishes

Following the Civil War, the United States began to experience problems in the Western and Southwestern territories. Indian uprisings became common practices. Much of this uprising occurred as a result of settlers moving into the West, which was considered an infringement on the Native American rights and territory. These many incidents led to the varied exploits of the "*Buffalo Soldiers*" who were military members, both regular and scouts, whom were involved in these actions from Arizona to the Dakotas. The Buffalo Soldiers were very successful in battling the Indians and in assisting in the settlement of the West. A committee was recently formed and a monument has been dedicated to the "Buffalo Soldiers—the African Americans who formed the ninth and tenth Calvary Regiments." The former Chairman of the Joint Chiefs of Staff, General Colin Powell, did the ribbon cutting at Fort Leavenworth, Kansas in the summer of 1992.

This period in the military history of the African American saw the beginning of a change in the availability of education to the career military man. Both the United States Academy at West Point, New York and the Naval Academy at Annapolis, Maryland admitted the first African American cadets to their programs.

The Spanish American War

By the time the Spanish-American War began, the African American was recognized as an integral part of the military—an integral part but not an equal. During this period many African Americans were trained in military tactics and received commissions. As a result of being commissioned, they were able to develop their leadership qualities and abilities. The African American officer came to the forefront during this period. He was recognized as a leader and was able to become an experienced leader of troops in and out of battle. The African American gained and maintained the respect of his fellow African American military members. An understanding of the needs and feelings of the African American could be identified since he was being led by one of his own who on many occasions had experienced the same frustration and depressed desires. Many African American troops served in Cuba and rode with Teddy Roosevelt and his "Roughriders." A little known fact is that the first troops to occupy San Juan Hill were African American. Many of these same troops also served with Roosevelt in the Philippines. They were called to arms and maintained an exemplary military record, although their service was considered minimal.

World War I

The period up to World War I saw a cessation in the activities of African Americans in the military. Only two regular army units remained on active duty. With the advent of World War I, African American troops were recruited and performed heroically, distinguishing themselves in the European Theater and in naval actions. More than 400,000 African American troops saw duty during World War I. These troops, though ill educated, overcame this as well as other obstacles, becoming decorated and held in high esteem by their foes. During this period, there were a limited number of commissioned African American officers and even fewer in leadership and command positions. After World War I, a number of African Americans remained in the active army to serve as laborers, stable-hands, black-smiths, performing menial tasks common to a non-mechanized military force. The Negro National Guard was formed during this period. And for the first time on record, an African American Colonel commanded this composite regiment.

WORLD WAR II

World War II called to arms many African American troops who served in all combat operations and all theaters of operation. During this period, the first pilot training program for African Americans was established. This pilot training was conducted in conjunction with officer training at Tuskeegee Institute in Alabama. Many of the senior officers of the military and highly decorated individuals were members of this select group. These pilots performed with exceptional knowledge and skill in all major operations.

Education was also an important factor for African Americans during World War II. Many were drafted, but there was an equally large group that volunteered for service. These troops performed duties in the areas of labor, quartermaster, and engineering. They have tremendous records as transportation supporters and truck drivers.

World War II also saw another change in the military forces. African American males were allowed to participate as infantrymen, parachutist/airborne, and tankers; furthermore, officers were allowed to lead troops on combat missions. A new day came to the forefront—the recognition that African American officers had developed leadership qualities although not always encouraged.

Another change took place in the military during WWII. African American professionals such as physicians, dentists, nurses, lawyers entered the ranks of those in uniform. The African American was now assuming more responsibility; some of the regular officers were advancing in rank, and the elimination of segregation was being considered. It should be noted that a black general officer could be counted among the active regular army officers at this time.

Again African Americans were highly decorated from Dorie Miller [a Pearl Harbor Navy hero], to the pilots who escorted bombers on raids, to the individual trooper in the foxhole. African Americans continued to prosper in the military and continued to preform in the military, and many made it their career upon completion of their initial tour of duty. They also saw the end of segregation in the military at this time.

KOREAN WAR

The African American continued to serve in defense of his country and world peace. With the advent of the Korean War, African Americans were again called to serve in the military. The younger men saw volunteering for duty as a way of being patriotic. African Americans constituted a large portion of the forces in Korea in all branches of the military. They served in all capacities n the uniform services. Many of the officers were real leaders by this time. They had been commissioned through one of the military academies or through the Reserve Officer Training Corps at colleges and universities. Others took what had been the traditional route through Officers Candidate School (OCS) and Officer Training School (OTS) with a few receiving direct commissions. Most of the officers came through the ROTC channels. This was possible because ROTC Detachments were established at many of the land grant colleges and was a requirement for all eligible and physically capable male college students. The new African American military members continued to emerge throughout the Korean War period. They were decorated with distinction and recognized for their accomplishments all over the world. They fought, died, and became prisoners of war, but held on to that pride and zeal expected and required by the code of conduct.

The African American continued his performance and lofty status as a fighting man. In the early part of the Korean War, an African American was awarded the Medal of Honor. The professional corps of African Americans also preformed service throughout the Korean War. The male and female individuals of this group became an integral part of the pattern that developed for those African Americans choosing the military as a career. The walls of segregation had been broken down and a sense of security existed for these individuals. Many left the active service to complete their education under the GI Bill, only to return in a more competitive capacity. Others remained on active duty and completed their education or advanced education through training in the military and its connection with civilian schools and other training facilities.

The African Americans were truly on their way. The military was a means of full-time employment with all benefits including retirement. The security that many African Americans had never experienced was now theirs. The challenge was to induce this desire for improving the education level of all members of the race. The military became an avenue of success for the African American. It trained individuals in service and provided funding for training for any skill or profession desired.

Subsequent to the Korean War, the military became very education conscious. Facilities known as Education Centers were opened at all camps, stations, and posts throughout the United States and abroad. Colleges and universities offered courses leading to certificates, degrees, and professional licenses. Individuals were afforded time and opportunity to attend classes to enhance their skills. Individuals nearing degree completion were given from twelve to twenty-four months full-time training with pay in support of this effort.

The Vietnam War

African Americans played a very key role in the Vietnam War. A totally new military force had emerged after the Korean War. The African American military member was no longer a laborer or unskilled individual who had to be assigned to menial tasks. For the first time in the military history of the United States Armed forces, African Americans were considered the critical link they have been for many years. They were given well deserved leadership positions and promotions equal to their performance. For the first time, African Americans were successful at being advanced to the critical ranks of Colonel and General Officer. In the enlisted rank, blacks became Command Sergeant Majors and First Sergeants who had critical positions in leading troops and training the badly needed replacements.

As the African American advance in rank and position in troop units, the same thing was occurring in the service sector of the military. African Americans became hospital commanders, chief-nurses, chiefs of surgery, and other highly skilled professionals. They were recognized by their peers and contemporaries as being fully qualified for the positions they held.

The African American in the military became a symbol of success. They became people their peers could look up to as role models, and the community gave them credit for being leaders. African Americans in Vietnam were proof that, given equal opportunity, unlimited success could be attained.

Post-Vietnam War

Since the end of the Vietnam War there has been continued success for the African American in the military. Many of the individuals who served honorably during the war remained on active duty and completed a successful career. Many attained the rank of General Officer or senior levels of the enlisted rank. Some of these individuals have advanced to the highest post in the military such as: Chairman of the Joint Chiefs of Staff, Chief of the Nurse Corps, Chief of the Medical Service Corps, Chief of the Ordinance Corps, and the Military Police. These positions have been or are presently being held by African American military members.

African American military personnel were the first of their race to be selected for participation in the space program. One of the pilots of a space vehicle was an African American military member. The knowledge and skills obtained through the military or with assistance from the military have been invaluable assets to the success of former military members and the success of society. Unlimited careers have opened up to a group of people who were not considered capable of functioning in a military environment by some of the pioneers of our country.

African Americans can look back on their role in the Revolutionary War through Desert Storm and be proud of the accomplishments. The dedication to the defense of this country as well as other friendly countries should have a very important place in the history of this nation. It should also be kept in mind that the military services have been the best employer around for African Americans.

Selected Readings:

Charles E. Francis, *The Tuskegee Airmen.*

William A. Gladstone, *United States Colored Troops, 1863–1867.*

Robert E. Greene, *Black Defenders of America, 1775–1973.*

Mary P. Motley (Ed.), *The Invisible Soldier: The Experience of the Black Soldier, World War II.*

Benjamin Quarles, *The Negro In The Civil War.*

Joseph T. Wilson, *The Black Phalanx.*

STUDY GUIDE 22

Give the war or conflict in which each person below gained prominence:

1 Crispus Attucks

2 Dorie Miller

3 Salem Poor

4 Peter Salem

5 What was the highest military office Gen. Colin Powell held?

6 In what state is West Point located?

7 In what state is the Naval Academy located?

8 Give the "leader" of the "Roughriders."

9 Where was the first pilot training program for blacks established?

10 Expand the abbreviation ROTC.

23

Black Music In America

Black music in America is a true reflection of this country's social history. In its legacy lies the historical foundation of the black man, his struggles, and those acts of persecution and deprivation which have been a way of life since 1619 when the first twenty Africans arrived in the American colonies at Jamestown as indentured servants.

In order for Americans and members of the international community to become more aware of the black man's involvement in societal activities as well as his achievements, one must study various aspects of the African and African American culture. A study of the music traditionally performed by blacks is just one way of gaining a broader perspective of those social issues which have forever been captured in song.

There are a variety of song forms which have received a great deal of recognition. Time and again, many song forms are viewed from the standpoint of their beauty and entertainment possibilities. In contrast to this viewpoint, black vocal literature must be viewed and analyzed as it relates to its social implications. From such a perspective, the history of the black man in the making of America can be seen.

Of the music literature which should be studied, the Negro work song, spiritual, blues, jazz and rhythm and blues are most essential. The work song was viewed as a song which served as a means for the release of tension or merely an instrument used to help time pass by the slaves. However, there is much to be learned from reviewing the work song. A vivid example of such can be obtained from the following.

WORKSONGS

I

Nigger go to white man
Ask him fo' work
White man say to nigger

Get out o' yo' shirt
Nigger threw off his coat
Went to work pickin' cotton
When time come to git pay
White folks give him nothin'

Li'l bees suck de blossoms
Big bees eat de honey
Nigger raise the cotton an' corn

White folks gits de money

Here sit de woodpecker
Learning how to figure
All fo' de white man
Nothin' fo' de nigger

Slabery an' freedom
Dey's mos' de same
No difference hardly
Cep' in de name

II

Went to Atlanta
Neber been dere afo'
White Folks eat de apple
Nigger wait fo' core

Went to Charleston
Neber been dere afo'
White folks sleep on featherbed
Nigger on de flo'

Went to Raleigh
Neber been dere afo'
White folks war de fancy suit
Nigger de over-o

Went to Heben
Neber been dere afo'
White folks sit in Lawd's place
Chase nigger down below

In contrast to how individuals may interpret the inner feeling of the work song, the two aforementioned clearly delineate the slaves' realization that he was being treated in an unjust manner.

A study of the Negro spiritual presents the analyst with vital information about the slave's life, fears and aspirations. Typically, the spiritual was a congregational song which expressed any number of societal (slave) problems. Many spirituals were sentimental, while others spoke of God's love for His children. Indeed, the emphasis on content varied from one song to another. For more than three hundred years the spiritual has kept an accurate account of the social problems of both the African and Afro-American. It has described their loves, fears and other humanistic characteristics which have been a part of the African American way of life since her/his arrival to the American colonies in 1619. There are so many sociological implications found in the spiritual that one needs not search in great depth. Furthermore, there is the spiritual's effect on other folk music of black Americans. This includes such song styles as the blues, gospel and popular music.

Even with the social implications which are prevalent in the spiritual, many people do not have a true understanding of its textural meaning. In most instances, the interpretation is that of the African's desire to die in order to join their God in heaven. There are a few isolated cases in which this may be the only interpretation of a spiritual. However, this interpretation should not be considered or accepted as the final analysis. For, one must not accept the impracticality of any proud race whose sole desire of happiness is to leave this earth due to incarceration, abuse, punishment, lack of respect or any other form of mistreatment.

An analysis of several spirituals solidifies the concept that this song, while in its early stages represents one of the African Americans major forms of communications. Through the Africans' singing of these songs, a true perspective of her/his life, problems, desires and daily activities can be determined. In addition to the story of the life(s) of the slave, the spiritual can be viewed as a song of rebellion. Merriam-Webster defines 'rebellion' as an open defiance of or resistance to an established dominance. Furthermore, rebellion implies open, organized, and often armed resistance to authority. This rebellion may involve mutiny as a form of insubordination or insurrection. It is through the definition of rebellion as defined by Merriam-Webster that the Negro spiritual can be analyzed.

Deep River, my home is over Jordan,
Deep River, Lawd, I wan' to cross
over into the camp ground
O' don'; you wan' to go
To that Gospel feast
That promised Land and,
where all is peace

ANALYSIS:

"Deep River" is a song of defiance which is often misinterpreted. In many instances the listener foresees the African expressing a desire to acquire death or a song which if sung in a morbid state depicts the death of an individual. On the contrary, the slave is mentally rebelling. The phrase, "my home is over Jordan," actually represents the north (home) and the Ohio River (Jordan). Likewise, the phrase "that promised land where all is peace" refers to the freedom of the north. Deep River was an uplifting spiritual which unlike its present status of being sung in a minor key was often sung in a major key. Not only was the use of a major key significant, but, it raised the hope and aspirations of the slave(s) that one day they would be freed.

Go Down Moses
When Israel was in Egypt's Land
Let my People go!
Oppressed so hard they could
not stand
Let my People go!
Go Down Moses
Way Down in Egypt's Land
Tell ole Pharaoh
Let my People go!

ANALYSIS:

"Go Down Moses" is one of the most moving of all spirituals. The lyrics and text express the slaves' understanding of the biblical stories about Moses, Pharaoh and the Jewish slaves. From the slaves' understanding of the plight of the Jews, they (African slaves) were unable to make adjustments in this spiritual to fit their situation. Moses, as sung in the Negro spiritual is a substitute or code word to represent Harriet Tubman, *et al.* Furthermore, this spiritual indicates, a further understanding of previous encounters of the institution of slavery. Therefore, this song portrays the African's view that Harriet Tubman (Moses) will enter Egypt's Land (the South) and actively assist in the slaves acquiring their freedom (let my people go). Again, this spiritual exemplifies the rebellious attitude of the slave towards his incarceration and his plight in bondage. The song further depicts the rebellious attitude of resistance to an established dominance.

My Lord, What A Morning:
My Lord, What A Morning
My Lord, What A Morning
My Lord, What A Morning
When de stars begin to fall

You'll hear de trumpet
sound to wake de nations
underground
Look into God's night hand,

When de stars begin to fall
You'll hear de sinner
moan to wake de
nations underground
Look into God's right hand,
When de stars begin to fall

ANALYSIS:

"My Lord, What A Morning" is considered one of the most beautiful Negro spirituals because of its smooth and melodious flow, its lack of percussive accentuation and driving force. "My Lord What A Morning" is generally falsely viewed by the listener. In the undercover of this song many listeners fail to note that the slaves were instructed to pay attention to the structure of the stars and the direction in which they fell. The direction of their falling served as a guide to escaping to the North. You'll hear de sinner moan refers to the slave owner (sinner). In retrospect, the sinners' moan is an indication that the slave owner is not in a position to interfere with their attempt for escapism. In addition, the sinners (slave owners) inability to interfere is also a signal for the underground railroad (abolitionist) to awaken. This awakening basically identifies the abolitionist's initial step to assist in the escape process of the slaves.

Swing Low, Sweet Chariot

Swing Low, Sweet Chariot
Comin' fo' to carry me home
Swing Low, Sweet Chariot
Comin' fo' to carry me home

I looked over Jordan and
what did I see
Comin' fo' to carry me home
A ban' of Angels a comin'
after me
Comin' fo' to carry me home

ANALYSIS:

"Swing Low, Sweet Chariot" is another spiritual which typifies a form of rebellion. Again, this song represents a form of escapism as portrayed in the statement 'A band of Angels comin' after me.'

Angels, in this instance refers to the abolitionist. "Swing Low, Sweet Chariot does not identify with any form of wagon, but, a means of transporting slaves to free land by crossing the Ohio River (Jordan). The slaves used this song in an organized manner to inform each other that the abolitionists were in fact coming to transport them to freedom.

De Gospel Train

Get on board, little chillun
Get on board, little chillun
Get on board, little chillun
dere's room for many a more

De gospel train's a comin'
I hear it just at hand
I hear de car wheels movin'
An' rumblin' thro' the land

De far is cheap, and all can go
De rich an' poor are there
No second class aboard dis train
No difference in de fare

ANALYSIS:

"De Gospel Train" is another spiritual which shows an organized pattern to rebel against slavery. The slaves are informed throughout this song that the abolitionists are near and they should prepare to leave. As the slave rebels in this song through his determination to escape, he establishes a pattern which will cause various problems for the slave owner. The rebel against slave society is to rebel against the schematic structure of the southern economic tradition. A loss of a slave was a loss of money, man power and productivity.

Steal Away

Steal away, steal away, steal away
to Jesus
Steal away, steal away home
I ain't got long to stay here

My Lord calls me, He calls me by
the Thunder
The trumpet sounds within 'a my
soul
I ain't got long to stay here

My Lord calls me, He calls me by
the lightning
The Trumpet sounds within 'a my soul
I ain't got long to stay here

ANALYSIS:

This is a most interesting spiritual. To steal away (leave undercover) is definitely a statement which refers to departing from the plantation. There is an immediacy about this particular spiritual because of the phrase 'He calls me by the thunder' and 'he calls me by the lightning.' Jesus is used very seldom in this spiritual. Thus, blending somewhat into the total structure of this song which addresses escaping to freedom. The desire of the slaves to refrain from using 'Jesus' is significant in that the listener and slave owner fail to note that the undercurrent personality being disguised is Harriet Tubman. To rebel against the institution of slavery means that one's major form of communication (song) must also be an insurrectionist form.

During the civil rights movement of the 1960s the spiritual was revamped to fit the social protest against segregation. Get on Board, Children, taken from a spiritual was utilized to draw blacks in the State of Mississippi to rebel against the social structure. This song received popular attention by the Mississippi Freedom Democratic Party during the Civil Rights Movement.

"Go Tell It On The Mountain," another popular spiritual, experienced a number of major changes during the civil rights movement. This respective spiritual has a number of linguistic correlations with "Go Down Moses" and "Wade in the Water." Fannie Lou Hamer, in her singing of "Go Tell It On The Mountain," utilizes this spiritual to herald the oncoming Civil Rights struggle.

"We'll Never Turn Back" was another freedom song performed during the civil rights movement. Many of the phrases in the text are derived from Nathaniel Detts' spiritual "I'll Never Turn Back No More" (1918). This spiritual, turned protest song, became the theme of the SNCC movement efforts in Mississippi.

Other spirituals which addressed the civil rights movement include "Walk With Me, Lord" which was in the same tradition as "Lord, Hold My Hand," and "Freedom Train" which is based on the hymn. "Old Ship of Zion." These spirituals and many others were revamped by musicians, black ministers and the black community for use during the civil rights movement.

For years, the spiritual has been viewed as a song sung for pleasurable purposes by the slave. Only in recent years have ethnomusicologists studied its inner parts. The study of the spiritual has revealed a number of major factors. First, this song goes beyond the realm of just a song sung for pleasure. Second, the spiritual touches on life and, finally, the spiritual has a rebellious nature. This rebellion is not derived from physical violence but, through the mental upheaval of defying the slave owner through the acquisition of freedom by means of the underground railroad.

The blues is another great song form which exemplifies social concerns of the black man during the early 1900s. These songs, as sung by such artists as Billie Holiday, Blind Lemon Jefferson, Big Bill Broonzy, Huddie Ledbetter, Albert King, B.B. King, Alberta Hunter, Gertrude "ma" rainey, Bessie Smith, Clara Smith, Mamie Smith, Bobby "Blue" Bland and Ethel Waters clearly delineate the black man's plight in the United States.

As a general rule, the blues relate to the most immediate concern of the black man. Among the most common concerns, as expressed through the blues are: unemployment, lack of money, love, unfair treatment by whites, and any other issue which was a problem of that time. The blues also expressed the poor living conditions of blacks in the rural south more than any other area of the country.

Jazz has been a part of American society since the late 1880s. Many musicians who acquired international reputation used this form and style of music to address social issues. Edward Kennedy "Duke' Ellington was one of the first jazz musicians to use his art to trace the history of the black man and address social issues. His composition, "Black, Brown and Beige" was a tone poem based on the history of the American Negro. Another selection of the Duke's which had social implications was "Black and Tan Fantasy."

The bebop era (1950s) was another period in which musicians used their musical skills to address social issues. Jazz artists such as John Burkes Gillispie (Dizzy), Thelonious Monk and Charlie Parker spoke often of the negative experiences blacks encountered on a daily basis. Their music and that of their peers struck out at the so-called establishment of the swing era (1940s); the exploitation of the black jazz musician by the recording industry; the lack of finances provided blacks for their performances as compared to their white counterparts; the forced participation of blacks in World War II; and the lack of racial sensitivity. Bebop music can clearly be seen from a social standpoint as a manifest of irate black musicians who are determined to end the further exploitation of themselves and their music.

Many other jazz musicians displayed their temperament toward the desire for social equality through the title of their songs and the implications therein. Jazz saxophonist, Sonny Rollins produced the album "The Freedom Suite" in 1958. This recording was a musical depiction of the Afro-American struggle for liberation from oppression. Charlie Parker's "Now's The Time" was directed toward abolishment of discrimination, oppression, racism and the Jim Crow image with which the black man had been saddled. And, one can not forget Max Roach's "We Insist: The Freedom Now Suite." This music exemplified what was felt by many to be the surge of political black nationalism.

The civil rights movement of the mid 1950s through the 1990s was an era which experienced an extensive amount of social and political unrest. As this era in American history heightened, a number of non-professional ensembles sang "freedom songs." Many performers felt that these songs exemplified the language of the black struggle. The foundation for many of these songs were derived from contemporary songs and styles prior to the 1900s. Unlike many songs which emphasized the soloist, these songs were mainly for large groups.

Many songs became household tunes because of the visibility they received through constant performance by vocalist involved with the Student Non-violent Coordinating Committee (SNCC). Songs such as "We Shall Overcome," "We're Marching On To Freedom Land," "Ballad of Medgar Evers," "We Shall Not Be Moved," "Dog, Dog" and, "Woke Up This Morning with my Mind on Freedom" are just a few which are representative of the civil rights movement. For an extensive period of time, Freedom songs were mainstream music for blacks. The freedom songs expressed the innermost feeling of blacks as they related to the class system in the United States. Many of these songs became so popular among blacks that recording companies marketed several noted selections.

The civil rights movement and the influence of Dr. Martin Luther King's presence brought a greater awareness and respect for blacks. Black awareness and pride was transmitted to all sectors of the performance medium. Artists such as James Brown (noted as the 'Godfather of Soul') promoted black pride. His songs, "Say It Loud, I'm Black and I'm Proud" (1968), "I Don't Want Nobody to Give Me Nothin'" (1969) and "Escapism" (1971) all placed a major thrust on black pride. Another selection, "Don't be a Dropout" (1965) was a step taken through song in an attempt to influence black youth to complete their education. James Brown, by far the greatest contributor of black songs during this era, clearly paved the way for black artists of the future.

Although civil rights has always been a concern in America, this country has witnessed a number of other problems which have no barrier as they would relate to ethnicity. Two of such social concerns have been the Vietnam conflict and narcotics. Although the Vietnam conflict was extremely controversial, there was one song which expressed the view of the public. That song, "Bring The Boys Home" by Freda Payne became quite popular. Various other black artists followed suit and recorded major selections which addressed the Vietnam conflict.

The growing problem with narcotics in the United States has also received a great deal of attention from black and white artists. The problems associated with drugs has had no class limitation. Its effect has disrupted many lives, caused the erosion of many families, and, has been one of the leading contenders in the cause of crime and death. Black musicians have been among those whose lives were affected due to the use of drugs. Jimi Hendrix, Billie Holiday and Charlie Parker are just a few of the fatalities.

The impact of the drug market had such an effect on blacks that numerous artists sang about this problem. The Temptations were successful with the song "Psychedelic Shack." Artists such as Curtis Mayfield produced "Superfly," "Stone Junkie," "Freddie's Dead," "Underground and Hell Down Below." Each of the songs was directed toward making the public aware of the social problems incurred through the involvement with drugs.

As witnessed through those songs previously mentioned, black music reflects those events taking place in America. Within these events, one can also find references to the social history of the black man. Black music has most definitely exemplified the black man's struggle since 1619. It is because of the role which black music has had in reference to this ethnic group that dictates its being viewed for more than its entertainment capabilities.

A great amount of attention has been given music achievements of rhythm and blues performers. Although notoriety of this nature should be made public, attention must also be given to major achievements of all black musicians. Limiting the recognition of black achievements from the early 1900s to the present will most assuredly rob black America of some of its greatest history.

A few of the black man's music achievements which are seldom presented to the general public include:

1 Edward Kennedy "Duke" Ellington's involvement with sixty-six (66) movies. In most instances, Ellington wrote the sound track. There are numerous movies where he and his band made cameo appearances.

2 Harold Wheeler was the co-producer of the sound tracks to the movies "Star Wars" and "Close Encounters."

3 William Grant Still won first prize in an international competition for the theme song of the New York World Fair (1939–40).

4 James Bland is the only black composer to have a song adopted as a state song—"Carry Me Back To Ole Virginny."

5 George Augustus Polgreen Bridgetower performed the "Kreutzer Sonata." This competition was written especially for him by Ludwig Von Beethoven.

6 Harry Lawrence Freeman was the first black man to conduct his own competition before a major symphony orchestra (1907).

7 Lionel Hampton introduced the vibraphone as a jazz instrument.

8 Arthur Lewis Herndon was the first black tenor to be permanently engaged in a German Opera House.

9 Earl Hines developed the trumpet style of playing the piano.

10 Elizabeth Maddox Huntley wrote, "Behold Thy Mother." On June 19, 1951, this song was adopted by Congress as the national Mother's Day Song.

11 Noble Sissle and Eubie Blakes's musical "Shuffle Along" (1921) was the first show produced by blacks to perform on Broadway.

12 Scott Joplin wrote the first ragtime opera, "Guest of Honor," in 1903. He later wrote "Treemonisha" in 1907.

13 Roberta Flack wrote the first song which openly referred to sex permissiveness—"First Time Ever I Saw Your Face."

14 Issac Hayes wrote the theme song to the movie "Shaft." This movie was the first in history to be totally controlled, produced and promoted by blacks.

15 Fisk [University] Jubilee Singers were the first collegiate ensemble to make a successful international tour with a repertoire of Negro Spirituals.

These achievements represent just a few of many which have been accomplished by black musicians. Because of the little attention given major achievements, it is necessary that musicians, educators and societies involved in the arts provide as much visibility as possible. Efforts of this nature cannot be overlooked. If recognition is not presented in a positive and informative way, a unique heritage could be swept away, never to be recovered.

STUDY GUIDE 23

1–7 Give the subtle (slave resistance) meaning of each word/phrase below:

1 Angels

2 Egypt's land

3 Jordan River

4 Let my people go

5 Moses

6 Sinner

7 Steal away

8–11 Name the composer of each song below:

8 "Carry Me Back To Ole Virginny"

9 "I'll Never Turn Back No More"

10 "Shaft"

11 "Treemonisha"

12 In what year did the first Africans arrive in the English mainland colonies on a permanent basis?

13 Where did the first Africans arrive in the above (12) question?

14–18 Give some forms of black musical selections/literature.

19 "Freedom Train" is based on what song?

20 Expand the abbreviation SNCC.

21 Give the "Godfather of Soul."

22 Who popularized the anti-Vietnam War tune "Bring The Boys Home?"

23 Who produced "Superfly"?

24 Who produced the song "The First Time Ever I Saw Your Face"?

25 The "Jubilee Singers" were associated with what school?

24

The Seventies

The signals seemed very cross when the nineteen-seventies opened. On the one hand, conservative G. Harold Carswell of Florida was being nominated to the U. S. Supreme Court by Republican President Richard Nixon. There was fear that he was going to show the real meaning of "Law and Order." And in California, the event that would be making the news involving activist Angela Davis was occurring. At the same time, in Newark, New Jersey, Kenneth A. Gipson was winning the Mayoral election. But, could this latter event have simply meant that because of the "white flight from the city," the tax base in Newark and elsewhere was declining. Things were certainly confusing.

In 1970, at Kent State University in Ohio, four students were killed by the national guard in an anti-Vietnam protest. This made the national news then, and it is constantly written about in general American History books now, but shortly afterwards two students were killed [May 14, 1970] on the campus of Jackson State University in Mississippi. Somehow the lives of these black students seemed not to be as important. Eventually Lynch St., running through the campus of Jackson State, where the killings had occurred was blocked off. This was similar to what had occurred earlier at Texas Southern University in Houston, another H.B.C.U., where after the 1970 riot, the campus was blocked off and no longer ran end-to-end through the campus. Both situations seemed to say black lives were not as important as white lives. This same year saw U. S. President Richard Nixon reluctantly extending the Voting Rights Act (1965) until 1975. The conservative reaction period had definitely sat in. And at San Rafael Courthouse in Bay area California an outbreak occurred [August 7, 1970] and a young lady by the name of Angela Davis became the center of attention. Mainly in the south, but also elsewhere, school districts were refusing to desegregate.

President Nixon years [1968–76] were years of reaction to what had been social progress. Sometimes, this previous period has been referred to as the "Second Reconstruction." But, as with the "First Reconstruction," this "Second Reconstruction," was being brought down, in part, due to white reaction which promoted a wave of conservatism.

A member of the "Big Four" of the Civil Rights movement of the late '60s and early '70s was lost in Lagos, Nigeria to a drowning accident. This was Whitney M. Young, Jr. who had headed the National Urban League. In the same year, 1971, Walter Fauntroy became Washington, D. C.'s first non-voting U. S. Congressional delegate. And Jesse Jackson's new group "Operation PUSH" was founded. This group, People United To Save Humanity was to be led by the former activist of SCLC.

In1972, things moved on with the first National Black Political Convention convening in Gary, Indiana. Gary's mayor, a black man, Richard Hatcher, became the leader of this group. In November, Barbara Jordan from Texas and Andrew Young from Georgia became the first black persons from the south elected to Congress since the "fall" of Reconstruction. Also in 1972, a little known fact of a major catastrophe occurred: Frank Wills, a black man, foiled the break-in of the Democratic National Convention Headquarters at the Watergate Hotel in Washington, D. C. Eventually this incident brought down an American President. But the immediate problem that made the news was the acquittal of activist Angela Davis in California. One of the "downers" of the year was the release of three white Mississippians who had been convicted of the 1964 Philadelphia area slaying of Mississippi-Chaney, Goodman, and Schwerner, three Civil Rights workers. The killers served only two of the three years for which they had been sentenced.

In 1973, the war in Vietnam came to a diplomatic close. North Vietnam and the "commies" defeated America. This war had changed many Americans, both black and non-blacks. On the six o'clock news, for example, reports were not just a matter of being given some statistics and told how many persons in Vietnam had been "napalmed," but the American viewer watched the war victims running down the roads in Vietnam with their tattered clothing on fire. Minorities in America began to link the problems of the "have-nots" (low income people) in North Vietnam to the problems of "have-nots" in America. But at least three signs of hope appeared in the African American community. In May, Tom Bradley was elected Mayor of Los Angeles, California; during his campaign, he had been pictured as a leftist to scare off potential white voters. Los Angeles was a city with a white majority population, but the city's mayor was a black man. In October, Maynard Jackson was elected as the first black mayor of Atlanta, Georgia, a city with a black majority population. Jackson had grown up as a part of the black "middle class." In November, Detroit, another black majority city, elected Coleman Young as its first black Mayor. Detroit was one of the "white flight" cities plagued by crime, but it has given Motown Recording Industry and Aretha Franklin.

1974 proved to be a year when Americans would truly show their "colors." Whether it was desegregation of the public schools in Boston, Massachusetts; the U. S. Senate attaching a rider to the appropriation bill denying the use of federal funds for busing programs; or a study in *Psychology Today* showing that Americans voted on Mayoral candidates on the basis of their being of a similar race as the voters. Racism was alive and well and kickin' high! Things like Hank Aaron becoming the new homerun king by hitting number 715 in major league baseball became footnotes to the catastrophe. To hit number 715 meant that he bypassed Babe Ruth. Barbara Jordan distinguished herself with her robust voice as she reported the impeachment charges against U. S. President Richard Nixon in the Congressional Hearings. And in June of 1974, one of the released "Watergate Tapes" showed President Nixon calling Supreme Court Justice Thurgood Marshall a "jackass." Fortunately for the black community (where he never had any real support) Nixon resigned the Presidency and was succeeded by Gerald Ford.

The biggest news in the African American community in the middle of the decade was Arthur Ashe winning the 1975 men's single Wimbledon Tennis Championship. Earlier Althea Gibson had won the Women's single at Wimbledon. Two "big" men also died that year: Elijah Muhammad who had founded the "Black Muslims" and A. Phillip Randolph who had founded the first black labor union. And in several newspaper reports (although this was not "new news" for the black community) it was pointed out that both the FBI (Federal Bureau of Investigations), headed by Herbert Hoover, and the CIA (Central Intelligence Agency) had been spying on prominent African Americans. The spy list included Martin Luther King, Jr. and entertainer Eartha Kitts who had insulted Lady Bird Johnson, the wife of U. S. President Lyndon B. Johnson, at a luncheon in 1968. Vernon Jordan, President of the National Urban League later commented that "all across the board, black people lost out in 1975."

In 1976, things began to look brighter politically when Jimmy Carter from Georgia was elected as President, because for the first time since LBJ in '68, a Democrat won the White House. In other news, Ben Hooks was named to succeed Roy Wilkins as leader of the NAACP. And, Andrew Young was named as the Chief United Nations Ambassador for the United States; for a black to hold this position was another first. President Jimmy Carter made a first when he appointed a black woman, Patricia Roberts Harris, to his Cabinet; she became the Secretary of the Department of Housing and Urban Development (HUD).

In 1977 an important thing happened: Ernest Morial, a black man, was elected Mayor of New Orleans. Then, the National Aeronautic and Space Administration (NASA) named several black men as Astronauts—Major Guion Bluford, Major Frederick Gregory and Dr. Ronald McNair. But the biggest event of the year occurred on television—Alex Haley's "Roots" was shown several nights. People were glued to their televisions. People liked and identified with the show so much that they named their babies "Kizzy" and "Kunte Kinte." This television mini-series also turned many people into genealogical buffs. Folks became anxious to know their own roots. Family reunions became hot items. Even the U. S. Senate praised the showing of "Roots." The show was felt to have produced more racial understanding in America. The "downer" of 1977 was the announced results of a Case Western University study, which reported that homicide was the number one killer of black men in the 25–34 age group.

The conservative reaction grew throughout the country, however, when the *Regents of the University of California v. Bakke* ruling was handed down. The *Bakke* case outlawed the use of racial quotas, saying they instituted nothing more than reverse discrimination. To many conservatives, this ruling was like reversing the 1954 *Brown* case. There were other dark clouds left on the 1978 horizon as well. Lt. Gov. Mervyn Dymally (Dem.) was defeated for re-election in California. And in Massachusetts, U. S. Sen. Edward W. Brooke (Rep.) was also defeated for re-election. To add to this bleakness, Rev. Jim Jones, a white evangelist, led his "believers" (who included many black Californians) from the United States to Jonestown, Guyana, where he convinced them to drink poison and commit mass suicide.

AIDS (Acquired Immune Deficiency Syndrome) reached epidemic proportions in 1979. Rumors ran rampant that this ailment had occurred because the United States government was experimenting with a "concoction" to rid itself of blacks, but it instead came to affect gays. At first, there was an hysteria that this disease was borne from monkeys in Africa and transmitted to man. Naturally, if it was an African disease, then it was reasoned that black Americans were the vehicles carrying AIDS from Africa to the United States.

The night became darker when Andrew Young was forced to resign from his United Nations Post. The battle might have been lost, but not the war; because another black man replaced Young. Also, the city that had gained the most negative image during the civil rights campaign, Birmingham, Alabama, elected a black man, Richard Arrington, as its mayor. And, Mrs. Rosa Parks, the "Mother of the Civil Rights Revolution," ended up winning the NAACP's Spingarn Award, which is presented to the person who best exemplified the ideas of their organization.

SUGGESTED READINGS:

Alton Hornsby Jr., *Chronology of African American History.*

The World Almanac and Book of Facts, 1996.

STUDY GUIDE 24

1	Kenneth A. Gipson served as Mayor of what city?
2	At what Mississippi school were students killed in 1970?
3	At what University in Ohio in 1970 were students killed while protesting the Vietnam War?
4	Name the black woman indicted as a co-conspirator in the San Rafael, California 1970 jail break.
5	In 1968, who began serving as U. S. President?
6	Which group was headed by Whitney Young?
7	Who headed PUSH?
8	Expand the abbreviation PUSH.
9	Richard Hatcher served as Mayor of what city?
10	What state was represented in part by Barbara Jordan in the U. S. House of Representatives?
11	What state was represented in part by Andrew Young in the U. S. House of Representatives?
12	In what city is Watergate?
13	Which black man foiled the Watergate break-in?
14	Who generally are "Have Nots?"
15	Maynard Jackson served as Mayor of what city?
16	Tom Bradley served as Mayor of what city?
17	Coleman Young served as Mayor of what city?
18	Give the highest governmental position held by Thurgood Marshall.
19	Who succeeded Richard Nixon as President of the United States?
20	With what group is the name Elijah Muhammad associated?
21	With what group is the name A. Phillip Randolph associated?
22	Which black woman first won the women's singles at Wimbledon?
23	Which black man first won the men's singles at Wimbledon?
24	Which Democrat was elected as U. S. President in 1976?
25	Expand the abbreviation NASA.
26	Who succeeded Roy Wilkins as head of the NAACP?
27–28	Name any two of the black men announced as astronauts in 1977.
29	Name the author of *Roots.*
30	What court case outlawed the use of racial quotas?
31	Name the black man who formerly served as Lt. Governor of California.
32	Name the black man who formerly served as U. S. Senator from Massachusetts.
33	Where did the mass suicide led by Jim Jones occur?
34	Expand the abbreviation AIDS.
35	What black man first served as the mayor of Birmingham, Alabama?

25

The 1980s

The state of the African American community underwent a number of substantial changes from the 1960s to the 1980s. There has been considerable debate over the degree of activism and the level of commitment by the African American community and some African American leaders with regard to social, political, and economic improvement in the decades following the civil rights era. Comparison is often made to the more active years of the civil rights movement (particularly the 1960s) where struggle was clear and unambiguous, and goals and objectives were not obscured by social and political maneuvering. Gone from the 1980s were the marches and demonstrations that characterized the struggles of the '60s and early '70s. And gone from the public's attention were the militant personalities and organizations that cried out against injustice and differential treatment of African Americans. But perhaps more importantly, gone was the charismatic leadership that was capable of galvanizing the African American community into a force that could "demand" a more equitable application of the civil liberties guaranteed to all citizens under the Constitution.

The other side of the debate maintained that the strategies of the '60s and early '70s had outlived their usefulness—African Americans could sit at restaurant counters, they could legally attend schools with white children (although the issue of segregated school facilities was far from resolved), and African Americans could vote in all public elections at the local, state, and national levels. Some members of the African American community argued that what was needed during the "post" civil rights years was political and economic empowerment. This chapter will take the position that the struggle for political, social, and economic equality has not lessened since the civil rights era, but has, in fact, taken on new strategies to attempt to engage the new tactics utilized by the forces of racism and reaction. The move away from marches and demonstrations as the primary strategies for social and political change was prompted by those with more sophisticated strategies who wished to maintain the status quo. This chapter will examine some of the events of the 1980s and the repercussions they have had on the African American community. Particular attention will be given to the domestic policies of the Ronald Reagan [1980–1988] Administration and their impact on the African American community. Some attention will also be given to the early years of the George Bush [1988–1992] Administration. However, this chapter can not address all the significant events of an entire decade affecting the African American community.

The present offensive against the rights and liberties gained during the civil rights era finds its genesis not during the Reagan Administration as posited by some scholars, but rather during the twilight of Lyndon Johnson's "Great Society." Richard Nixon conveyed an unmistakable message in his 1968 presidential campaign—he would not support further desegregation of the public schools if elected to the office of president. It should be noted that in 1968 school desegregation was still a robustly contested issue, confined almost exclusively to the South. Not until *Keyes v. School District No. 1 Denver, Colorado* 413 U. S. (1973) did a significant desegregation case involve a northern school district. Prior to *Keys*, desegregation was perceived as a southern problem, a consequence of *dejure* segregation practices.

Upon gaining the White House in 1968, Nixon immediately began to use policies to slow the desegregation process. The Nixon Administration's position was so clearly anti-desegregation that the Supreme Court felt compelled to challenge the government's retreat from desegregation. In his 1972 presidential campaign, Nixon made opposition to busing for desegregation a primary plank in his campaign platform. However, as consistently as Nixon utilized the issue of "forced busing" to enhance his position with mainstream white America, the succeeding Presidents, Gerald Ford and Jimmy Carter were just as persistent in not making it an issue in their presidential campaign for 1976.

Moreover, neither Ford (during his replacement of Nixon) nor Carter (during his term in the White House) were particularly active in the area of school desegregation. It was not until Reagan that the issue of school desegregation, or, for that matter, of civil rights, drew "Executive" attention. Many African American scholars contend that the Reagan years in the White House brought about a resurgence in racism. While this strong assertion is strong, it should be noted that during Regan's campaign for a second term in office, the Ku Klux Klan felt comfortable enough with the Reagan Administration's domestic policies to endorse his candidacy. Reagan's ultra conservative policies have been credited with the tremendous upsurge in racist and vigilante violence all over the country during his two terms in office. Manning Marable has suggested that the Reagan Administration sponsored a political agenda that attempted to promote and institutionalize right wing conservatism. He put together a cadre of conservative legal experts that helped him to redefine the role of the Department of Justice; which in turn allowed him to undermine affirmative action, purge the Civil Rights Commission of critics, altering its mission; and to impede school desegregation while concurrently advocating tuition tax credits and voluntary integration. Changing the Department of Justice role also allowed Regan to reduce the activities of the Office of Federal Contracts Compliance Programs where enforcement against discriminatory practices in the awarding of federal contracts have historically occurred; additionally, it enabled him to purge the welfare rolls of poor African Americans and Latino families. These counter-offensives took place along side the Administration's efforts to reduce food stamp allocations, reduce health care benefits, and to virtually end all meaningful construction on new public housing units.

Busing to achieve desegregation was an area consistently opposed by the Reagan Administration. Although it was perhaps the most effective tool in transporting reassigned students to specific schools in a school district (and sometimes across school districts). William Bradford Reynolds, Assistant Attorney General of the Civil Rights Division of the Department of Justice, stated the Administration's position on desegregation before the House Subcommittee on School Desegregation. He indicated that the President, the Vice President, the Secretary of Education, the Attorney General and himself were all in opposition to mandatory busing. Yet, The State Of Black America, 1987 argued that the most damaging example of the Reagan Administration's policy toward school desegregation was that districts, once having implemented a court-ordered plan for desegregation, became "unitary" and were then entitled to: (a) have existing court orders withdrawn and (b) have implemented new plans which, in effect, allowed districts to resegregate their schools.

The mainstay of affirmative action was the Department of Justice and Title VII of the 1964 Civil Rights Acts. Title VII, the Equal Employment Opportunity Commission, and the Department of Justice were suppose to mitigate long standing patterns of discrimination. During the decades of the '60s and much of the '70s, the three branches of the federal government advocated and supported affirmative action. Both Republican and Democratic administrations advanced and enforced affirmative action regulations and guidelines. Affirmative action was established as a preventive procedure designed to minimize the probability of discrimination. Similarly to its retreat in the enforcement of civil rights in school desegregation, the Reagan Administration, through the Department of Justice, launched an attack upon affirmative action. The administration called into question some of the basic principles upon which discrimination could be proven. One such principle was the "Griggs rule," which required employers to demonstrate the relevancy of "tests" used to make job-related decisions. It should be noted that a common practice among employers bent upon carrying out discriminatory employment practices was to base hiring and promotion upon tests that had no relationship to job performance.

Title VII prohibited intentional discrimination and forbade employers to limit, classify, or segregate applicants or employees in any way that would deprive or limit them in employment opportunities. Congress affirmed the "Griggs rule" as early as 1972, extending Title VII coverage to the local, state, and federal governments. The Supreme court upheld the principle in *Albemarle Paper Company v. Moody,* 1975. Opposition to affirmative action and the EEOC Guidelines came from some of the most powerful sectors of the economy. Early in the inaugural year of the Reagan Administration (1981), the Department of Justice initiated a campaign to roll back the victories of the last three years of the Carter Administration. William Bradford Reynolds again articulated the Administration's position when he argued before Congress in 1981 that the Administration would not seek affirmative action remedies for groups who had been discriminated against if such remedies (as they believed) were in conflict with the Constitution. Reynolds stated that he believed "racial preferences, even to overcome past discrimination . . . are at war with the American ideal of equal opportunity." In 1982, the Department of Justice again opposed affirmative action, and in a friend-of-the-court brief, suggested to the High Court that the "last-hired, first-fired" seniority system could not be superseded to protect minorities and women hired under affirmative action.

Although the Department of Justice was the primary agent in the onslaught against affirmative action under the Reagan Administration, the Labor Department also softened its enforcement of affirmative action.

During the 1986–1987 term, *Paradise v. Prescott,* another affirmative action case, was argued before the Supreme Court. The Department of Justice initiated the suit, arguing that the Alabama State Patrol had engaged in "pervasive past discrimination." For almost four years the State Patrol had excluded Blacks from employment opportunities, especially in the upper ranks. The District Court resolved that for each non-minority promoted to the higher ranks, one minority should also be promoted until each rank achieved twenty five percent minority representation (or until the State Patrol could effectively demonstrate that it had developed an unbiased procedure for filling open positions in the ranks). Nevertheless, the Department of Justice again reversed its position, maintaining that the discriminatory acts by the Alabama State Patrol did not warrant the remedy proposed by the District Court because the violations entailed hiring and not promotional discrimination. The Department of Justice also argued that affirmative action should not be utilized as a "catch up" measure to remedy "longstanding imbalances in the patrol's upper ranks, despite the fact that such imbalances are a consequence of past discrimination.

The offensive to dismantle the civil rights struggle was, in part, moved inside the U. S. Commission on Civil Rights. Ronald Reagan purged the Commission of his critics and replaced them with Commissioners who were more in line with his views. Under former Chairperson Arthur S. Flemming, the U. S. Commission on Civil Rights openly criticized policies of the Reagan Administration that the Commission felt were oppositional to the tenets upon which the Commission was founded. In response to this criticism, Reagan began a process of restructuring the U. S. Commission on Civil Rights. In the spring of 1983, Reagan nominated three Commissioners, but he restructured Commission was more predisposed to the Reagan Administration's policies. The black conservative Chairperson of the Commission was Clarence M. Pendleton Jr. of California. Commissioner Mary F. Berry, a progressive black woman, was appointed by House Majority Leader James C. Wright Jr., a Texas Democrat. Eventually, Reagan fired Mary F. Berry and Blandina Cardenas Ramirez who were both critical of his policies. However, Democratic Congressional leaders reappointed them to positions on the Commission. A consequence of restructuring the Civil Rights Commission, which was affirmed in 1984 by a 6–2 vote, was that Commission was no longer bound to respect previous policy decisions. The Civil Rights Commission joined the Department of Justice in arguing against the use of quotas as a strategy in remedying past discrimination.

As a result of the Civil Rights Commission concurring with the anti-civil rights policies of the Reagan Administration, the NAACP, the National Organization for Women (NOW), and two Hispanic organizations all joined with the Hispanic, Black, and Women's congressional caucuses in arguing before Congress for the "discontinuation" of the U. S. Commission on Civil Rights. This union was a significant and bold step attempted by that coalition, especially given that the Commission was historically perceived as a bulwark in the civil rights struggles of minorities and women. Within the restructured Commission, a pattern of partisan voting emerged: Mary F. Berry and Blandina Cardenas Ramirez, representing the minority perspective, often opposed policies contrary to prior policy decisions; and the remaining members represented the "new" ideology along with the majority perspective.

The incidents of racial violence dramatically increased during the Reagan years. Manning Marable contends that this increase was a result of the Reagan Administration's offensive against civil rights. Accordingly, the Administration's policies produced a social and political climate where racists felt comfortable enough to step out of the closet to perform blatant acts of institutional and vigilante racism. Other observers also point to the lack of enforcement of civil rights as a major cause in the upsurge in racism. The Department of Justice concluded that over thirty major racial incidents occurred at American colleges and universities from 1983 to 1987.

The contemporary struggle by African Americans and other harried groups represents the latest counter offensive against racism and the denial of civil rights. This fighting back has been manifested in a number of ways: it has been reflected in the efforts of civil rights organizations and, and as equally significant, has been the historically erratic support of the Legislative, Executive and Judicial branches of the federal government. The Judiciary has perhaps been the most consistent supporter of minority rights in the civil rights struggle. This support does not imply, however, that the courts have been steadfast in their position of protecting civil rights. It should be noted that the Supreme Court initially supported the constitutionality of slavery; and prior to the turn of the century contrived and sanctioned the "separate but equal" doctrine that became the law of the land for the next fifty-eight years. Nevertheless, since the 1954 *Brown* decision, the courts have been more consistent in supporting the cause of civil rights than have been the Legislative and the Executive branches. This unbalanced support is the primary reason why so many civil rights organizations have become recently concerned when presidents Reagan and Bush have attempted to stack the Supreme Court with justices politically grounded in right wing conservatism.

Perhaps the most significant development in what some observers view as a national grassroots counter offensive to the anti-civil rights policies of the Reagan Administration has been the emergence of an African American as a serious contender for the highest office in the land. Disregarding the temptation to establish a third political party—one that would be more responsive to the needs of minorities and the poor—the Reverend Jesse Jackson, along with his Rainbow Coalition, forged a position of requisition and prominence within the leadership of the Democratic Party.

On November 3, 1983 the Reverend Jesse L. Jackson announced his candidacy for the presidency of the United States. Jackson's announcement was not enthusiastically received by certain groups, organizations, and politicians. Interestingly, much of the opposition was generated within the African American community. Much of the recognized African "establishment" recoiled at Jackson's announcement. Thinking Jackson a charlatan, Jackson's announcement to run for president proved a dilemma for some leaders in the African American community to give their support.

During Jackson's bid for the 1988 Democratic Party's presidential nomination, much appeared to have change on the surface. Most notable was the demonstrable support by the African American leadership for Jackson's candidacy. The grassroots, consisting of many working class and young whites, made manifest their support for Jackson along with masses of black folk. This constituency, especially the African American support, sent a clear message to the African American leadership that their support for Jackson was unwavering. Accordingly, most of the African American leader ship—whether they were in agreement with Jackson's candidacy or not—gave ostentatious support before the public. There was no overt or virulent criticism of Jackson's pronounced candidacy for the presidency for 1988.

On the contrary, much of the black opposition to Jackson in 1984 openly supported his candidacy. For example, during the 1988 Democratic Convention held in Atlanta, Georgia, Coretta Scott King, who had robustly opposed Jackson's candidacy during the previous campaign, joined Jackson on the podium with raised hands, following the candidate's dramatic speech. Charles Rangel, a democratic Representative from New York who had also opposed Jackson's previous campaign, maintained in his interviews at the Convention that he was a staunch supporter of Reverend Jesse Jackson.

What troubled much of the white establishment were the issues that Jackson was addressing in his campaign platform. Consequently, he was forcing other candidates to address some of the same issues. This approach to the issues was not the conventional way that politicians tried to gain mass appeal. Jackson had dared to address the Middle East question as both a moral and political issue; he raised the issue of a Palestinian homeland (with self-determination); he advocated more pronounced sanctions against South Africa as a strategy to initiate the dismantling of Apartheid; and he raised issues concerning Nicaragua, El Salvador, Panama, drugs, the homeless, etc. However, a focal point of Jackson's campaign (established in his 1984 effort) was "peace abroad and justice at home."

The decade of the 1980s represented a period of unique struggle within the African American community. The Rainbow Coalition represented, along with Jesse Jackson, a tremendous endeavor by the progressive and liberal forces to address the ultra conservative policies of the Reagan Administration. The struggle also involved some of the traditional institutions in American society. While the federal courts could be considered remiss in furthering the cause of affirmative action, school desegregation, and other areas of civil rights, they nevertheless refused to permit the Reagan Administration from completely dismantling the hard won gains of the civil rights era. In addition, Congress, while passing what some civil rights advocates presume to be irresponsible legislation, fought to prevent certain Reaganites from obtaining key political, administrative, and judicial positions (*e.g.*, Robert Bork to the Supreme Court and Witliam B. Reynolds as Associate Attorney General).

SUGGESTED READINGS:

Derrick A. *Bell, Race, Racism and American Law.*

Julius L. Chambers, "The Law and Black Americans: Retreat From Civil Rights," *The State of Black America,* 1987.

The Cincinnati Herald, April 26, 1986.

Citizens Commission on Civil Rights, "There Is No Liberty," *A Report on Congressional Efforts To Curb the Federal Courts and to Undermine the Brown Decision.*

Sheila D. Collins, *The Rainbow Challenge: The Jackson Campaign and the Future of U. S. Politics.*

Nathan Glazer and Daniel P. Moynihan, *Beyond The Melting Pot: The Negroes, Puerto Ricans, Jews, and Irish of New York City.*

Higher Education Daily, September 24, 1981.

Institute for the Study of Educational Policy, *Howard University, Affirmative Action for Blacks in Higher Education: A Report,* 1978.

Manning Marable, *The Black Scholar: Journal of Black Studies and Research,* Vol. 14, No. 6, Nov.-Dec., 1983.

United States Commission On Civil Rights, *Affirmative Action in the 1980s: Dismantling the Process of Discrimination,* November, 1981.

The Wall Street Journal, January 10, 1983, p. 6.

STUDY GUIDE 25

1 Who served as U. S. President 1980–88?

2 Who served as U. S. President 1988–92?

3 Whose Presidential administration was known as the "Great Society?"

4 Was the Nixon administration for or against "forced busing?"

5 What Presidential administration noticeably attacked affirmative action?

6 Name the black woman who served as a Commissioner of the U.S. Commission on Civil Rights and proved to be a thorn in Reagan's side.

7 Clarence Pendleton represented what state?

8 Expand the abbreviation NOW.

9 What blackman was a major Presidential candidate in 1984 and 1988?

10 What became the name of the supporting group of the above person (#**9**)?

26

The 1990s

THE NINETIES

African Americans are the largest and most visible ethnic minority group in the United States. Because of their population size (thirty million in 1991), along with their legacy of slavery and legal subjugation, African Americans occupy a special niche in the United States society.

The African American population has made remarkable progress since the 1960s. They are now more educated, earn higher salaries, work in more prestigious jobs and participate more fully in politics. But the remarkable progress of the post civil rights era appeared to have slowed during the 1980s, even regressed in some areas. Many observers feel that Ronald Reagan's presidential administration, which dominated national politics during most of the 1980s, was particularly harmful to Black Americans' socio-economic advancement erasing civil rights gains and promoting a general anti-black climate. Many view the administration of George Bush during the 1990s as a continuation of the Reagan politics of the 1980s.

Statistics show that in the 1990s black Americans ranked below white Americans on nearly every measure of socio-economical status. Studies also document the increase in institutional racism, overt racism and hate crimes on America's black population. This chapter will not reiterate the disadvantaged status of African Americans. Instead, the major focus of this chapter will be the collective response on behalf of the black community in the progress of bringing about change. Black American life today reflects a series of sweeping and significant changes, whether in educational reform, political participation, the striving for economic independence, or in a heightened sense of self-worth and oneness.

Historically, the African-American has looked to the public schools as vehicles for upward mobility. But the promise of equal education envisioned in 1954 is still unfulfilled in the 1990s. Many school system districts are desegregated, but few are truly integrated institutions. The over-representation of black students among the failures, underachievers and the drop-outs is often cited in the newspapers and the electronic media. The education of young black males too often is viewed as a special dilemma for the public school system. It has to be understood that the under education of black children does not exist in a vacuum. The school is not an isolated social institution, but a mirror of the broader society.

The black community today is responding to the failures of the traditional programs of the public school system in educating many young black males. Many programs today are actively and positively "reclaiming" the African American male through formal and informal education. The following are examples of programs that are providing leadership in this area.

1. *African-American Adolescent Male Development Center*: The National Urban League in 1985 started its first male-focus program—the Male Responsibility Program—a pregnancy prevention program for African American males. Based upon a commitment to be holistic in addressing the problems facing the black male, the National Urban League recently established the African American Male Development Center. The Center serves as a national clearinghouse, and provides information about programs that encourage the healthy development of black males and their families.

2. *Sigma Programs*: Phi Beta Sigma Fraternity offers programs for black males, ages 6–18, that address educational achievement, leadership development, self-pride, cultural awareness and community responsibility. The ultimate goal of the Sigma Programs is to help produce a future generation of well-rounded black American men capable of assuming leadership roles in their families, communities, nation and the world. In carrying out its goals, the Los Angeles Chapter of Phi Beta Sigma sponsors an annual retreat for young black males, ages nine to fourteen.

3. *Center for Educating African-American Males*: This program which is based at Morgan State University (Baltimore, Maryland) has for its goal the development of programs that create a learning environment in city schools in which Black school age boys are encouraged and expected to succeed academically.

The aforementioned are only examples of the many programs sponsored by groups based in the black community addressing the needs of the young black males of the 1990s. Many African Americans are reacting to the grim statistics generated by the public schools relative to the academic achievement of black males through developing culturally sensitive programs.

The need and the function of the historically black institution have produced up to seventy percent of all of the black graduates of colleges since the inception of this nation. Based upon projections, these institutions will produce in excess of 300,000 college graduates every ten years. The fact that historically public and private black colleges enroll less than twenty percent of black undergraduates but confer one-third of all baccalaureate degrees is a testament to the importance of such institutions to the black community and the American society. In the areas of graduate and professional training, the statistics are equally as impressive: two black colleges account for forty percent of all blacks earning degrees in dentistry, two account for twenty-two percent of all blacks in medicine, four accounts for sixteen percent of all blacks in law, and one account for eighty-two percent in veterinary medicine.

The historically and predominantly black institutions are a vital resource and the backbone of African American leadership. These institutions are the custodianship of the African American culture. They have been important repositories of African American literature, history and culture. A commitment to their survival is a commitment to maintaining a critical part of the black and the American experience.

The black church of the 1990s continues to hold the allegiance of large numbers of African Americans and exerts great influence over their behavior. Beyond its clearly religious function, the black church has been characterized by many as a social service center, political academy and financial institution.

Liberation theology underscores the focus of the Black church of the 1990s. This focus is based upon the premise that the church must address itself to the resolution of deep-seated inequities in the social order and that the church should be a resource base for needed change.

The black church as a social institution interacts with and influences two other important social institutions in today's Black community—the family and the school. The activities of Shiloh Baptist Church, a large inner city Church located in Washington, D. C., is a striking example of this interactive functioning of church, family and school. Through the Family Life Center, the church provides a wide range of activities which are facilitated for the whole family. Among the activities is the Male Youth Health Enhancement Program. This program involves young males of the community in after school and week-end programs stressing life issues and African American history.

The aforementioned is only one of the many black churches addressing the needs of the family and the school through a collaborative effort. The Congress of National Black Churches, an umbrella association of churches in the eight historically black denominations, operate a number of outreach programs involving parents and children after school and on weekends and holidays.

Many black churches as a part of their programming for the 90s are returning to one of their historical missions—creating schools. For example, Concord Baptist Church in Brooklyn operates its own private elementary school. So too, does the Allen A.M.E. Church in Queens and the St. Paul Community Baptist Church in Brooklyn. The 1990s will witness a more extensive network of private church related schools as alternatives or supplements to the education available to black youths at public schools.

Another aspect of the black experience receiving special attention during the 1990s is the role of black women in this country's past. Until recently, those who studied or wrote in the field of African American Studies tended to concentrate on the black forefathers, saying little about the black foremothers. Too often when these researchers discussed black women, they cast them in subordinate roles. Today, there is an increasing awareness that African American women have played significant roles in the ongoing struggle for freedom and equality. Beginning with the abolitionist movement and continuing through the Civil Rights movement of the 1960s, they have organized and led struggles for suffrage, anti-lynching laws and international human rights laws.

Any account of the history and the culture of the United States of America is incomplete without a discussion of the role and contributions of black women. Such women would include, Ida B. Wells, Mary McLeod Bethune, Zora Neale Hurston, Ella Baker and Fannie Lou Hamer. Darlene Clarke Hine, Joyce Ladner, Bernice Johnson-Reagan and Paula Giddings, are among the many black women scholars that are responsible for providing the missing pages of African American history and American history relative to black women.

Black women of the 1990s are assuming responsibility and making contributions in all areas of our society. Government and politics, education, science, medicine, business and theology are among the areas of their involvement.

Politics is one area in which the increasingly heterogeneous African American population of the 1990s may still share common interests. They are overwhelmingly allied with the Democratic party and they tend to support African American candidates.

While the number of black elected officials still represents a tiny fraction of the membership in city, state and federal legislative bodies, the number has skyrocketed over the past two decades. Blacks today have better luck winning in local races because national U. S. elections are characterized by racially polarized voting. While blacks account for only a small share of the national electorate, many city and congressional district populations have a majority black population. Although the racial composition of a jurisdiction is believed to be the strongest indicator of black electoral success, the 1990s witnessed blacks being elected from jurisdictions and cities in which blacks were a minority. Denver, Colorado; Seattle, Washington; New York City and Kansas City, Missouri are all examples of cities with a minority black population that elected a black mayor. The ability of black candidates to articulate issues relative to black Americans and the American people in general, is one of the major factors responsible for their success in winning elections in such areas.

There is a long history of black owned and operated businesses in the black community. Economic growth through the 1990s is expected to be modest compared with the experience of the last decade. The continuing problem of a large federal budget deficit, along with major problems in real estate and financial institutions, will hamper economic growth which, in turn, will affect the opportunities available to black business owners. But the nation's largest black owned businesses have shown their ability to adapt and prosper in good times as well as bad times. Studies show that sales for the nation's largest black owned businesses have climbed from sales of less than half a million in 1972 to nearly $8 billion in 1991. Moreover, during the last twenty years, seven black owned companies have managed to rank among the top one hundred every single year.

The interest of black Americans in Africa, its present and past, and their awareness of their African heritage retention in music, the arts, and literature, is taking hold of the 1990s. Increasingly, an Afrocentric approach is replacing the traditional Eurocentric approach in explaining the reality of the black experience in America. The black community is seeking cultural anchoring and reconnecting to the African past. The annual celebration of Kwanzaa is an example of a step in this process.

African American students today are well aware that the exclusion of African Americans from "mainstream" courses gives all students a distorted picture of American society and rob black Americans of their appreciable heritage. College and university students are returning to some of the strategies of the late 1960s and are demanding that courses specifically devoted to the unique experience of African Americans be offered, and that formal departments, programs and institutes of African American Studies be created.

Despite incredible odds, the African Americans of the 1990s are finding ways of overcoming the obstacles and are making remarkable contributions to all of humankind. The remarkable resilience of the African American is due in large measure to the survival of the most basic values of the African American cultural heritage. These values include spirituality, high achievement aspiration, respect for the elders and commitment to family. A commitment to these values coupled with strong leadership and community efforts will continue to serve African Americans well during the 1990s and beyond.

Suggested Readings:

Carl T. Rowan, *Dream Makers, Dream Breakers, The World of Thurgood Marshall.*

STUDY GUIDE 26

1–3 What were some of the major problems the black community faced as a result of the policies of the Reagan and Bush years?

4 In what state is Morgan State University lcated?

5 Centering academic work on an African background is known as what?

Significant Events in African-American History

1492 At the time that Christopher Columbus laid claims to the "New World," Africans were on his voyage. One such was supposedly, **Pedro Alonso Nino**.

1517 Bartolome de Las Casas suggested that Spaniards be allowed to import Africans as workers to the "New World."

1539 *Esteban* was among the group of explorers who set out looking for the Seven Cities of Cibola.

1619 Twenty Africans arrived in Jamestown to become the first of their people in the English mainland colonies on a permanent basis.

1640 **John Punch**, a black servant, along with two white indentured servants ran away and were returned to Maryland. The two white servants were given an added year to serve their master, whereas **Punch** was sentenced to serve his master for the rest of his natural life.

1655 England took control of Jamaica from Spain

1660 Virginia began referring to its African population in non-human terms and in law, simply treating it as a labor force.

1664 Maryland passed a law to prevent white women from marrying black men.

1741 The so called "Slave Plot" in New York City resulted in thirteen blacks being burned alive, eighteen blacks hanged, and seventy blacks were transported to the West Indies.

1761 **Jupiter Hammon**, a New York poet, became the first African-American to have his work published. His best known work became

"An Evening Thought." Another work was "Salvation By Christ with Penitential Cries."

1770 **Phillis Wheatly**, a Massachusetts poet, published her first poem entitled "On the Death of Reverend George Whitefield."

Crispus Attucks was slain in the Boston Massacre.

1773 The first black Baptist Church was established in Silver Bluff, South Carolina. Roger Williams had founded the American Baptist Church in Rhode Island in 1639.

1775 In Philadelphia, the first abolitionist society was organized.

There were both black and white men who fought against the British at Lexington and Concord.

Peter Salem and **Salem Poor** became heroes in the Battle of Bunker Hill. **Peter Salem** killed the British Commander, Major Pitcairn.

In Virginia, Lord Dunmore, the British Governor, invited blacks to fight the British(?) and thereby gain their freedom.

The Americans ordered that only white men could fight in the American Army.

1776 In a little over a month, Americans changed their minds and reissued an order for free black men to join the American Army.

Prince Whipple and **Oliver Cromwell** were with George Washington when he crossed the Delaware River on Christmas Day.

A Baptist Church for blacks was established at Petersburg, Virginia.

1779 **Pompey**, a spy who was black, helped make it possible for Anthony Wayne to win the Battle of Stony Point.

George Liele founded First Baptist Church of Savannah, Georgia. This was done prior to **Liele** leaving the United States to Settle in Jamaica.

1780s **James Derham**, born a chattel in Philadelphia in 1762, became one of the first black physicians in America. He began to practice in New Orleans.

1780 Pennsylvania instituted gradual abolition.

1781 Over half of the settlers who founded Los Angeles, California this year were of African descent.

1784 Connecticut and Rhode Island instituted gradual abolition.

1786 **Richard Allen, Absalom Jones, William White**, *et. al.*, blacks were pulled from their knees in prayer at St. George's Church in Philadelphia and told that blacks would only be allowed to kneel in prayer after all whites had finished praying first.

1787 **Prince Hall**, a Barbados immigrant and Methodist Minister, received a charter from the English Grand Lodge and established black Masonry in America. **Hall**, an American Revolutionary War veteran, had been initiated in 1775 by some of General Gage's men.

1790 **Jean Baptist Ponté DuSable** became the first permanent settler at what was to become Chicago.

1792 **Joshua Bishop** was named pastor of First Baptist Church for whites in Portsmouth, Virginia.

1794 The cotton gin was patented by **Eli Whitney**.

Bethel A.M.E. Church, better known as "Mother Bethel" was organized in Philadelphia by **Richard Allen**.

Absalom Jones organized the African Episcopal Church by establishing St. Thomas Protestant Episcopal Church of Philadelphia.

1796 The A.M.E. Church was founded in New York City when members of John Street M.E. Church felt themselves discriminated against and decided they wanted to worship separately from whites. The leaders of this movement were **Peter Williams, James Varick, George Collins**, and **Christopher Rush**.

1799 Bryan Baptist Church, named after **George Liele's** successor, **Andrew Bryan**, was organized at Savannah.

New York instituted gradual abolition.

1800 **Gabriel Prosser** led a slave uprising in Henrico County, near Richmond, Virginia.

1804 Haiti under **Toussaint L'Overature's** successor, **Jean Jacques Dessalines**, came to the forefront as the second republic in the "New World."

New Jersey instituted gradual slave abolition.

1807 **John Gloucester** organized First African Presbyterian Church in Philadelphia.

1808 After January 1, 1808, no more African bondsmen were legally allowed to be brought into the United States.

Reverend **Thomas Paul** founded Abyssinia Baptist Church in New York City.

1815 The Corp d'Afrique fought in the Battle of New Orleans under General Andrew Jackson.

Paul Cuffe, a wealthy shipbuilder, merchant, and sea captain, who was black, financed an expedition transporting thirty-eight African Americans "back to Africa." They went to Sierra Leone as part of a colonization scheme.

1816 The African Methodist Episcopal Church was organized.

The American Colonization Society was organized. One aim of this group became to found a home in Africa for freed African Americans

1817 Some Philadelphia blacks met to protest the colonization movement. One argument against this movement was that this was simply an attempt to make things quieter and more acceptable for slave holders by freeing the country of all free black men.

1822 Blacks from America were settled on the shores of what would eventually become Liberia.

Denmark Vesey was found guilty of having plotted a slave revolt in Charleston, South Carolina.

1823 **Alexander Twilight** became the first African American to receive a degree from an American college. He graduated from Middlebury College in Vermont.

1826 **John Russwurm** graduated from Bowdoin College. He too became one of the early American black college graduates.

1827 *Freedom Journal*, the first African American newspaper was published by **John Russwurm** and Reverend **Samuel Cornish**. In this year, *Freedom Journal* attacked the idea of colonization.

1829 Dixwell Avenue Congregational Church in New Haven, Connecticut was organized as the first black Congregational Church.

David Walker published his *Walker's Appeal*, a pamphlet calling on slaves to rise up and slash their master's throats. Georgia put up a bounty of $10,000 for him alive and $1,000 for him dead.

1830-1860

The "Underground railroad" existed.

1830 The First "National Negro Convention convened in Philadelphia at "Mother Bethel."

1831 William Lloyd Garrison and his partner, Isaac Knap, published, in Boston, the first issue of the abolitionist newspaper, *The Liberator*.

Nat Turner of Virginia led the most prominent slave revolt.

1833 The Maryland Colonization Society founded the colony of Maryland in Liberia.

1834 **Henry Blair** became the first black man to receive a patent. He received a patent for the corn harvester and in 1836, for the cotton planter.

The British Empire abolished slavery.

1836 **Alexander L. Twilight** was probably the first elected African American Official. He was elected to the Vermont State Legislature.

1838 *Mirror of Liberty*, the first African American magazine was published by **David Ruggles**.

1839 African slaves mutinied aboard the *Amistad*. They were captured by a U. S. warship. The U. S. Supreme Court eventually declared them free in 1841.

1841 Slaves on board the *Creole*, sailing from Hampton, Virginia to New Orleans, revolted and sailed to the Bahamas. There they were freed by the British government.

1843 **Peter Ogden** received a charter from England establishing the Grand United Order of Odd Fellows.

1845 Frederick Douglass wrote and published *Narrative of the Life of Frederick Douglass: An American Slave.*

Macon B. Allen became the first black man to be admitted to the bar to practice law. He passed the bar exam in Worcester, Massachusetts.

1846 **Norbert Rillieux** invented a vacuum pan evaporator, referred to as the "Jamaican Train," that revolutionized the sugar industry.

Frederick Douglass, who had escaped from slavery in Maryland in 1838, received his own "bill of sale" from his former "slave owner."

1847 Frederick Douglass began publishing his abolitionist newspaper, *The North Star*.

Liberia gained its independence.

1849 **Harriet Tubman**, destined to become known as the "Moses of her people," escaped from slavery in Maryland. She eventually returned some nineteen times and freed approximately 300 slaves.

Benjamin Roberts filed the first school desegregation suit on behalf of his daughter, **Sarah**, who had been denied admission to white schools in Boston. The Massachusetts Supreme Court rejected the suit and established the controversial "separate but equal" precedent.

1850 **Aaron Ashworth** of Jefferson County, Texas was the largest cattle rancher in his county. In 1846, he owned 4,578 acres of land. In 1850, he owned 2,470 head of cattle. Another East Texas black, **William Goings** of Nacogdoches, had a white wife and grew wealthy from land speculations. **Goings** employed nine slaves and several whites in his blacksmith shop.

A Fugitive Slave Law was passed by Congress requiring all Americans, anywhere in the country, to be responsible for returning slaves (chattels). This law incensed Ralph Waldo Emerson, Henry David Thoreau, *et al.*

Because of the passage of the Fugitive Slave Act, 5,000 African Americans emigrated to Liberia.

Cyprian Ricard purchased an estate in Iberville Parish, Louisiana for $225,000. Ninety-one slaves were part of the property.

1852 Harriet Beecher Stowe published *Uncle Tom's Cabin.*

1853 **William Wells Brown** became the first, African American novelist publishing *Clotel.*

1854 Lincoln University, the first (HBCU) African American College, had its beginnings in Oxford, Pennsylvania as Ashmun Institute.

1855 **John Mercer Langston** was elected as the Clerk of Brownhelm township—Lorain County, Ohio.

1856 Pro-slavery men staged a deadly raid on Lawrence, Kansas.

In retaliation for the Lawrence, Kansas raid John Brown led a raid on Pottawatomie Creek, Kansas.

Wilberforce University of Ohio was founded by the Methodist Church.

1857 **Dredd Scott** in his suit for freedom forced a Supreme Court decision declaring black people ineligible for American citizenship.

1858 **William Wells Brown**, the novelist, became the first black playwright after writing the play, "The Escape."

1859 John Brown led an unsuccessful raid on Harper's Ferry, Virginia.

The last ship with African slaves (chattels) brought to America landed at Mobile, Alabama in December.

1860 **Thomy Lafon** was perhaps the wealthiest individual African American. At his death, he had amassed a fortune of some $500,000 in real estate. Free black people in New Orleans owned some $15,000,000 in taxable property.

Abraham Lincoln was elected President of the United States of America.

South Carolina, on December 20, became the first of eleven states to secede form the Union.

1861 The seven seceding states met at a convention in Montgomery, Alabama and fashioned themselves into the Confederate States of America. They chose as President, Jefferson Davis of Mississippi. Alexander H. Stephens, of Georgia, was chosen as the Vice President. Eventually these seven states were joined by four others. The eleven states that formed the C.S.A. were: Alabama, Arkansas, Florida, Georgia, Louisiana, Mississippi, North Carolina, South Carolina, Tennessee, Texas and Virginia. The four slaveholding states, Delaware, Kentucky, Maryland, and Missouri, remained within the Union. These four states became known as the "Border States."

The military phase of the Civil War began on April 12, 1861 when C.S.A. forces fired upon Union forces at Fort Sumpter, South Carolina under the command of Major Robert Anderson.

U. S. General John C. Fremont issued a proclamation freeing bondsmen in Missouri. President Abraham Lincoln nullified this proclamation as well as the edict of Ben Butler and all other union officials interested in freeing the bondsmen.

A school for blacks opened at Fortress Monroe, Virginia.

Slavery was abolished in Washington, D. C.

1862 U. S. General Benjamin Butler began organizing free blacks in New Orleans into the U. S. Army.

U. S. General David Hunter issued a proclamation freeing bondsmen in Florida, Georgia and South Carolina. President Abraham Lincoln nullified this proclamation.

Robert Smalls took the *Planter* and gave it to the U. S. Navy.

A black delegation met with President Lincoln to discuss Lincoln's proposal for black migration to some place outside the USA, preferably some place in Central America.

The Battle of Antietam (MD) was fought.

President Lincoln issued his preliminary Emancipation Proclamation.

During the fall, the South Carolina Colored Regiment of the Union Army was attacked by bloodhounds at Pocatalago Bridge.

The First Kansas Colored Volunteers fought victoriously in its first military engagement.

1863 President Lincoln issued the Emancipation Proclamation.

The Governor of Massachusetts authorized the recruiting of the 54th Massachusetts.

The C.S.A. ordered that black troops of the USA be killed rather than taken as P.O.W.'s.

Union troops fought and lost the Battle of Port Hudson (LA). Major **Andre Cailloux** of the Louisiana Colored Volunteers distinguished himself.

In June and July, C.S.A. troops invaded the North. The Gettysburg Campaign took place.

Black people were indiscriminately set upon by white mobs in the New York City draft mobs. Federal troops fighting the Civil War now had to be diverted to put down these riots.

The 54th Massachusetts lost a number of its men in futile attempts to charge Fort Wagner (Charleston Harbor, SC).

On July 30, President Lincoln issued an order to kill rebel troops if black troops were summarily killed rather than taken as P.O.W.'s by the C.S.A. This, unofficially, caused the "rebs" to counter their previous order.

1864 At Mobile, Alabama, the Knights of Pythias was established.

C.S.A General Nathan Bedford Forrest captured Fort Pillow, Tennessee and the Confederacy killed black soldiers rather than take them as P.O.W.'s.

The U. S. Congress finally passed a bill equalizing army pay for black and white soldiers.

The "Wade-Davis Bill" advocating Congress' version of "Radical" Reconstruction was put forth. President Lincoln pocket vetoed the bill.

Atlanta, Georgia fell and Union General William T. Sherman began his "March to the Sea."

The first black daily newspaper, *The New Orleans Tribune*, was founded by **Dr. Louis C. Roudanez**.

General William T. Sherman began settling blacks on forty acre tracts in the Charleston, South Carolina area.

The XIII Amendment, abolishing slavery, was passed by Congress.

Congress established the Bureau of Refugees, Freedmen and Abandoned Lands (aka. Freedmen's Bureau) on March 3.

The C.S.A authorized the use of blacks as soldiers.

C.S.A. General Robert E. Lee surrendered to U. S. General Ulysses Grant at Appomattox Courthouse, Virginia ending the military phase of the Civil War.

President Abraham Lincoln was fatally shot at the Ford Theater in Washington, D. C.

On the White's Ranch, in Texas, the last skirmish of the Civil War was fought on May thirteenth.

Father Patrick Healy became the first African American to be awarded a Ph.D. He earned his degree from the Louvain in Belgium.

Pennsylvania U. S. Congressmen Thaddeus Stevens advocated a policy of giving blacks forty acres.

Mississippi started the process of enacting black codes restricting the rights of the freedmen.

Atlanta University was founded.

1866 The so-called "Radicals" began to charter the directions of Reconstruction.

Congressman Thaddeus Stevens proposed an addition to the Freedmen's Bureau Bill giving each freedman a forty-acre plot of land.

The Freedmen's Bureau Bill extended the life of the Freedmen's Bureau.

Congress passed the Civil Rights Bill protecting the freedmen.

Congress overrode President Johnson's veto of the Civil Rights Bill.

The Joint Committee on Reconstruction reported out what would eventually become the 14th Amendment.

The Memphis, Tennessee race riot took place.

Congress passed the 14th Amendment.

The New Orleans race riot occurred.

President Johnson vetoed the Freedmen's Bureau Bill. The veto was narrowly sustained by Congress. This was to be the last of President Johnson's successes in controlling reconstruction.

Congress passes a new Freedmen's Bureau Bill. Now, Congress overruled the President.

"Radicals" won the hotly contested Congressional elections.

1867 Morehouse College was founded in Augusta, Georgia.

A Reconstruction Act was passed, dividing the former C.S.A states into five military districts.

Congress passed the "Tenure of Office Act."

Howard University was founded.

Congress passed the Army Appropriation Act requiring that all Army orders be issued through the General of the Army. This act was deliberately meant to tie the hands of President Johnson.

St. Augustine College in Raleigh, North Carolina was founded by the Episcopalian Church.

President Johnson removed Secretary of war Edwin M. Stanton from Office without Senate approval.

The Louisiana Constitutional Convention met in New Orleans with supposedly forty-nine black and forty-nine white delegates.

1868 The South Carolina Constitutional Convention met and had a majority of black delegates.

With U. S. Grant having resigned after the Senate refused to accept the resignation of Secretary of War Stanton, President Johnson now stubbornly appointed General Lorenzo Thomas.

The U. S. House of Representatives voted to impeach (President Andrew Johnson. Johnson's trial began shortly afterwards.

Francis L. Cardozo was elected Secretary of State for the State of South Carolina.

Oscar I. Dunn was elected Lieutenant Governor of Louisiana.

President Johnson was saved from removal from office by one vote.

Congress voted to readmit Alabama, Florida, Georgia, Louisiana, North Carolina and South Carolina to the Union.

The 14th Amendment to the U. S. Constitution, defining citizenship, was ratified.

Pennsylvania U. S. Congressman Thaddeus Stevens died.

New Orleans was the scene of a race riot.

John Willis Menard of Louisiana became the first African American elected to the U. S. House of Representatives.

U. S. Grant won the U. S. Presidency.

1869 President Grant appointed **Ebenezer Don Carlos Bassett** as Minister to Haiti.

Congress voted to readmit Alabama, Florida, Georgia, Louisiana, North Carolina, and South Carolina to the Union.

In the case of *Texas v. White*, the Supreme Court restated Lincoln's theory of the Union, saying that the Union was indissolvable.

1870 **Hiram Revels** was elected as a U. S. Senator from Mississippi.

Jonathan I. Wright was elected as a State Supreme Court Justice in South Carolina.

The 15th Amendment, defining suffrage, was ratified.

The enforcement Act was passed by Congress. This Act guaranteed the suffrage of African Americans.

Mississippi, Texas and Virginia were voted to be readmitted.

Alonzo J. Ransier was elected Lieutenant Governor of South Carolina.

The C.M.E. (Colored Methodist Episcopal) Church was organized at Jackson, Tennessee.

1871 The Second Congressional Act, not law, placed Congressional election under the federal government rather than the states wherein they occurred.

The Third Enforcement Act or the Ku Klux Klan Act protected the Civil Right of blacks in the former C.S.A. states.

1872 **Charlotte E. Ray** became the first practicing black female attorney.

For forty-three days, P. B. S. Pinchback served as Governor of Louisiana.

1874 **Blanche K. Bruce** was elected as a Senator from Mississippi.

The Freedmen's Bank failed.

Father Patrick Healy became the President of Georgetown University.

U. S. Senator Charles Sumner, of Massachusetts, died.

1875 **Blanch K. Bruce**, from Mississippi, became the first African American to serve a full term in the U. S. Senate.

James Healy was consecrated a Bishop in the Catholic Church.

The "Mississippi Plan" occurred. To get whites back into political control, any means of violence was used. It started in Mississippi and spread to other formerly **C.S.A.** states.

The first Kentucky Derby was run and the winning jockey was a black man, **O. Lewis**.

1876 **P. B. S. Pinchback**, elected U. S. Senator from Louisiana, was refused his seat by the U. S. Senate.

Prairie View A&M University was founded.

In the *U. S. v. Cruishank* case, the meaning of the 14th Amendment was limited by the U. S. Supreme Court.

Rutherford B. Hayes and Samuel J. Tilden vied for the U. S. Presidency. Tilden came up short of the necessary electoral votes on opening ballot and eventually lost to Hayes. One of the "compromises" giving Hayes the victory was the "Wormley Agreement."

1877 In South Carolina, federal troops were withdrawn and Democrats (Conservatives) took control of the state government. In Louisiana, on April 20, ten days after the South Carolina events, the same thing happened.

1879 The "Exodus Movement" began. It was led by **Benjamin "Pap" Singleton** and **Henry Adams. Adams** headed the Louisiana wing and **"Pap" Singleton** headed the Tennessee branch.

1880 Southern University was founded in New Orleans.

In the case of *Virginia v. Rives,* the courts decided that just because black people were absent from a jury, this did not necessarily mean blacks were being denied due process.

1881 **Booker T. Washington** established Tuskegee Institute in Alabama.

In Georgia, Spelman College and Morris Brown College were founded.

1882 Virginia State College was established.

John F. Slater (educational) Fund was established.

1883 In the Civil Rights cases, the U. S. Supreme Court declared void the Civil Rights Act of 1875 which provided for equal accommodations for all people in public inns, etc.

In *United States v. Harris,* the U. S. Supreme Court declared null and void the Klu Klux Klan Act.

1884 The Berlin Conference was held and formally organized the partitioning of Africa into colonies.

Isaac Murphy was the winning jockey in the Kentucky Derby. He also won in 1890 and 1891.

Moses Fleetwood Walker was the first African American in major league baseball.

1887 Florida A&M University was founded.

1890 Savannah State College was founded.

The Texas Farmers' Colored Association proposed the creation of an independent all black state.

The second Morrill Act was passed authorizing the creation of land grant colleges that were black.

T. Thomas Fortune spearheaded the founding of the African American National League.

1891 North Carolina A&T was founded.

The Baltimore Afro-American Newspaper was founded.

1893 At Provident Hospital in Chicago, **Dr. Daniel Hale Williams** performed the world's first successful open heart operation.

1895 **Frederick Douglas** died.

Booker T. Washington delivered his "Atlanta Exposition Speech," referred to by some as the "Atlanta Compromise."

The National Baptist Convention was established.

The National Medical Association was founded.

Ft. Valley State College was founded in Georgia.

In the *Plessy v. Ferguson* case, the U. S. Supreme Court established the "separate but equal" rule.

South Carolina State College was founded.

1897 Langston University in Oklahoma was founded.

1898 Some twenty or more black Americans lost their lives in the explosion of the battleship Maine in the Havana, Cuba harbor.

The Spanish-American War began.

In the court case of *William v. Mississippi* the courts accepted as valid the literacy test that was discriminatingly used in voting.

The "grandfather clause" was included in Louisiana's new constitution as a means of curtailing black voters.

African Americans were among the American troops that landed in Cuba.

Black troops charged El Caney in the Spanish-American War.

North Carolina Mutual Insurance Co. was founded in Durham, North Carolina.

The African American Presbyterian Church was organized.

1899 The Improved Benevolent and Protective Order of Elks was founded.

1900 Booker T. Washington helped in the founding of the National Negro Business League.

"Lift Ev'ry Voice and Sing" was composed by **James Weldon Johnson** and his brother, **I. Rosamond Johnson.**

Bill Pickett became a noted cowboy with "bulldogging."

1901 Congressman **George H. White** of North Carolina ended his term in Congress. His tenure was that of the last black serving in Congress during the Reconstruction era.

Booker T.Washington dined at the White House.

In Georgia, Spelman College and Morris Brown College were founded.

Grambling College of Louisiana was founded by **Charles P. Adams**, *et al.*

William Monroe Trotter launched his *Guardian* newspaper.

1903 **W.E.B. Du Bois** published *The Souls of Black Folk.*

Maggie L. Walker began to head the St. Luke Bank and Trust Co. in Richmond, Virginia.

1904 **Mary McLeod Bethune** founded her school in Daytona Beach, Florida.

1905 The Niagara Movement was begun. This movement was spearheaded by **W.E.B. Du Bois** and **Monroe Trotter.**

The Chicago Defender was founded.

1906 The Brownsville, Texas race riot occurred.

Alpha Phi Allah fraternity, Inc. was founded.

1907 Quaker, Anna T. Jeanes founded the Rural School Fund.

1908 The Springfield, Illinois race riot occurred. This riot helped to pave the way for the coming of the NAACP.

Jack Johnson became the World's Heavy-weight Boxing Champion.

At Howard University, Alpha Kappa Alpha Sorority was founded.

1910 The NAACP was organized on a permanent basis.

W.E.B. Du Bois published the first issue of *The Crisis*, the official organ of the NAACP.

A city ordinance was passed in Baltimore which required separate black and white residential areas.

The Pittsburgh Courier was founded.

What became the National Urban League was launched.

1911 Kappa Alpha Psi Fraternity was founded.

In Jamaica, **Marcus Garvey** founded the Universal Negro Improvement Association (U.N.I.A.).

1913 Delta Sigma Theta Sorority was founded.

1914 Omega Psi Phi Fraternity was founded.

"Chief" Alfred Sam created rumbles, especially in Oklahoma, when he proposed sending black people "back to Africa."

1915 In *Guinn v. United States*, the U. S. Supreme Court voided the "grandfather clause."

The U. S. Marines landed in Haiti, which became an American Protectorate.

Carter G. Woodson spearheaded the founding of the Association for the Study of Negro Life and History.

Booker T. Washington died.

The "Great Migration" of black people from the South to the North began.

The showing of "Birth of A Nation" was protested.

1916 The first volume of *The Journal of Negro History* was published.

1917 America entered WWI. Some twenty thousand black people were part of the regular Army.

Black people held a protest march down 5th Avenue in New York City.

The Houston, Texas race riot occurred.

Marcus Garvey reorganized the U.N.I.A. in Harlem.

At least thirty-eight black people were lynched this year.

1918 The George Peabody (education) Fund was liquidated.

On November 11, WWI ended.

By the end of the year, more than 1,000,000 black people had migrated from the South.

1919 The First Pan-African Congress met in Paris, France.

The "Red Summer" occurred. Race riots took place in Longview, Texas; Washington, D. C.; Chicago, Illinois; etc.

1920 **Marcus Garvey's** U.N.I.A. held its National Convention in New York City.

The first black Executive Secretary of the NAACP was appointed in the person of James Weldon Johnson.

Zeta Phi Beta Sorority was founded.

1921 "Shuffle Along" opened in New York City.

1922 The Dyer Anti-lynching Bill failed in Congress.

1923 **Marcus Garvey** was sentenced to prison by the U. S. Government.

Due to Klan violence, Martial law was declared illegal in Oklahoma.

Bethune-Cookman College was founded in Florida.

1925 **A. Philip Randolph** helped to organize the Brotherhood of Sleeping Car Porters labor union.

Xavier University was founded.

1926 **Carter G. Woodson** inaugurated "Negro History Week."

1927 The U. S. Supreme Court voided the Texas white primaries, in the case of *Nixon v. Herndon*.

Marcus Garvey was deported to Jamaica.

1928 **Oscar DePriest**, from Chicago, became the first African American elected to Congress from a Northern state.

1929 On October 29, the stock market collapsed initiating the "Great Depression."

1931 The Scottsboro Trials began.

1933 *The Atlanta Daily World* became a daily newspaper.

1934 **Arthur Mitchell**, a democrat from Chicago, became the first black Congressman.

1935 The National Council of Negro Women was founded.

1936 At the Berlin Olympics, Jesse Owens won four Gold Medals.

1938 **Crystal Bird Fauset** became the first black woman elected as a state legislator. She served in the Pennsylvania Legislature representing a part of Philadelphia.

In the Constitutional case of *Missouri ex rel Gaines v. Canada*, the U. S. Supreme Court ruled that states must provide black citizens with equal educational facilities.

1939 **Marian Anderson** sang at the Lincoln Monument after the Daughters of the American Revolution had refused to grant her permission to sing at Constitution Hall in Washington, D. C.

The Legal defense fund and Educational Fund for the NAACP were incorporated.

1940 *Native Son*, a novel by **Richard Wright**, was published.

In England, **Dr. Charles Drew** was appointed head of the blood plasma project.

Benjamin O. Davis, Sr. became a U. S. Army General.

Hattie McDaniel received an Oscar for "Best Supporting" role.

President Franklin D. Roosevelt issued Executive Order 8802, which forbade racial discrimination in war industries.

The U. S. Army Flying School was set up at the Tuskegee Institute in Alabama.

On December 7, **Dorie Miller** became a hero at the Battle of Pearl Harbor.

1942 The "Durham Manifesto," calling for racial changes throughout America, was issued.

C.O.R.E. was organized.

The Beaumont, Texas race riot occurred.

1943 A race riot in Detroit, Michigan occurred.

C.O.R.E. was "defined" as a national group.

A race-riot occured in Harlem, New York.

The *Smith v. Allwright* court case decision was handed down by the U. S. Supreme Court. It abolished all white Democratic primaries.

The U.N.C.F. was incorporated. This organization had been founded by **Franklin D. Patterson**, *et al.*

1945 President Franklin D. Roosevelt died at Warm Springs, Georgia.

In May, V.E. Day occurred with the surrender of Germany.

Colonel Benjamin O. Davis, Jr. was named as Commander of Godman Field, Kentucky. Thus, he became the first black man to head the U. S. Air Force Base.

Jackie Robinson was signed to the Brooklyn Dodgers contract by Branch Rickey. **Robinson** became the black man who desegregated modern major league baseball.

John H. Johnson published *Ebony* magazine's first issue.

In December, V.J. Day occurred with the surrender of Japan. This concluded WWII.

Nat "King" Cole became the first black person with a network radio show.

1946 A race riot occurred at Columbia, Tennessee.

William H. Hastie was inaugurated, becoming the first black Governor of the Virgin Islands.

The U. S. Supreme Court banned segregation on interstate bus travel in the case of *Irene Morgan v. Commonwealth of Virginia.*

A race riot occurred at Athens, Alabama.

1947 Texas Southern University was founded.

"Freedom Riders" began to be sent throughout the South.

Sipuel v. Oklahoma State Board of Regents desegregated the state-run law school.

State courts prevented from enforcing racial restrictive covenant in the case of *Shelly v. Kraemer.*

Oliver Hill was elected to the Richmond, Virginia City Council.

Executive Order #9981, ordering branches of the armed services to provide black people with "equality of treatment and opportunity" was issued by President Harry Truman.

1949 **Ezzard Charles** became the new World's Heavyweight Boxing Champ by defeating **Jersey Joe Walcott.** This followed the retirement of Joe Louis, another 1949 event.

The first black owned radio station, WERD, took to the airwaves in Atlanta, Georgia.

William Hastie became the first African American member of the U. S. Circuit Court of Appeals.

1950 The *Sweaff v. Painter* case was announced by the U. S. Supreme Court which required the state of Texas to provide professional education facilities for its black residents. This case helped with the foundations of segregation. Similar destructions of segregational foundations had taken place in the cases *McLaurin v. Oklahoma State Regents* and *Henderson v. United States.*

As the first African American noted by the Pulitzer Prize Committee, poet **Gwendolyn Brooks** received the Pulitzer Prize for her book of verse, *Annie Allen.*

Ralph J. Bunche was awarded the Nobel Peace Prize for having served as a mediator for the Palestinian Conflict.

1951 **Z. Alexander** was elected to the Nashville, Tennessee City Council.

A race riot occurred in Cicero, Illinois. It was spurred in an attempt to keep Cicero an all white city.

Jet magazine was founded.

1952 The first black student was admitted to the University of Tennessee.

Tuskegee University reported that for the first time since 1881, there were no lynchings in America.

1953 The U. S. Supreme Court banned segregation in restaurants in Washington, D. C.

The President of Dillard University in New orleans, Louisiana, **Albert W. Dent**, was elected as President of the National Health Council.

A bus boycott was begun in Baton Rouge, Louisiana.

Reverend J. H. Jackson of the Olivet Baptist Church in Chicago was elected as President of the National Baptist Convention.

Dr. Rufus Clement, President of Atlanta University, was elected to the Atlanta Board of Education.

Hulen Jack became President of the Manhattan Borough.

1954 In a unanimous decision, the U. S. Supreme Court ruled segregation as unconstitutional in the *Brown v. Board of Education of Topeka, Kansas* case, reversing the 1896 *Plessy v. Ferguson* ruling.

At Indianola, Mississippi, the first White Citizens Council was organized.

Washington, D. C. and Baltimore, Maryland began school desegregation.

Benjamin O. Davis, Jr. became the first African American General in the Air Force.

Charles C. Diggs, Jr. became Michigan's first African American Congressman.

1955 Opera singer, **Marian Anderson**, debuted at the "Met." She became the first African American in the history of the Company.

Roy Wilkins became the new Executive Director of the NAACP. He succeeded **Walter White** who had died earlier (March 21, 1955).

The Bandung, Indonesia Conference of People of Color was held.

Mary McLeod Bethune died.

The U. S. Supreme Court said that school desegregation must proceed with "all deliberate speed."

Emmett Till, a Chicago teenager vacationing in Mississippi, was lynched in Money, Mississippi.

The "Interstate Commerce Commission banned segregation in interstate travel.

Rosa Parks, a seamstress who was simply tired, refused to give up her seat and paved the way for the Montgomery, Alabama Bus Boycott. Mrs. Parks thus became known as "The Mother of the Modern Civil Rights Movement."

The Montgomery Bus Boycott began and this movement brought **Martin Luther King, Jr.** to the forefront of the Civil Rights Movement.

1956 The Montgomery, Alabama home of Martin Luther King, Jr. was bombed.

Autherine Lucy was admitted to the University of Alabama. She was suspended on February 7, 1956, following a riot, and on February 29, 1956, she was expelled.

A manifesto denouncing desegregation was signed by 100 U. S. Senators and Representatives from Southern states.

White supremacists attacked singer **Nat "King" Cole** on a performance stage in Birmingham, Alabama.

In Tallahassee, Florida, a bus boycott began.

A Federal court ruled that segregation on buses in Montgomery, Alabama was in violation of the U. S. Constitution.

In Mansfield, Texas, a white mob prevented the enrollment of black students in the public school.

A race riot at Clinton, Tennessee was sparked by attempted school desegregation.

The Montgomery Bus Boycott was called off. The next day, December 21, 1956, Montgomery, Alabama buses were desegregated.

In Birmingham, Alabama, the home of **Reverend Fred Shuttlesworth**, a local protest leader, was bombed.

Nat "King" Cole became the first black person with a network television show.

1957 In New Orleans, the Southern Christian Leadership Conference (S.C.L.C) was organized. **Martin Luther King, Jr.** became its President.

Ghana became an independent nation.

At Wimbledon, **Althea Gibson** won the Women's Tennis Singles Championship.

Congress passed a Civil Rights Bill that empowered the government to seek injunctions against voting infractions.

Gov. Orval Fabus used the Arkansas National Guard to bar students from desegregating an all white high school in Little Rock.

In Nashville, the Hattie Cotton Elementary School was destroyed by dynamite after a (one) black student attended the school.

U. S. President Dwight Eisenhower ordered Federal Troops to Little Rock due to the school desegregation crisis.

President Eisenhower now ordered regular Army personnel to Little Rock to calm the white mob, which was trying to prevent school desegregation.

President Eisenhower ordered more troops to Little Rock to escort nine black students in their attempts to desegregate Central High School.

In late November federal troops pulled out of Little Rock.

Dorothy Heights was elected President of the National Council of Negro Women.

1958 **Dr. Clifton Wharton** was named as the U. S. Minister to Rumania.

In Pennsylvania, **Robert N. C. Nix** was elected to Congress.

In New York City, a deranged black woman stabbed **Martin Luther King, Jr.**

In Washington, D. C., at least 1,000 young people participated in a "Youth march" for desegregated schools. The march was led by **Harry Belafonte, A. Philip Randolph** and **Jackie Robinson.**

1959 When "A Raisin In the Sun" opened on Broadway, it produced a series of "firsts." This was the first play on Broadway with an African American playwright, **Lorraine Hansberry**. It was also a first for a play with a black director, **Lloyd Richards.**

The lynching of **Mack Parker** took place in Poplarville, Mississippi.

The Prince Edward County, Virginia public schools closed down in an attempt to prevent school desegregation.

Barr Gordy, Jr. established Motown Records.

1960 "Sit-ins" started at Greensboro, North Carolina by four North Carolina A&T University students.

Students from Alabama State University held the first sit-ins in the Deep South.

Early in the following month, nine students at Alabama State were expelled for having participated in the sit-ins.

Southern University expelled eighteen students for sit-in demonstrations.

The Student Non-Violence Coordinating Committee was organized! at Shaw University.

Federal Judge J. Skelly Wright ordered the New Orleans schools to desegregate.

Zaire gained its independence.

Somalia gained its independence.

Dahomey gained its independence.

Niger gained its independence.

Church "keel-ins" began in Atlanta, Georgia featuring black and white students.

The Ivory Coast gained its independence.

The Congo (Brazzaville) gained its independence.

Senegal gained its independence.

Ten days of sit-ins in Jacksonville, Florida were followed by a race riot.

Nigeria gained its independence.

Massachusetts Senator John F. Kennedy was elected as the President of the United States.

The schools in New Orleans began the process of desegregating.

1961 A riot at the University of Georgia occurred following the admission of **Charlayne Hunter** and **Hamilton Holmes**.

"Because" of student demonstrations, Southern University was closed.

Clifton R. Wharton was sworn in as the Ambassador to Norway.

Sierra Leone gained its independence.

A bus of "Freedom Riders" was bombed near Anniston, Alabama.

In Montgomery, Alabama, "Freedom Riders" were attacked by a white mob.

Martial Law was declared in Montgomery.

Whitney Young, Jr. became the Executive Director of the National Urban League.

Orders to bar segregated interstate bus facilities were issued by the I.C.C.

Ossie Davis's play, "Purlie Victorious" opened on Broadway.

In McComb, Mississippi, "Freedom Riders" were attacked by a white mob.

In Albany, Georgia, hundreds of Civil Rights demonstrators were arrested. **Martin Luther King, Jr.** was among those arrested.

1962 In New Orleans, Archbishop Joseph Rummell excommunicated three parishioners for their fierce opposition to school desegregation.

1963 **Carl T. Rowan** was named the American Ambassador to Finland.

Martin Luther King, Jr. opened the Birmingham, Alabama desegregation movement.

Medgar Evers was assassinated in Jackson, Mississippi. He was the NAACP's Field Secretary for Mississippi.

W.E.B. Du Bois died in Accra, Ghana.

The "March on Washington" occurred and culminated with **Martin Luther King, Jr.'s** "I have a Dream" speech.

In Birmingham, Alabama, four black girls were killed in the racist bombing of the 16th Street Baptist Church.

In Dallas, Texas, U. S. President John F. Kennedy was assassinated.

Kenya gained its independence.

"Freedom of Choice" plans (started appearing throughout the South in the school desegregation movement.

1964 The 24th Amendment to the U. S. Constitution, barring poll taxes, was ratified.

Cassius Clay (Muhammad Ali) won the World Heavyweight Boxing Championship.

Malcom X cut his ties with the Nation of Islam.

The Civil Right Bill of 1964, calling for open public accommodations and equal employment was signed by President Lyndon B. Johnson.

Bodies of Civil Rights activist, **James Chaney**, Andrew Goodman and Michael Swerner were found near Philadelphia, Mississippi.

Martin Luther King, Jr. was awarded the Nobel Peace Prize.

Sidney Poitier received an Oscar as "Best Actor of the Year" for his role in "Lilies of the Field."

1965 The Selma, Alabama, voter registration drive began.

Playwright **Lorraine Hansberry** died.

Singer **Nat King Cole** died.

Malcom X was assassinated.

In Alabama, Civil Rights Activists **Jimmy Lee Jackson** died from injuries allegedly inflicted by law officials.

In the Selma, Alabama movement, Civil Rights workers were viciously attacked and a white Unitarian minister, Reverend James J. Reeb, later died from those injuries.

Under the protection of federal troops, **Martin Luther King, Jr.** led marchers from Selma to Montgomery. The march began March 21 and culminated with a rally at the Alabama State Capitol. After this rally, white Civil Rights advocate, Mrs. Viola Liuzzo was slain on U. S. Highway 80 while transporting some of the marchers back home.

Benjamin O. Davis, Jr. was promoted to Lieutenant General in the U. S. Air Force, becoming its first black General.

Patricia Roberts Harris was appointed as the U. S. Ambassador to Luxembourg.

Vivian Malone, one of the first black students at the University of Alabama, graduated from the same.

The Voting Rights Bill became law paving the way for mass black voter registration.

The Watts (Los Angeles, California) Riots occurred.

Thurgood Marshall was confirmed as the Solicitor General of the United States.

The West Side of Chicago became embroiled in a race riot.

1966 With the departure of **James Farmer**, it was announced that the new National Director of C.O.R.E. would be **Floyd B. McKissick.**

Harold R. Perry was ordained as the second black American Catholic Bishop in the history of the United States.

The Georgia State Legislature denied a seat to Julian Bond due to his opposition of the Vietnam War.

Robert C. Weaver was sworn in as the first African American Secretary in the Cabinet of the President of the United States. **Weaver** became Secretary of the Department of Housing and Urban Development.

Andrew F. Brimmer, born in Louisiana, became the only African American to become Governor of the U. S. Federal Reserve Board.

Emmett Ashford became the first African American to become a Major League Baseball umpire.

Bill Russell, born in Louisiana, by becoming the Head Coach of the Boston Celtics, became the first black man to coach a professional sports team in modern times.

Stokely Carmichael (Kwame Touree) was replaced as leader of S.N.C.C.

A White House Conference on Civil Rights was held with over two thousand people in attendance.

James Meridith was shot by a sniper along Highway 51 on his "March" from Memphis to Jackson, Mississippi.

A riot occurred in Omaha, Nebraska.

A riot occurred in Chicago, Illinois.

A riot occurred in Cleveland, Ohio.

A riot occurred in Lansing, Michigan.

A riot occurred in Waukegan, Illinois.

With the confirmation of **Constance Baker Motley** as a Federal Judge, she became the first black woman to become a Federal Judge.

A riot occurred in Dayton, Ohio.

A riot occurred in Atlanta, Georgia.

Huey Newton and **Bobby Seale** spear-headed the founding of the Black Panther Party in Oakland, California.

Edward W. Brooke (Rep.) was elected as a U. S. Senator from Massachusetts.

1967 U. S. Representative **Adam Clayton Powell, Jr.** was unseated as Chairman of the House of Education and Welfare Committee. He was charged with misappropriation of government funds.

Julian Bond was seated in the Georgia State Legislature.

In Tuskegee, Alabama, **Lucius D. Amerson** was sworn in as the Sheriff, becoming the first African American Sheriff in the South in the twentieth century.

U. S. Representative **Adam Clayton Powell, Jr.** was expelled from the U. S. House of Representatives. He was then re-elected to the House by his Harlem District.

Muhammad Ali, because of his draft refusal, lost the recognition of the W.B.A. and the New York State Athletic Commission.

H. Rapp Brown of Louisiana replaced **Stokely Carmichael** (Kwame Toure) as leader of S.N.C.C.

A riot occurred in Boston, Massachusetts.

In the court case of *Loving, et al., v. Virginia*, a ban on interracial marriage was ruled unconstitutional.

A riot occurred in Cincinnati, Ohio.

President Lyndon B. Johnson named U. S. Solicitor General **Thurgood Marshall** as a Judge on the U. S. Supreme Court.

A race riot occurred in New York.

Major Robert H. Lawrence became the first African American Astronaut.

A race riot occurred in Tampa, Florida.

A riot occurred in Newark, New Jersey.

A riot occurred in Cairo, Illinois.

A riot occurred in Durham, North Carolina.

A riot occurred in Memphis, Tennessee.

The first "Black Power Conference" was held in Newark, New Jersey.

A riot occurred in Cambridge, Maryland.

A riot occurred in Milwaukee.

Thurgood Marshall was confirmed by the Senate as a Judge on the bench of the U. S. Supreme Court.

Walter E. Washington was appointed by President Lyndon B. Johnson as mayor of Washington, D. C.

Richard G. Hatcher was elected mayor of Gary, Indiana.

Carl B. Stokes was sworn in as mayor of Cleveland, Ohio.

Mayor **Robert Lawrence**, the first African American astronaut, was killed in an airplane accident.

1968 At South Carolina State College, three students were slain in a demonstration protesting segregation.

Alcorn State College was the site of a racial segregation demonstration.

The "Kerner Commission" reported that America was growing toward two unequal societies.

M.L.K. announced plans for the "poor peoples Campaign." (held later despite of the death of Rev. King)

At Howard University, students seized the Administration Building, demanding certain campus changes.

An uprising occurred at Cheney State College of Pennsylvania.

A race riot occurred at Memphis, Tennessee.

A student revolt occurred on the campus of Bowie State College.

On April 4, M.L.K. was assassinated in Memphis.

Tuskegee Institute's students demanded campus changes.

On April 9, funeral services were held for M.L.K.

Ralph David Abernathy became the successor of M. L. K. as leader of S.C.L.C.

A Civil Rights Bill banning housing discrimination and administering punishment for inciting a riot passed.

"Resurrection City" part of the "Poor People's Campaign" was erected on the site of the Lincoln Memorial in Washington, D. C.

The alleged assassin of M.L.K. was captured in London at the airport.

Over 50,000 marchers participated in the "Poor People's Campaign" march on Washington, D. C.

Massachusetts U. S. Senator, **Edward W. Brooke** was named Temporary Chairman of the Republican National Convention meeting in Miami.

A riot occurred in Miami.

A riot occurred in Cleveland, Ohio.

A riot occurred in Gary, Indiana.

At the Democratic Convention in Chicago, **Reverend Channing E. Phillips** of Washington, D. C. was nominated as candidate for President of the United States.

Arthur Ashe became the first black man to win the U. S. Open title in Tennis.

In the Olympic Games at Mexico City, **John Carlos** and **Tommie Smith** raised their fists in a black power salute following their 200 meter victory.

Shirley Chisolm became the first black woman elected to the U. S. Congress. By being elected, she became a member of the largest black delegation ever to serve in Congress. Others in this group were U. S. Senator **Edward W. Brooke** (Rep.) of Massachusetts. In the House of Representatives (all Democrats): **Adam Clayton Powell, Jr.** of New York, **William L. Dawson** of Illinois, **Charles C. Diggs** of Michigan, **Augustus Hawkins** of California, **Robert N. C. Nix** of Pennsylvania, **John Conyers** of Michigan, **Louis Stokes** of Ohio, **William L. Clay** of Missouri, and others.

1969 Even though there was a controversy, the U. S. Congress seated **Adam Clayton Powell, Jr.** as a Representative from New York.

A student was slain in a demonstration at North Carolina A&T State University.

The U. S. Supreme Court ruled against the House unseating the Congressman **Adam Clayton Powell, Jr.**

Warren Burger was appointed to the Supreme Court as Chief Justice, succeeding Earl Warren.

A riot occurred in Baton Rouge, Louisiana.

A riot occurred in Ft. Lauderdale, Florida.

A riot occurred in Hartfort, Connecticut.

Dr. Clifton Wharton was elected President of Michigan State University.

In the case of *Alexander v. Holmes*, originating in Mississippi, the Courts finally abandoned the "all deliberate speed" principle and called for a unitary school district.

In a police raid in Chicago, Black Panther leaders Mark Clark and Fred Hampton were slain.

1970 **Joe Frazier**, by defeating **Jimmy Ellis**, became W.B.A. Heavyweight Boxing Champion.

The nomination of **G. Harold Carsell** to the U. S. Supreme Court was defeated by the U. S. Senate.

A race riot occurred in Augusta, Georgia.

On the campus of Jackson State University, an uprising occurred and two students were killed.

Kenneth A. Gipson was elected mayor of Newark, New Jersey.

President Richard Nixon signed an extension of the Voting Rights Act to last until 1975.

Charles Rangel defeated **Adam Clayton Powell, Jr.** for a Congressional seat from Harlem (NYC) in a Democratic Primary.

A riot occurred at Hartford, Connecticut.

San Rafael, California (Marie County) courthouse break occurred. **Angela Davis** became prominent as a result of this incident.

A confrontation between Black Panther Activists and Philadelphia, Pennsylvania police occurred.

There was a shootout between black activists and police in New Orleans.

Angela Davis was arrested in New York City.

Among the newly elected African American were **George Collins (Ill), Ronald Dellums** (CA), **Ralph Metcalfe (Ill), Mitchell** (MD), and **Charles Rangel** (NY).

A riot occurred in Daytona Beach, Florida.

William L. Dawson, Congressional Democrat from Illinois, died.

General **Benjamin O. Davis, Sr.** died.

1971 The Congressional Black Caucus was organized.

A riot occurred in Wilmington, North Carolina.

Whitney M. Young, Jr. drowned in Lagos, Nigeria.

The Congressional Black caucus met with President Richard Nixon.

Reverend Walter Fauntroy became Washington, D.C's nonvoting Congressional Delegate.

The U. S. Supreme Court ruled that it was constitutional for the use of school busing to achieve school desegregation.

Samuel Gravely, Jr. became the first African American to be promoted to Admiral in the U. S. Navy.

President Nixon rejected the "Demands" placed on him by the Congressional Black Caucus.

According to Pentagon reports, of the total American forces in Vietnam, eleven percent were African Americans. Of all the deaths, 12.5 percent were black soldiers.

A riot occurred in Chattanooga, Tennessee.

Vernon Jordan became the new Executive Director of the National Urban League.

A racial riot occurred in Columbus, Ohio.

The U. S. Supreme Court overturned the draft evasion of **Muhammad Ali.**

Louis Armstrong died.

A confrontation between members of the Republic of New Africa and the police in Jackson, Mississippi resulted in the death of some policemen and the arrest of **Imari Obadele** and some of his followers of the R.N.A.

George Jackson, a "Soledad Brother," was killed in an attempt to breakout of San Quetin, California prison.

Attica prison in New York was seized by inmates.

A race riot occurred in Memphis, Tennessee.

Ralph Bunche retired from his position as a U.N. Ambassador. A few months after his retirement, **Ralph Bunche** died. **Reverend**

Jesse Jackson spearheaded the founding of P.U.S.H.

1972 A riot occurred in Baton Rogue, Louisiana.

Singer **Mahalia Jackson** died.

Shirley Chisolm began her unsuccessful presidential candidacy.

The first national black political convention was held in Gary, Indiana.

Former Congressman **Adam Clayton, Jr.,** died.

Kwame Nkrumah of Ghana died.

A white jury acquitted **Angela Davis** of charges relating to the 1970 Marin County Courthouse shoot out.

Republicans breaking into the Democratic Party Headquarters at Watergate in Washington D. C. were foiled by the actions of guard **Frank Wills.**

Yvonne Braithwaite Burke of California was approved as Co-Chairperson of the National Democratic Part Convention that went on to nominate George McGovern for President of the United States.

In a 5:4 decision, the U. S. Supreme Court ruled that the death penalty constituted "cruel and unusual punishment" and was a violation of the 8th Amendment of the U. S. Constitution.

In Alabama, **Johnny Ford** (Tuskegee) and **A. J. Cooper** (Pritchard) were elected as mayors.

The Secretary of the Army finally expunged the records of over 100 black soldiers instigated in the 1906 Brownsville, Texas riot.

Baseball pioneer **Jackie Robinson** died.

Sixteen black people were elected to Congress. The newly elected were **Andrew Young** (Atlanta, Georgia), **Barbara Jordan** (Houston, Texas), and **Yvonne Braithwaite Burke.**

At Southern University (Baton Rogue), two students were killed in an uprising.

Congressman **George Collins** (Illinois) died in an airplane crash.

1973 **Tom (Thomas) Bradley** was elected mayor of Los Angeles, California.

Cardiss Collins was elected to succeed her husband as Congressperson from Chicago.

Maynard Jackson was elected as mayor of Atlanta, Georgia.

Coleman Young was elected mayor of Detroit, Michigan.

Hank Aaron of the Atlanta Braves became "Home Run King" by hitting number 715.

The U. S. House of Representatives Judiciary Committee started holding hearings to decide whether or not to impeach President Richard Nixon. **Barbara Jordan** distinguished herself as a member of this body.

Mrs. Martin Luther King, Sr. was shot and killed by **Marcus Chennault**.

1973 President Richard Nixon resigned his office. Gerald Ford succeeded him as the New President of America.

Frank Robinson became the first black to become manager of a big baseball team. He took over the Cleveland Indians.

Muhammad Ali defeated **George Foreman** in the "Rumble in the Jungle" prize fight fought in Kinshasa, Zaire.

Mervyn Dymally, a State Senator, was elected Lieutenant Governor of California. In Colorado, State Senator **George L. Brown** was elected Lieutenant Governor.

In Washington, D. C., **Walter E.Washington**, who had been appointed mayor by then U. S. President Lyndon B. Johnson, was elected mayor.

Harold Ford (Dem.) was elected to the U. S. House of Representatives from Memphis, Tennessee.

U. S. President Gerald Ford appointed **William T. Coleman** as Secretary of Transportation.

1975 The leader of the Nation of Islam, **Elijah Muhammad**, died.

Singer **Josephine Baker** died.

The first African American to compete in the Masters Golf Tournament, **Lee Elder**, failed to qualify to finish the final two rounds.

James B. Parsons from Chicago became the first African American to be named Chief Judge of the Federal District Court.

Chemist **Dr. Percy Julian** died.

Civil rights and labor leader **A. Philip Randolph** died.

Former boxer **Ezzard Charles** died.

The U. S. Supreme Court ruled in the *Weber v. Kaiser Aluminum* case that the establishment of quotas and voluntary programs to help minorities in employment were acceptable.

Arthur Ashe became the first black man to win the Men's Wimbledon Singles Tennis Title.

Saxophonist **Julian "Cannonball" Adderly** died.

Joanne Little, accused of murdering a white jailer who made sexual advances, was acquitted.

1976 Singer **Paul Robeson** died.

Kenneth Gipson, mayor of Newark, NJ, became the first African American to serve as President of the U. S. Conference of Mayors.

Congresswoman **Barbara Jordan** of Texas became the first black person to deliver the keynote address at a national political convention. She addressed the Democratic Convention.

Mordecai H. Johnson, the first black President of Howard University, died.

Clarence "Willie" Norris, the last of the "Scottsboro Boys," finally received a full pardon from Governor George Wallace of Alabama.

Georgia's Jimmy Carter, the choice of black American voters, was elected President of the United States.

The NAACP named **Benjamin Hooks** as its Executive Director to succeed **Roy Wilkins**.

Andrew Young, Congressman from Georgia, was named United States Chief Ambassador to the United Nations.

President Jimmy Carter named **Patricia Harris** as Secretary of Housing and Urban Development.

1977 "Roots," based on a novel by **Alex Haley**, was shown on ABC on television during the week of January 23–30.

The first African American Secretary of the U. S. Army was confirmed.

Henry L. Marsh III was elected mayor of Richmond, Virginia.

The Catholic Diocese of Biloxi, Mississippi installed **Joseph Howze** as its Bishop.

Dr. Clifford R. Wharton, Jr. became Chancellor of the State University of New York.

Ernest Morial was elected mayor of New Orleans.

Major **Guion Blufford,** Major **Frederick Gregory**, and **Dr. Ronald McNair** were all named as Astronauts by NASA.

Muhammad Ali was defeated by **Leon Sphinx** for the title as the World's Heavyweight Boxing Champion.

The Bakke case, issuing "reverse discrimination," was promulgated by the U. S. Supreme Court.

In September, **Muhammad Ali** won back the title of the World's Heavyweight Boxing Champion by defeating **Leon Sphinx** in a rematch.

Congressman **Ralph L. Metcalfe** of Illinois, died in Chicago.

The New Congressmen elected included **William Gray** (PN), **Bennett Stewart** (IL), **Julian Dixon** (CA), and **George "Mickey" Leland** (TX).

In California, Lieutenant Governor **Mervyn Dymally** was defeated for reelection. And in Massachusetts, U. S. Senator **Edward W. Brook** (Rep.) was defeated.

In Guyana, the "Jonestown Massacre" occurred.

Max Robinson became network television's first black news anchorman.

Frank Peterson, Jr. was promoted to General in the U. S. Maine Corps.

1979 The Southern Conference on Afro-American Studies, Inc. was founded.

Patricia "Pat" Harris, Secretary of HUD, was reappointed by President Jimmy Carter as Secretary of Health, Education, and Welfare.

James P. Lyke was ordained as Auxiliary Bishop of the Cleveland, Ohio Catholic Diocese.

Following clamors for his resignation, **Andrew Young** resigned as the U.N. Ambassador. This followed in the wake of his having unauthorized meetings with P.L.O. officials.

Donald McHenry was named to replaced **Andrew Young** as U.N. Ambassador.

Lou Brock, a native of Arkansas and a product of Southern University, became the "baseball big league base stealers" when he stole his 935th.

Richard Arrington was elected mayor of Birmingham, Alabama.

In Greensboro, North Carolina, Klansmen fired on an anti-Klan rally, killing five people.

Princeton University professor **Arthur Lewis** was awarded the Nobel Prize in Economics.

1980 Racial unrest broke out in Idabell, Oklahoma.

Jesse Owens, the hero of the 1936 Berlin Olympic Games, died.

In a coup in Liberia, Sergeant **Samuel Doe** overthrew and killed President **William Tolbert**.

A race riot occurred in Miami, Florida.

President of the National Urban League, **Vernon Jordan, Jr.,** was wounded in an assassination attempt.

Race riots continued in Miami, Florida.

1981 President Ronald Reagan appointed **Samuel Pierece** as Secretary of HUD.

Boxer **Joe Louis** died.

The National Bar Association elected its first woman President, Attorney **Arnette Hubbard**.

Roy Wilkins, former NAACP leader, died.

Upon resignation of **Vernon Jordon, John E. Jacob** became the new leader of the National Urban League.

Over 300,000 people participated in a "Solidarity Day" march protesting the racial policies of the Reagan Administration.

Andrew Young was elected mayor of Atlanta, Georgia.

Edward McIntyre was elected mayor of Augusta, Georgia.

James Chase was elected mayor of Hartford, Connecticut.

Coleman Young was reelected mayor of Detroit, Michigan.

The new faces in the Congressional Black Delegation were: **Mervyn Dymall** (CA), **Augustus Savage** (IL), **Harold Washington** (IL), and **George Crockett, Jr.** (MI).

1982 **Wayne Williams** was convicted for a series of slaying of youths in Atlanta, Georgia.

1983 In October, **Jesse Jackson** announced his democratic candidacy for U. S. President.

Jesse Jackson went to Syria and secured the release of Lieutenant Robert Goodman, a navigator whose airplane had been shot down over Syria.

Alice Walker won a Pulitzer Prize for her novel, *The Color Purple*.

1984 In the Los Angeles Olympic games, 1960 Olympian **Rafer Johnson** carried the Olympic Torch for the opening ceremony.

1986 Astronaut **Ronald McNair** was killed in the "Challenger" space craft explosion in which all hands were lost.

1988 **Toni Morrison** won a Pulitzer Prize for *Beloved*.

1989 Texas Congressman **George "Mickey" Leland** was killed in an airplane crash in Ethiopia.

Colin Powell became the first African American to become Chairman of the U. S. Joint Chiefs of Staff.

L. Douglas Wilder became the Governor of Virginia.

1990 **David Dinkins** became the first black mayor of New York City.

Sharon Pratt Dixon became the mayor of Washington D. C.

THE AFRICAN BACKGROUND: SOCIOLOGICAL

NAME:____________________ DATE:________ ACTIVITY:__________ APPROVAL:_______

1 ____________________
2 ____________________
3 ____________________
4 ____________________
5 ____________________
6 ____________________
7 ____________________
8 ____________________
9 ____________________
10 ____________________
11 ____________________
12 ____________________
13 ____________________
14 ____________________
15 ____________________
16 ____________________
17 ____________________
18 ____________________
19 ____________________
20 ____________________
21 ____________________
22 ____________________
23 ____________________
24 ____________________
25 ____________________
26 ____________________
27 ____________________
28 ____________________
29 ____________________
30 ____________________
31 ____________________
32 ____________________
33 ____________________
34 ____________________
35 ____________________
36 ____________________
37 ____________________
38 ____________________
39 ____________________
40 ____________________
41 ____________________
42 ____________________
43 ____________________
44 ____________________
45 ____________________
46 ____________________
47 ____________________
48 ____________________
49 ____________________
50 ____________________

THE AFRICAN BACKGROUND: GEOGRAPHICAL AND ECONOMICAL

NAME:____________________ **DATE:**________ **ACTIVITY:**________ **APPROVAL:** ________

1	________________	26	________________
2	________________	27	________________
3	________________	28	________________
4	________________	29	________________
5	________________	30	________________
6	________________	31	________________
7	________________	32	________________
8	________________	33	________________
9	________________	34	________________
10	________________	35	________________
11	________________	36	________________
12	________________	37	________________
13	________________	38	________________
14	________________	39	________________
15	________________	40	________________
16	________________	41	________________
17	________________	42	________________
18	________________	43	________________
19	________________	44	________________
20	________________	45	________________
21	________________	46	________________
22	________________	47	________________
23	________________	48	________________
24	________________	49	________________
25	________________	50	________________

THE AFRICAN BACKGROUND: POLITICAL

NAME:__________________________ DATE:________ ACTIVITY:________ APPROVAL: ________

1 ______________________________
2 ______________________________
3 ______________________________
4 ______________________________
5 ______________________________
6 ______________________________
7 ______________________________
8 ______________________________
9 ______________________________
10 ______________________________
11 ______________________________
12 ______________________________
13 ______________________________
14 ______________________________
15 ______________________________
16 ______________________________
17 ______________________________
18 ______________________________
19 ______________________________
20 ______________________________
21 ______________________________
22 ______________________________
23 ______________________________
24 ______________________________
25 ______________________________
26 ______________________________
27 ______________________________
28 ______________________________
29 ______________________________
30 ______________________________
31 ______________________________
32 ______________________________
33 ______________________________
34 ______________________________
35 ______________________________
36 ______________________________
37 ______________________________
38 ______________________________
39 ______________________________
40 ______________________________
41 ______________________________
42 ______________________________
43 ______________________________
44 ______________________________
45 ______________________________
46 ______________________________
47 ______________________________
48 ______________________________
49 ______________________________
50 ______________________________

THE ENSLAVEMENT PROCESS

NAME:____________________ **DATE:**________ **ACTIVITY:**________ **APPROVAL:** ________

1 __________	26 __________
2 __________	27 __________
3 __________	28 __________
4 __________	29 __________
5 __________	30 __________
6 __________	31 __________
7 __________	32 __________
8 __________	33 __________
9 __________	34 __________
10 __________	35 __________
11 __________	36 __________
12 __________	37 __________
13 __________	38 __________
14 __________	39 __________
15 __________	40 __________
16 __________	41 __________
17 __________	42 __________
18 __________	43 __________
19 __________	44 __________
20 __________	45 __________
21 __________	46 __________
22 __________	47 __________
23 __________	48 __________
24 __________	49 __________
25 __________	50 __________

THE DIASPORIA

WORKSHEET A

NAME:____________________ **DATE:**________ **ACTIVITY:**________ **APPROVAL:** ________

1 ____________________
2 ____________________
3 ____________________
4 ____________________
5 ____________________
6 ____________________
7 ____________________
8 ____________________
9 ____________________
10 ____________________
11 ____________________
12 ____________________
13 ____________________
14 ____________________
15 ____________________
16 ____________________
17 ____________________
18 ____________________
19 ____________________
20 ____________________
21 ____________________
22 ____________________
23 ____________________
24 ____________________
25 ____________________
26 ____________________
27 ____________________
28 ____________________
29 ____________________
30 ____________________
31 ____________________
32 ____________________
33 ____________________
34 ____________________
35 ____________________
36 ____________________
37 ____________________
38 ____________________
39 ____________________
40 ____________________
41 ____________________
42 ____________________
43 ____________________
44 ____________________
45 ____________________
46 ____________________
47 ____________________
48 ____________________
49 ____________________
50 ____________________

THE DIASPORIA

WORKSHEET B

NAME:________________ **DATE:**________ **ACTIVITY:**________ **APPROVAL:** ________

1	____________	26	____________
2	____________	27	____________
3	____________	28	____________
4	____________	29	____________
5	____________	30	____________
6	____________	31	____________
7	____________	32	____________
8	____________	33	____________
9	____________	34	____________
10	____________	35	____________
11	____________	36	____________
12	____________	37	____________
13	____________	38	____________
14	____________	39	____________
15	____________	40	____________
16	____________	41	____________
17	____________	42	____________
18	____________	43	____________
19	____________	44	____________
20	____________	45	____________
21	____________	46	____________
22	____________	47	____________
23	____________	48	____________
24	____________	49	____________
25	____________	50	____________

EIGHTEENTH CENTURY AFRICAN AMERICAN ACCOMPLISHMENTS

NAME:____________________ DATE:________ ACTIVITY:________ APPROVAL: ________

1 ____________________
2 ____________________
3 ____________________
4 ____________________
5 ____________________
6 ____________________
7 ____________________
8 ____________________
9 ____________________
10 ____________________
11 ____________________
12 ____________________
13 ____________________
14 ____________________
15 ____________________
16 ____________________
17 ____________________
18 ____________________
19 ____________________
20 ____________________
21 ____________________
22 ____________________
23 ____________________
24 ____________________
25 ____________________
26 ____________________
27 ____________________
28 ____________________
29 ____________________
30 ____________________
31 ____________________
32 ____________________
33 ____________________
34 ____________________
35 ____________________
36 ____________________
37 ____________________
38 ____________________
39 ____________________
40 ____________________
41 ____________________
42 ____________________
43 ____________________
44 ____________________
45 ____________________
46 ____________________
47 ____________________
48 ____________________
49 ____________________
50 ____________________

COLONIAL AMERICA TO THE UNITED STATES OF AMERICA

NAME:__________ **DATE:**_____ **ACTIVITY:**_____ **APPROVAL:** _____

1 __________
2 __________
3 __________
4 __________
5 __________
6 __________
7 __________
8 __________
9 __________
10 __________
11 __________
12 __________
13 __________
14 __________
15 __________
16 __________
17 __________
18 __________
19 __________
20 __________
21 __________
22 __________
23 __________
24 __________
25 __________
26 __________
27 __________
28 __________
29 __________
30 __________
31 __________
32 __________
33 __________
34 __________
35 __________
36 __________
37 __________
38 __________
39 __________
40 __________
41 __________
42 __________
43 __________
44 __________
45 __________
46 __________
47 __________
48 __________
49 __________
50 __________

NINETEENTH CENTURY ANTEBELLUM AFRICAN AMERICAN ACCOMPLISHMENTS

NAME:__________________________DATE:________ACTIVITY:________APPROVAL: _________

1 ________________________________
2 ________________________________
3 ________________________________
4 ________________________________
5 ________________________________
6 ________________________________
7 ________________________________
8 ________________________________
9 ________________________________
10 ________________________________
11 ________________________________
12 ________________________________
13 ________________________________
14 ________________________________
15 ________________________________
16 ________________________________
17 ________________________________
18 ________________________________
19 ________________________________
20 ________________________________
21 ________________________________
22 ________________________________
23 ________________________________
24 ________________________________
25 ________________________________
26 ________________________________
27 ________________________________
28 ________________________________
29 ________________________________
30 ________________________________
31 ________________________________
32 ________________________________
33 ________________________________
34 ________________________________
35 ________________________________
36 ________________________________
37 ________________________________
38 ________________________________
39 ________________________________
40 ________________________________
41 ________________________________
42 ________________________________
43 ________________________________
44 ________________________________
45 ________________________________
46 ________________________________
47 ________________________________
48 ________________________________
49 ________________________________
50 ________________________________

THE COMING OF THE CIVIL WAR, 1820–1860

NAME:________________ **DATE:**________ **ACTIVITY:**________ **APPROVAL:** ________

1 ____________________
2 ____________________
3 ____________________
4 ____________________
5 ____________________
6 ____________________
7 ____________________
8 ____________________
9 ____________________
10 ____________________
11 ____________________
12 ____________________
13 ____________________
14 ____________________
15 ____________________
16 ____________________
17 ____________________
18 ____________________
19 ____________________
20 ____________________
21 ____________________
22 ____________________
23 ____________________
24 ____________________
25 ____________________
26 ____________________
27 ____________________
28 ____________________
29 ____________________
30 ____________________
31 ____________________
32 ____________________
33 ____________________
34 ____________________
35 ____________________
36 ____________________
37 ____________________
38 ____________________
39 ____________________
40 ____________________
41 ____________________
42 ____________________
43 ____________________
44 ____________________
45 ____________________
46 ____________________
47 ____________________
48 ____________________
49 ____________________
50 ____________________

THE AFRICAN AMERICAN AND THE CIVIL WAR

NAME:____________________ **DATE:**________ **ACTIVITY:**________ **APPROVAL:** ________

1 ____________________
2 ____________________
3 ____________________
4 ____________________
5 ____________________
6 ____________________
7 ____________________
8 ____________________
9 ____________________
10 ____________________
11 ____________________
12 ____________________
13 ____________________
14 ____________________
15 ____________________
16 ____________________
17 ____________________
18 ____________________
19 ____________________
20 ____________________
21 ____________________
22 ____________________
23 ____________________
24 ____________________
25 ____________________
26 ____________________
27 ____________________
28 ____________________
29 ____________________
30 ____________________
31 ____________________
32 ____________________
33 ____________________
34 ____________________
35 ____________________
36 ____________________
37 ____________________
38 ____________________
39 ____________________
40 ____________________
41 ____________________
42 ____________________
43 ____________________
44 ____________________
45 ____________________
46 ____________________
47 ____________________
48 ____________________
49 ____________________
50 ____________________

RECONSTRUCTION

WORKSHEET A

NAME:__________ **DATE:**______ **ACTIVITY:**______ **APPROVAL:** ______

1 __________
2 __________
3 __________
4 __________
5 __________
6 __________
7 __________
8 __________
9 __________
10 __________
11 __________
12 __________
13 __________
14 __________
15 __________
16 __________
17 __________
18 __________
19 __________
20 __________
21 __________
22 __________
23 __________
24 __________
25 __________
26 __________
27 __________
28 __________
29 __________
30 __________
31 __________
32 __________
33 __________
34 __________
35 __________
36 __________
37 __________
38 __________
39 __________
40 __________
41 __________
42 __________
43 __________
44 __________
45 __________
46 __________
47 __________
48 __________
49 __________
50 __________

RECONSTRUCTION

WORKSHEET B

NAME:________________ **DATE:**________ **ACTIVITY:**________ **APPROVAL:** ________

1 ____________________

2 ____________________

3 ____________________

4 ____________________

5 ____________________

6 ____________________

7 ____________________

8 ____________________

9 ____________________

10 ____________________

11 ____________________

12 ____________________

13 ____________________

14 ____________________

15 ____________________

16 ____________________

17 ____________________

18 ____________________

19 ____________________

20 ____________________

21 ____________________

22 ____________________

23 ____________________

24 ____________________

25 ____________________

26 ____________________

27 ____________________

28 ____________________

29 ____________________

30 ____________________

31 ____________________

32 ____________________

33 ____________________

34 ____________________

35 ____________________

36 ____________________

37 ____________________

38 ____________________

39 ____________________

40 ____________________

41 ____________________

42 ____________________

43 ____________________

44 ____________________

45 ____________________

46 ____________________

47 ____________________

48 ____________________

49 ____________________

50 ____________________

**FROM THE FALL OF RECONSTRUCTION
TO THE DAWN OF THE 20TH CENTURY**

NAME:________________________ **DATE:**________ **ACTIVITY:**________ **APPROVAL:** ________

1 ____________________
2 ____________________
3 ____________________
4 ____________________
5 ____________________
6 ____________________
7 ____________________
8 ____________________
9 ____________________
10 ____________________
11 ____________________
12 ____________________
13 ____________________
14 ____________________
15 ____________________
16 ____________________
17 ____________________
18 ____________________
19 ____________________
20 ____________________
21 ____________________
22 ____________________
23 ____________________
24 ____________________
25 ____________________
26 ____________________
27 ____________________
28 ____________________
29 ____________________
30 ____________________
31 ____________________
32 ____________________
33 ____________________
34 ____________________
35 ____________________
36 ____________________
37 ____________________
38 ____________________
39 ____________________
40 ____________________
41 ____________________
42 ____________________
43 ____________________
44 ____________________
45 ____________________
46 ____________________
47 ____________________
48 ____________________
49 ____________________
50 ____________________

NINETEENTH CENTURY BLACK NATIONALISM

NAME:____________________ **DATE:**________ **ACTIVITY:**________ **APPROVAL:** ________

1 ____________________
2 ____________________
3 ____________________
4 ____________________
5 ____________________
6 ____________________
7 ____________________
8 ____________________
9 ____________________
10 ____________________
11 ____________________
12 ____________________
13 ____________________
14 ____________________
15 ____________________
16 ____________________
17 ____________________
18 ____________________
19 ____________________
20 ____________________
21 ____________________
22 ____________________
23 ____________________
24 ____________________
25 ____________________
26 ____________________
27 ____________________
28 ____________________
29 ____________________
30 ____________________
31 ____________________
32 ____________________
33 ____________________
34 ____________________
35 ____________________
36 ____________________
37 ____________________
38 ____________________
39 ____________________
40 ____________________
41 ____________________
42 ____________________
43 ____________________
44 ____________________
45 ____________________
46 ____________________
47 ____________________
48 ____________________
49 ____________________
50 ____________________

THE AGE OF BOOKER T. WASHINGTON

NAME:______________________ DATE:________ ACTIVITY:________ APPROVAL: ________

1 ________________	26 ________________
2 ________________	27 ________________
3 ________________	28 ________________
4 ________________	29 ________________
5 ________________	30 ________________
6 ________________	31 ________________
7 ________________	32 ________________
8 ________________	33 ________________
9 ________________	34 ________________
10 ________________	35 ________________
11 ________________	36 ________________
12 ________________	37 ________________
13 ________________	38 ________________
14 ________________	39 ________________
15 ________________	40 ________________
16 ________________	41 ________________
17 ________________	42 ________________
18 ________________	43 ________________
19 ________________	44 ________________
20 ________________	45 ________________
21 ________________	46 ________________
22 ________________	47 ________________
23 ________________	48 ________________
24 ________________	49 ________________
25 ________________	50 ________________

BLACK AMERICA'S RESPONSE TO WORLD WAR I

NAME:____________ **DATE:**________ **ACTIVITY:**________ **APPROVAL:** ________

1 __________	26 __________
2 __________	27 __________
3 __________	28 __________
4 __________	29 __________
5 __________	30 __________
6 __________	31 __________
7 __________	32 __________
8 __________	33 __________
9 __________	34 __________
10 __________	35 __________
11 __________	36 __________
12 __________	37 __________
13 __________	38 __________
14 __________	39 __________
15 __________	40 __________
16 __________	41 __________
17 __________	42 __________
18 __________	43 __________
19 __________	44 __________
20 __________	45 __________
21 __________	46 __________
22 __________	47 __________
23 __________	48 __________
24 __________	49 __________
25 __________	50 __________

HARLEM RENAISSANCE: A HISTORICAL PERSPECTIVE

NAME:__________ DATE:__________ ACTIVITY:__________ APPROVAL: __________

1 __________
2 __________
3 __________
4 __________
5 __________
6 __________
7 __________
8 __________
9 __________
10 __________
11 __________
12 __________
13 __________
14 __________
15 __________
16 __________
17 __________
18 __________
19 __________
20 __________
21 __________
22 __________
23 __________
24 __________
25 __________
26 __________
27 __________
28 __________
29 __________
30 __________
31 __________
32 __________
33 __________
34 __________
35 __________
36 __________
37 __________
38 __________
39 __________
40 __________
41 __________
42 __________
43 __________
44 __________
45 __________
46 __________
47 __________
48 __________
49 __________
50 __________

BETWEEN THE WARS AND WORLD WAR II

WORKSHEET A

NAME:____________________ DATE:________ ACTIVITY:________ APPROVAL: ________

1 ____________________
2 ____________________
3 ____________________
4 ____________________
5 ____________________
6 ____________________
7 ____________________
8 ____________________
9 ____________________
10 ____________________
11 ____________________
12 ____________________
13 ____________________
14 ____________________
15 ____________________
16 ____________________
17 ____________________
18 ____________________
19 ____________________
20 ____________________
21 ____________________
22 ____________________
23 ____________________
24 ____________________
25 ____________________
26 ____________________
27 ____________________
28 ____________________
29 ____________________
30 ____________________
31 ____________________
32 ____________________
33 ____________________
34 ____________________
35 ____________________
36 ____________________
37 ____________________
38 ____________________
39 ____________________
40 ____________________
41 ____________________
42 ____________________
43 ____________________
44 ____________________
45 ____________________
46 ____________________
47 ____________________
48 ____________________
49 ____________________
50 ____________________

BETWEEN THE WARS AND WORLD WAR II

WORKSHEET B

NAME:__________ **DATE:**__________ **ACTIVITY:**__________ **APPROVAL:** __________

1 __________
2 __________
3 __________
4 __________
5 __________
6 __________
7 __________
8 __________
9 __________
10 __________
11 __________
12 __________
13 __________
14 __________
15 __________
16 __________
17 __________
18 __________
19 __________
20 __________
21 __________
22 __________
23 __________
24 __________
25 __________
26 __________
27 __________
28 __________
29 __________
30 __________
31 __________
32 __________
33 __________
34 __________
35 __________
36 __________
37 __________
38 __________
39 __________
40 __________
41 __________
42 __________
43 __________
44 __________
45 __________
46 __________
47 __________
48 __________
49 __________
50 __________

THE IMMEDIATE YEARS OF THE BROWN CASE

NAME:__________________ DATE:________ ACTIVITY:________ APPROVAL: ________

1 ____________________
2 ____________________
3 ____________________
4 ____________________
5 ____________________
6 ____________________
7 ____________________
8 ____________________
9 ____________________
10 ____________________
11 ____________________
12 ____________________
13 ____________________
14 ____________________
15 ____________________
16 ____________________
17 ____________________
18 ____________________
19 ____________________
20 ____________________
21 ____________________
22 ____________________
23 ____________________
24 ____________________
25 ____________________
26 ____________________
27 ____________________
28 ____________________
29 ____________________
30 ____________________
31 ____________________
32 ____________________
33 ____________________
34 ____________________
35 ____________________
36 ____________________
37 ____________________
38 ____________________
39 ____________________
40 ____________________
41 ____________________
42 ____________________
43 ____________________
44 ____________________
45 ____________________
46 ____________________
47 ____________________
48 ____________________
49 ____________________
50 ____________________

THE KING ERA AND TURMOIL

NAME:____________________ DATE:________ ACTIVITY:________ APPROVAL: ________

1 ________________	26 ________________
2 ________________	27 ________________
3 ________________	28 ________________
4 ________________	29 ________________
5 ________________	30 ________________
6 ________________	31 ________________
7 ________________	32 ________________
8 ________________	33 ________________
9 ________________	34 ________________
10 ________________	35 ________________
11 ________________	36 ________________
12 ________________	37 ________________
13 ________________	38 ________________
14 ________________	39 ________________
15 ________________	40 ________________
16 ________________	41 ________________
17 ________________	42 ________________
18 ________________	43 ________________
19 ________________	44 ________________
20 ________________	45 ________________
21 ________________	46 ________________
22 ________________	47 ________________
23 ________________	48 ________________
24 ________________	49 ________________
25 ________________	50 ________________

TWENTIETH CENTURY BLACK NATIONALISM

NAME:________________________ DATE:________ ACTIVITY:________ APPROVAL: ________

1 ______________________	26 ______________________
2 ______________________	27 ______________________
3 ______________________	28 ______________________
4 ______________________	29 ______________________
5 ______________________	30 ______________________
6 ______________________	31 ______________________
7 ______________________	32 ______________________
8 ______________________	33 ______________________
9 ______________________	34 ______________________
10 ______________________	35 ______________________
11 ______________________	36 ______________________
12 ______________________	37 ______________________
13 ______________________	38 ______________________
14 ______________________	39 ______________________
15 ______________________	40 ______________________
16 ______________________	41 ______________________
17 ______________________	42 ______________________
18 ______________________	43 ______________________
19 ______________________	44 ______________________
20 ______________________	45 ______________________
21 ______________________	46 ______________________
22 ______________________	47 ______________________
23 ______________________	48 ______________________
24 ______________________	49 ______________________
25 ______________________	50 ______________________

A SURVEY OF AFRICAN-AMERICAN LITERATURE FROM THE PAST TO THE PRESENT

NAME:__________ DATE:________ ACTIVITY:________ APPROVAL:________

1	__________	26	__________
2	__________	27	__________
3	__________	28	__________
4	__________	29	__________
5	__________	30	__________
6	__________	31	__________
7	__________	32	__________
8	__________	33	__________
9	__________	34	__________
10	__________	35	__________
11	__________	36	__________
12	__________	37	__________
13	__________	38	__________
14	__________	39	__________
15	__________	40	__________
16	__________	41	__________
17	__________	42	__________
18	__________	43	__________
19	__________	44	__________
20	__________	45	__________
21	__________	46	__________
22	__________	47	__________
23	__________	48	__________
24	__________	49	__________
25	__________	50	__________

AFRICAN AMERICANS IN THE MILITARY

NAME:____________________ DATE:________ ACTIVITY:________ APPROVAL: ________

1 ____________________	26 ____________________
2 ____________________	27 ____________________
3 ____________________	28 ____________________
4 ____________________	29 ____________________
5 ____________________	30 ____________________
6 ____________________	31 ____________________
7 ____________________	32 ____________________
8 ____________________	33 ____________________
9 ____________________	34 ____________________
10 ____________________	35 ____________________
11 ____________________	36 ____________________
12 ____________________	37 ____________________
13 ____________________	38 ____________________
14 ____________________	39 ____________________
15 ____________________	40 ____________________
16 ____________________	41 ____________________
17 ____________________	42 ____________________
18 ____________________	43 ____________________
19 ____________________	44 ____________________
20 ____________________	45 ____________________
21 ____________________	46 ____________________
22 ____________________	47 ____________________
23 ____________________	48 ____________________
24 ____________________	49 ____________________
25 ____________________	50 ____________________

BLACK MUSIC IN AMERICA

NAME:____________________ **DATE:**________ **ACTIVITY:**________ **APPROVAL:** ________

1 ____________________
2 ____________________
3 ____________________
4 ____________________
5 ____________________
6 ____________________
7 ____________________
8 ____________________
9 ____________________
10 ____________________
11 ____________________
12 ____________________
13 ____________________
14 ____________________
15 ____________________
16 ____________________
17 ____________________
18 ____________________
19 ____________________
20 ____________________
21 ____________________
22 ____________________
23 ____________________
24 ____________________
25 ____________________
26 ____________________
27 ____________________
28 ____________________
29 ____________________
30 ____________________
31 ____________________
32 ____________________
33 ____________________
34 ____________________
35 ____________________
36 ____________________
37 ____________________
38 ____________________
39 ____________________
40 ____________________
41 ____________________
42 ____________________
43 ____________________
44 ____________________
45 ____________________
46 ____________________
47 ____________________
48 ____________________
49 ____________________
50 ____________________

1970s

NAME:__________ DATE:__________ ACTIVITY:__________ APPROVAL: __________

1 __________
2 __________
3 __________
4 __________
5 __________
6 __________
7 __________
8 __________
9 __________
10 __________
11 __________
12 __________
13 __________
14 __________
15 __________
16 __________
17 __________
18 __________
19 __________
20 __________
21 __________
22 __________
23 __________
24 __________
25 __________
26 __________
27 __________
28 __________
29 __________
30 __________
31 __________
32 __________
33 __________
34 __________
35 __________
36 __________
37 __________
38 __________
39 __________
40 __________
41 __________
42 __________
43 __________
44 __________
45 __________
46 __________
47 __________
48 __________
49 __________
50 __________

1980s

NAME:____________________ **DATE:**________ **ACTIVITY:**________ **APPROVAL:** ________

1 ____________________
2 ____________________
3 ____________________
4 ____________________
5 ____________________
6 ____________________
7 ____________________
8 ____________________
9 ____________________
10 ____________________
11 ____________________
12 ____________________
13 ____________________
14 ____________________
15 ____________________
16 ____________________
17 ____________________
18 ____________________
19 ____________________
20 ____________________
21 ____________________
22 ____________________
23 ____________________
24 ____________________
25 ____________________
26 ____________________
27 ____________________
28 ____________________
29 ____________________
30 ____________________
31 ____________________
32 ____________________
33 ____________________
34 ____________________
35 ____________________
36 ____________________
37 ____________________
38 ____________________
39 ____________________
40 ____________________
41 ____________________
42 ____________________
43 ____________________
44 ____________________
45 ____________________
46 ____________________
47 ____________________
48 ____________________
49 ____________________
50 ____________________

1990s

NAME:____________________ **DATE:**________ **ACTIVITY:**________ **APPROVAL:** ________

1 ____________________

2 ____________________

3 ____________________

4 ____________________

5 ____________________

6 ____________________

7 ____________________

8 ____________________

9 ____________________

10 ____________________

11 ____________________

12 ____________________

13 ____________________

14 ____________________

15 ____________________

16 ____________________

17 ____________________

18 ____________________

19 ____________________

20 ____________________

21 ____________________

22 ____________________

23 ____________________

24 ____________________

25 ____________________

26 ____________________

27 ____________________

28 ____________________

29 ____________________

30 ____________________

31 ____________________

32 ____________________

33 ____________________

34 ____________________

35 ____________________

36 ____________________

37 ____________________

38 ____________________

39 ____________________

40 ____________________

41 ____________________

42 ____________________

43 ____________________

44 ____________________

45 ____________________

46 ____________________

47 ____________________

48 ____________________

49 ____________________

50 ____________________